2012
The Transformation from the Love of Power to the Power of Love

By

Robert Roskind

Copyright 2008 by Robert Roskind
This edition published in 2008 by One Love Press

ISBN: 978-1-56522-101-7

Cover design by Jonathan Gullery

One Love Press
P.O. Box 2142
Blowing Rock, NC 28605
(828) 295-4610 FAX: (828) 295-6901
Website: www.onelovepress.com
Email: Roskind@boone.net

<u>Books by Robert Roskind</u>

The Beauty Path: A Native American Journey into One Love

Rasta Heart: A Journey into One Love

The Gathering of the Healers: The Healing of the Nations

Memoirs of an Ex-Hippie: Seven Years in the Counterculture

In the Spirit of Marriage: Creating & Sustaining a Loving Union

In the Spirit of Business: A Guide to Creating Harmony & Fulfillment in your Worklife

Building Your Own House

Order at:
www.onelovepress.com

Dedication

This book is dedicated to Mayan Elder Tata Pedro Cruz, who for over 50 years has tenaciously safeguarded the sacred wisdom and customs of his ancestors.

Acknowledgements

I would like to thank the following people. Without their generous and heartfelt help, this book could not have come about.

My wife, Julia, for sharing every step of the journey with me and reminding me always that the peace of God lives within each of us;

My daughters, Alicia and Julie, for making our travels so much fun and whose presence reminds me that the work we do is for future generations;

Chus Landa and Louise Rothwell, for their devotion to act as translators for all our reasonings with Tata Pedro;

Luis Arturo Gonzalez and Danilo Rodriguez, for their memorable tours of Tikal;

Dr. Rosita Arvigo, for generously sharing her knowledge of Mayan healing practices;

Danny Diaz, for always being there at just the right time;

Jonathan Gullery, for another inspired cover;

Cindi Courter and Lucy Freedman, for their excellent job as editors and proofreaders;

Joseph Moore, Tareyton Lewis, and Tami Parnell, for proofreading.

Preface

When I was young and learned of the pain and suffering in the world, I wondered, *Why can't we all just love each other more and how can I find some way to help*? One of the first people who helped me answer those questions was the woman who helped raise me. Louise was a black woman in the pre-civil rights South. She had seen much suffering. Sometimes we would discuss this problem late into the night and she would always conclude by saying, "The only problem we have on this Earth is we don't love ourselves enough." At some deep level, I knew this was true.

Over my life, witnessing the civil rights, anti-war, environmental, and women's movements, the fall of apartheid and the Soviet Union, the counterculture of the 1960s, and the growth of democracies to an all-time high, I sensed we were moving in the right direction. Now, six decades into this particular incarnation and more clearly understanding the mentality of many of the world's leaders and the power of the military-industrial complex and of the large corporations, I found myself wondering, *At our present rate of expansion of consciousness can we grow quickly enough for the human race to avoid even greater pain, perhaps even a global disaster*? For me, my research into the wisdom of the Maya, and my association with many others on this path, has answered this question and the answer is **YES!!**

But how can this transformation to love happen when the forces against it seem so powerful and so many still seem so asleep? The answer is simple and it is the key message of this book. Very simply stated the ancient Maya have explained that for the last five thousand years the "winds" of human consciousness have been blowing toward *duality*—toward exploitation, exclusion, corruption, dominance and competition. They have been blowing toward *the love of power*. If you were into duality, you had the wind at your back. According to their Mayan calendar, on December 21, 2012, these "winds" will change toward *unity*—toward equality, inclusiveness, integrity, sustainability and cooperation. These winds will be blowing toward *the power of love*.

In reality, we are *now* in the transformation from one *Great Cycle* to another. The shift in these winds started to express itself decades before this cosmic date in 2012. It was discernible through the efforts of Gandhi, Martin Luther King, Jr., Mandela and Archbishop Tutu, Bob Marley and other conscious artists, the environmental and appropriate technology movements, the West opening to the spirituality of the East, and many other expressions of unity that we have seen emerge and grow—in spite of the fact that they were still "flying into the wind."

So for several decades now, we have been living under the aura of an event that has yet to occur. If the Mayan calendar can be believed—and I think after reading this book you will agree it can— soon all expressions of unity and love will, after 5125 arduous years, have the wind at their backs. The world will not end. It will be *transformed*. To prepare ourselves, our families and our world for this transformation, we are only being asked to do one thing—to love and forgive as much as we can.

Is this really possible or just a naïve or delusional fantasy held by a few open-hearted but misguided dreamers? When you think it through, this will *not* happen by governmental laws, religious decrees or commercial endeavors. The *only* way this planet will heal itself through love is by enough individuals becoming more loving in their daily lives. That is *all* it will take and that is *all* we are all being asked to do.

Join us and welcome Home!

Author's note: Many of the ceremonies and reasonings described in this book can be viewed on www.YouTube.com. Just search under "Robert Roskind."

Chapter 1

A Spiritual Scavenger Hunt

Love is creating the biggest transformation in the human world. For thousands of years humans have repressed love. We forgot what love means . . . First, we have to become aware that we are asleep. Then we can awaken . . . This is the prophecy for the new humanity. Human beings will know who they are.
- Don Miguel Ruiz, *Toltec Prophecies*

Our journey to discover the wealth of the Maya—not their physical riches but their spiritual wealth—began around the Winter Solstice on December 21, 2005. That year, our family—my wife, Julia, and our grown daughters, Alicia and Julie—vacationed on Ambris Caye, a peaceful and somewhat remote small island off the coast of Belize, a country with a large Mayan population and many ancient Mayan cities. During that vacation, I was putting the final touches on my latest book, *The Beauty Path:A Native American Journey into One Love.* Like several of my previous books, it chronicles our latest search for messages of unconditional love, in this case from Native American tribes, especially the Hopi.

One day, while we were on Ambris Caye, I wandered alone around San Pedro, the small village on the island. There are only a few vehicles in the village so the pace is very laid back. Its main cobblestone street is lined with galleries and gift shops and an assortment of small beachfront hotels and restaurants. We had all fallen in love with the area as soon as we arrived. I dropped by a small art gallery filled with many Mayan paintings and sculptures. After spending a leisurely hour in the shop talking with the owner, who was in great awe of the Mayan culture, I left feeling a strong desire to visit the historical sites a few hours inland on the mainland where the Maya still lived. Since the beginning of my own spiritual search almost four decades earlier when I was in my twenties, I had occasionally heard about the Mayans and their sacred calendar that

1

mysteriously ended in 2012. *This could be my next book*, I thought. *Maybe the Mayans also had a message of love for the world.*

Inspired and over-caffeinated (sometimes it's hard for me to distinguish between the two), I went across the street to the internet cafe and spent a couple of hours researching the nearby Mayan sites and was delighted to find out there was going to be a gathering that included some Mayan elders the following week during the solstice. It was called Activation Maya 2005 and it was being held near Tikal in Guatemala, several hours inland from the Belize coast.

"I think I might stay a little longer and go seek out the Mayan elders at this gathering," I said to the girls that night over dinner. "You guys want to come?"

Our daughters had other plans that prevented them from extending their vacation. The idea of roaming around the lowlands for another week didn't sound that appealing to Julia, who never likes to be gone too long from our nest.

"Maybe I'll just put you guys on the return flight in Belize City and head out on my own," I said.

They tried to be supportive of my new plans, but I could tell by their looks, from stricken to disappointed, that they didn't cherish the idea of an international return trip without me—the tour guide and detail person of all our vacations. By the next day, not wanting to break up the annual family vacation and not entirely certain this *was* my next step, I had let the idea go, awaiting further guidance as to what to do next.

A few months later, *The Beauty Path* came out. It was our fourth book chronicling our 6-year journey to bring forward the wisdom of several indigenous cultures. Two of our books, *Rasta Heart* and *The Gathering of the Healers,* reveal the wisdom of Rastafari, reggae music and Bob Marley. *Memoirs of an Ex-Hippie* is on the wisdom of the counterculture of the 1960s and 1970s (I was a commune hippie back then and, between escapades, we were seeking—and often found—true wisdom).

Several months passed after the release of *The Beauty Path* and I had still received no guidance on the next book. Without another vision, I was starting to get edgy. In March, I got an email about a one-day seminar on the 2012 Mayan Prophecies to be held the following month in Sedona, Arizona. The seminar featured Mayan calendar researcher Jose Arguelles, the author of *The Mayan*

Factor. Figuring this would be a good way to learn more about the Mayan reality, I called the seminar organizers and asked if they might be interested in our making a presentation about our work, including video footage of both the Native American and Rasta elders. They enthusiastically agreed so we decided to head to Sedona near the Four Corners area of Arizona for the seminar the following month.

We knew this area of Arizona well. While writing *The Beauty Path,* we had been working very closely with Hopi and Havasupai elders whose reservations are near the Four Corners. Eleven miles from the closest road, the Havasupai live on the floor of the Grand Canyon. The Hopi, who have strong ties to the Havasupai, live a couple of hundred miles east on a very remote high mesa. Because of their extreme geographical isolation and their steadfast commitment to their traditional ways, the Hopi are considered the most culturally and spiritually intact of all the Native American tribes. This trip would be a good opportunity to meet with them again, especially with the Hopi elder, Radford Quamahongnewa, and his family. Radford, the "eyes, ears and tongue" of the spiritual leaders of Shungopavi, the Mother Village of the Hopis, is featured in *The Beauty Path.*

The day before the seminar, we flew into Phoenix and drove to Hopiland where we spent a pleasant day visiting Radford and his wife, Lorna, his daughter, Dawn, her husband, Dwayne, and their son, Rad. The next day, we headed to Sedona for our presentation.

Sedona is the "New Age capital" of the U.S., a distinction which is embraced by some locals while shunned by others. The small village is set in a wide valley with pristine Oak Creek running through the middle. Surrounding—and dwarfing—the town on almost all sides are mammoth brilliant rust-colored canyon walls. As soon as you enter the area, it becomes clear why the Indians knew this to be a power spot.

Julia and I checked into our hotel and drove over to a nearby resort where the seminar was being held. We spent an hour with Jose Arguelles before the gathering. At one point, I asked him what he thought about our doing a book on Mayan wisdom or perhaps on the Hawaiian message, another book we were considering. "I'm familiar with both cultures and if I were you, I'd do the book on Hawaiian wisdom," he said with no further elaboration. However, after hearing

3

his presentation later that day on the significance of the Mayan calendar as a harbinger of vast planetary changes, I was more intrigued than ever.

After our presentation, complete with a few brief technical snafus while trying to show our video footage, Lorna and Radford, who had driven down from Hopiland, joined us for dinner.

"You know my uncle, who was a spiritual leader in my village, told me that we are the Mayans' ancestors," Radford said over dinner under the beautiful Arizona sky, with the awe-inspiring red Sedona mountains as our backdrop. "He said that many of our people stayed behind after we migrated from that area in Mexico and Central America and we promised them that one day we would find them again."

The Hopi believe they emerged from the underground Third World into this Fourth World, through a sacred and still-secret passageway from one world to another, called the *sipapu*, in a remote area of the Grand Canyon. After emerging, they were instructed to continue to migrate until they reached their final home. Every few centuries, a certain celestial sign would appear. When that happened, they were instructed that they were to leave their villages, cities, orchards, and fields and continue their migrations. Some stayed, unwilling to leave the home they had known for centuries and everything they had accumulated over a lifetime. Others stayed due to age, infirmity or family situations. The most spiritually attuned continued on.

Radford's uncle had told him that the great Mayan culture and city-states that flourished in Mexico, Belize and Guatemala, were created by Hopis during their migration. When the sign came around 830AD while they were in Central America, many of the tribe deserted their large ceremonial cities in Tikal, Uxmal, Copan, Mayapan and other Central American locations and continued northward. Without their spiritual leadership and ceremonies, the tribe and the cities dissipated into the jungle. Archaeological evidence confirms this date as the time when these palatial ceremonial cities were inexplicably abandoned.

According to Hopi oral history, these spiritual tribal members then settled in the American Southwest and lived for a time as the Anasazi cliff-dwellers. They built villages and ceremonial sites at places like Chaco Canyon and Mesa Verde and when the celestial

4

sign reappeared, they deserted these cities as well (another phenomenon archaeologists have never been able to explain). Around 1100AD, after migrating for millennia through both North and South America, they arrived at their final home—Hopiland, "the Center of the Universe," a remote semi-arid high mesa near present-day Flagstaff, Arizona.

Like the Hopi, the Maya were known for their prophecies concerning major world changes as we transition from the "Fourth to the Fifth World." The Maya even had an exact date for the culmination of this transitional period. According to their ancient and very accurate calendar, the transition would reach its climax on the end date of the 5125-year "Great Cycle" that had begun in August 11, 3113BC (some researchers put the date at 3114BC or 3115BC). That end date was on the Winter Solstice, December 21, 2012.

The Hopi also had a thousand-year-old prophecy that said we would one day leave the Fourth World of conflict and separation and enter the Fifth World of spirituality and unity. However, unlike the Maya, the Hopi had no fixed date for this transition and as Radford had told us, "It could be tomorrow or it could be in a thousand years."

For months after the Sedona symposium and our dinner with Radford and Lorna, our guidance continued to lead us back to the Maya. Like a kid's search game where each clue directs you to the next clue, these synchronistic connections, "JAH-incidences" as Julia calls them, had always led us on our spiritual scavenger hunt.

Researching our books on Rasta and Bob Marley had led us from Jamaica to Arizona to the Hopis and the Havasupais. The Havasupais had adopted Bob Marley's music almost as a tribal drumbeat in the mid-1970s. The Hopis, too, were conscious reggae fans, hosting 72 reggae concerts on their reservations over the last two decades. Now, a new thread of our journey seemed to be emerging leading us from the Hopi to the Maya.

During that spring and summer, I started reading a few books on Maya. The more I read, the more I felt there might be ancient wisdom within their ceremonies, structures, initiations and calendars. We decided that for our next family vacation in December of 2006, we would go to Tikal near Flores, Guatemala. While there, we would see if we felt led to do a book on their wisdom.

5

After searching the web for our upcoming vacation, I found that Activation Maya 2006, their second yearly gathering in Tikal, was being held around the Winter Solstice, just as it had been the year before when I had found it on the web while we were in Belize. This time, our travel plans placed us in the area the same week.

I called the number on the website and told the man who answered that we were planning to vacation in nearby Flores and asked if it would be all right if we dropped by their event to meet some of the Mayan elders.

"No problem, my brother," he replied. "I know both of you. My name is LionFire. I was one of the presenters in Sedona when you were there at Jose Arguelles' seminar. In fact, I helped you fix your DVD player when it was giving you problems. Mayan elder Tata Pedro will be there. Come by and meet him and maybe you could give a presentation one night about your family's journey like you did in Sedona." *Another JAH-incident perhaps?*

Ajq'iij Pedro Cruz García (Tata Pedro as he is affectionately known) is a prominent member of the Mayan Council of the Ancients of Atitlan as well as the 2005 World Ambassador of Peace. This could be our first connection to the Maya.

∞∞∞∞∞∞∞∞∞∞∞∞∞∞∞∞∞∞∞∞∞∞∞∞∞∞∞∞∞∞∞∞∞∞∞

A few months later, in late December, our family flew to Flores. It's not easy to get there. You have to fly to Guatemala City or Cancun and then catch a small plane to nearby Santa Elena. Flores is a beautiful small island-village on Lake Petén Itzá connected to the mainland and the larger village of Santa Elena by a narrow bridge about a hundred yards long and ten yards wide. Three-wheeled taxis zoom back and forth—in their rush to go who knows where—shattering the otherwise relaxed pace.

Aside from that, Flores is very picturesque with ancient, narrow, cobblestone streets flanked by craft shops, and charming pastel-colored buildings. There are several small hotels, guest houses and restaurants, most with lake views and lakeside dining.

The Flores/Santa Elena area is now the capital of the Petén region, with a population of around 15,000. Flores' history is very deep and rich. The Itzá, a Guatemalan ethnic group of Maya

6

affiliation speaking the Itzá dialect, left the Yucatan region in the 13th century and built Flores, known as Tayasal, as their capital. They called it *Noh Petén*, or literally "City Island." It was here on the island of Flores on the shore of Lake Petén Itzá that the last independent state of the Maya civilization held out against the onslaught of the Spanish conquerors. In 1541, Spanish Conquistador Hernando Cortes came to the island on his way to Honduras, but, finding nothing of value, he did not try to conquer it. The Spanish did not subdue the island until 1697 when they marched in, attacked via boats and destroyed it. From the ruins of *Noh Petén* arose the post-conquest village of Flores.

Flores and Santa Elena, its grittier neighbor on the other end of the short causeway, are vibrant small villages catering to the locals as well as the tourists who often stay there when visiting Tikal, about an hour's drive away. Many restaurants open at four in the morning to catch the tourists before they head out to view Tikal at dawn.

The four of us wandered the streets together shopping for gifts and eating at a floating restaurant. The prices were very reasonable—Guatemala being one of the few good deals left for tourists as the U.S. dollar continues its decline. The evening was hot and muggy, but a pleasant wind was coming off the lake. The town seemed surprisingly quiet given that this was their tourist season.

We were enjoying the night, catching up on the details of each other's lives. After dinner, we walked across the bridge and decided to stop at a store to get a few supplies. We were directed by some locals to the largest store in Santa Elena, a block or two from our hotel.

We wandered over and entered the Santa Elena version of Wal-Mart, a high-ceilinged, brightly-lit box store about the size of a mid-sized grocery. They sold everything from food to bicycles to fans to televisions. It was a few days before Christmas and the store was packed with marimba music blaring loudly and everyone in the midst of their frantic Christmas shopping. We all immediately became disoriented. It was hard to imagine that peaceful Flores was only a few hundred yards away. Glad to be out of the commercial frenzy we thought we had left in the States, we quickly got what we needed and left, retreating to the quiet of our small lakefront hotel.

Our second night in Flores, Julia and I drove over to the Activation Maya gathering in a nearby village to make our presentation. We were both excited about meeting Tata Pedro and seeing where this connection might lead.

"Tata Pedro left yesterday," LionFire said as he greeted us, half-apologetically.

"You're kidding," I said, unable to conceal my disappointment, having just traveled over 2000 miles hoping to meet this man.

"It's complicated. Things got very intense before he left," LionFire said. "But everyone is looking forward to your presentation tonight."

About 40 or 50 people, mostly young Americans, were attending this 8-day gathering with "elders and shamans," some real, some self-appointed. We later learned that one of the organizers, Aum-Rak, wanted Tata Pedro to shorten his two-hour ceremonies, feeling they were too long for the attention span of many of the people gathered there and it would not encourage them to return in the following years. This was something Tata Pedro could not do. It would be like asking a priest to shorten the mass or a Native American elder to shorten the Sun Dance. Aum-Rak was adamant so Tata Pedro left—his dignity and ceremonies intact.

Everybody at the gathering was still struggling with the upsetting exit of the elder they had come so far to meet. They, like us, were disappointed to be deprived of access to his wisdom. *We've missed our chance to meet with the elder*, I thought. *Maybe we're not meant to write a book on Mayan wisdom.*

Most of the participants were staying at the Gringo Perdido, a modest backpacker hotel where we would be giving our talk shortly after dinner. The hotel was located in the small village of El Remate, twenty miles west of Flores, where we were staying. Both towns are situated on Lake Petén Itza, a beautiful 40-mile long lake set like a jewel in the rain forest and rolling hills of the Guatemalan lowlands. The hotel was one of the many in the area catering mostly to young backpackers and eco-tourists on a budget. Its modestly priced rooms included a bed with a mosquito net, a chair and small table, and a ceiling fan—just the necessities, nothing more. The dining room was an open pavilion area overlooking the lake.

After dinner, we moved the dining room tables aside and set

out chairs in a semi-circle around a computer screen set up to show video footage of our journey. The setting that night was ideal—an open-air gathering spot on a beautiful lake. The evening was cool and, after awhile, mosquito-free. The crowd seemed open-hearted and open-minded. There was nothing to break their attention and create angst for an early conclusion—no TV, no internet, no radio, no bars, no private air-conditioned rooms, no cellphone service—nothing! nada! With a captive audience, it was a storyteller's dream. I enjoyed every minute!

My presentation covered our spiritual odyssey to bring forth the wisdom of both the Rastas and the Native Americans, showing live footage of our reasonings with their elders. Also, we showed footage of our One Love concerts and events in Jamaica and the U.S. Since 2003, we had organized and hosted over 50 of these free concerts in Jamaica, often held at ghetto and rural schools, as well as large public concerts on Bob Marley's birthday (February 6). We had also hosted over 20 in the U.S. at Native American reservations, prisons, colleges and public venues. The concerts featured both local and internationally known conscious recording artists, such as Abijah, Luciano, Bunny Wailer, Culture and others. We also invited speakers known for their message of love. All donated their time and talent at no charge.

Some concerts were at small schools, others at large ones with thousands of students lining the courtyard. One of our most moving concerts was at Hopiland High School where we watched 850 Native American students rush the stage and sing in unison all the words to every Bob Marley song performed—the inspiring words of a man who had been long dead before any of them were born. Our largest concert was on February 6, 2005, Bob Marley's 60th birthday. It featured over thirty of the island's top conscious recording artists and speakers. The concert, held in the Kingston central business district and in conjunction with the Jamaican government, was attended by over 15,000 live with over two million watching on television or listening on radio across the island.

We ended our presentation at the Gringo Perdido with a videotaped reasoning of Radford, who in his calm, dignified and humble way, told us about his people's thousand-year old covenant with the Creator to become the first *Hopi*—the Peaceful People—to serve as a pattern for all humanity. We also relayed the message

9

Radford gave us before we left for Guatemala: that the Hopi would never forget their southern relatives and that one day they would seek them out.

As we headed out, several people came up to chat with us, including a handsome young Guatemalan man who introduced himself as Danny Diaz. Unfortunately, we had run over time and we knew the friend who had driven us over wanted to get home to his family so we were unable to really connect with anyone. We told Danny that we hoped we would see him again, perhaps a few days later on the Solstice at Tikal.

"You know, I really liked Danny," Julia said as we drove away. "I wish we had more time to connect with him. I hope we link up with him again."

∞∞∞∞∞∞∞∞∞∞∞∞∞∞∞∞∞∞∞∞∞∞∞∞∞∞∞∞∞∞∞∞∞∞∞∞∞

The concept that the Hopi were once the Mayans was given another mystical twist in a legend I began reading before our trip. It seems that within the prophecies of the some Native American tribes and within the Incas and Q'eros of Peru and the Runa of Mexico, is the story that one day the indigenous people of South America (metaphorically referred to as "the Condor of the South") would join again with the indigenous people of North America ("the Eagle of the North") to usher in a global purification and a new cycle. Some even say the quetzal bird of Central America is part of this myth.

This prophecy was retold at the *Encuentro*, The First Continental Meeting of Indigenous Peoples on the 500 Years of Indian Resistance. Held in Quito, Ecuador in 1990, it was attended by many tribes from North and South America including Yanomanis, Mapuches, Kunas, Quechuas, Caribs, Navajos, Hopis, Lummis, Lumbees, Osages, Inuits, Crees and Seminoles. According to the ancient Runa prophecy, the people of Mesoamerica passed through many trials and tribulations and were eventually dispersed into the four cardinal directions. Prophets instructed the elders to maintain their traditions during this diaspora and to search for a path to liberation.

Every 500 years, the prophecy stated, the life of the nation would be nourished and renewed. The tribulations began about 500

10

years ago when Cortez landed in the Yucatan in 1519, so *now* is a renewal period. In our time, the beginning of this liberation would be symbolized by the prophecy retold at the *Encuentro*: "When the Condor of the South and the Eagle of the North come together again, the union of their tears will heal the wounds of the Indian peoples and fortify their spirit, body and thought. A new generation will spring forth who will reach out their hands to end oppression, exploitation and injustice and will write the word *Liberty* in the sky." A life-size image of an eagle and a condor being joined together by a man is clearly etched into the cornerstone, which is dated to at least 1165AD, of the rarely-visited central pyramid at Mayapan on the Yucatan Peninsula near Merida, Mexico.

It is becoming clear that many indigenous people are bringing forward their wisdom in these times to assist with the re-unification. This ancient life-asserting, earth-honoring wisdom has the power to restore planetary balance and to assist others in making the transition from the old to the new world. The collective knowledge of the indigenous peoples of the Americas in these times is critical to successfully make this transition.

Since the 1990s, there have been many gatherings to bring together elders of North and South American tribes, many held in ancient Mayan cities in Central America and at Lake Titicaca in Peru. The prophecy is also playing itself out on a wider world-stage. In September of 2006, Bolivian President Evo Morales, the country's first indigenous president, arrived in New York to attend the United Nations General Assembly session. The first thing he did was to request a "frank and substantive" meeting with the Native American leaders including those from the Haudenosaunee (Iroquois), Lakota and Cree nations.

"It was a meeting between the eagle and the condor," said Tonya Frichner, founder of the New York-based American Indian Law Alliance, an indigenous rights group, which organized the meeting in collaboration with the United Nations Indigenous Peoples' Forum. "It was a very significant meeting in our struggles. For him to honor us by meeting with our traditional leaders is another step in the undeniable presence of indigenous peoples in international advocacy, especially human rights."

11

Chapter 2

Mayan Healing
Dr. Rosita Arvigo

Thus, as we arrive at the completion of creation . . . the divine reality will be clearly visible, and our vision will be unobscured by darkening filters. At that point we will simply know the truth and there will be no need for explanations. This truth will be evident as we see the light of God.
        -Carl John Calleman, *The Mayan Calendar: Solving the Greatest Mystery of Our Times*

The next day we left Julie and Alicia at our hotel in Flores and we hired a driver and drove two and a half hours over the border to the village of San Ignacio, Belize. We were heading to San Ignacio to meet with a world-renowned herbalist and healer, Dr. Rosita Arvigo. We had decided to add a trip to visit Dr. Arvigo because two different friends had told us about Rosita and her work studying with traditional Mayan healers. We figured it would be worthwhile to meet with her and to bring forward this vital piece of Mayan wisdom. I emailed her about coming to visit and she readily agreed.

I typically rent a car and to drive myself whenever we travel, preferring not to entrust our safety into the hands of local drivers—many of whom seem to have some kind of perverse death wish. However, in this case I had no choice. The rental company would not allow me to drive the car over the border.

The road was pretty good until about an hour from the border where it turned from a paved road with occasional potholes to a deeply rutted muddy road that bounced us all over the inside of the car and made us wonder if the trip was really worth it. Except for a

12

few large cargo trucks and a few small taxi vans heading to the border, there was almost no traffic.

"How do these trucks drive these hills in the rainy season?" I asked Willie, our driver. The hills were very steep and I knew the annual rains must turn the road into soup.

"You remember that large bulldozer we passed at the bottom of the big hill?" he replied. "Well, during the rainy season they use that to pull the trucks up the hill. Then they can make it."

The small border crossing went smoothly, with only one or two people in line. Willie had to stop on the other side to get a one-day insurance policy for driving in Belize. The half-hour drive from the border to San Ignacio, where Dr. Arvigo lived, continued on paved roads through the beautiful rolling hills. We passed through one small village with many Chinese restaurants and businesses. Willie had no idea how they happened to settle there.

I had been researching Dr. Arvigo on the Internet and learned a little of her history. Born in Chicago, with a degree in naprapathy (a branch of medicine that focuses on the evaluation and treatment of neuro-musculoskeletal conditions), Dr. Arvigo and her husband, Greg, along with their daughter, Crystal, moved to San Ignacio in the late 1970s. They bought six acres of the remote rainforest, at that time accessible only by a six-mile boat trip. She soon met Don Elijio Panti, a 90-year old Mayan shaman and healer, famous throughout that part of the Americas. He was the last recipient of the 1000-year oral knowledge of Mayan natural cures and remedies. At his peak, he treated 5000 people each year, mostly at no charge.

Don Elijio, who passed away in 1996 at the age of 103, took Rosita under his wing as his apprentice, beginning of her three-decade long devotion for learning and teaching the healing modalities of the Mayans. Dr. Arvigo also studied with Hortence Robinson, a 73 year-old herbal midwife of Belize who has been delivering babies since she was 13. Dr. Rosita Arvigo is now a naprapathic physician, a master herbalist and recognized authority on Mayan healing techniques and Central American medicinal plants.

It has been Dr. Arvigo's passion and quest to preserve traditional healing practices and rescue healing plants from areas where the rainforest is being destroyed. Through her seminars and classes, attended by healers from many countries, she is also

13

bringing the simple and safe healing techniques of the Central American *sobaderas* (healers) to North America and Europe, where they are so needed. Toward this goal, she has studied with dozens of traditional healers and midwives.

She was the founder and director of Ix Chel Tropical Research Foundation, an organization dedicated to the preservation and study of medicinal rainforest plants. Additionally, she worked for nine years with Dr. Michael Balick of The New York Botanical Garden to collect medicinal plants for research at The National Cancer Institute, sending them over 3000 plants to study. Given that only a few thousand of the planet's 250,000 plant species have been extensively screened for their therapeutic potential, and the few hundred plant-based prescription drugs are derived from under 100 species, this work is much needed.

She is also the founder and, until recently, president of The Traditional Healers' Foundation in Belize, which works to support traditional healers. She established the Rainforest Medicine Trail, which has since been taken over by the Lodge at Chaa Creek.

The newsletter, *The Tree of Life,* is about her work. She maintains her small private practice in Belize and now is mostly teaching and offering seminars and classes for other healers. Rosita has also authored several well-respected books, including: *Spiritual Bathing:Healing Rituals & Traditions from Around the World, Rainforest Remedies:100 Healing Plants of Belize, Sastun:My Apprenticeship with a Maya Healer,* and *Rainforest Home Remedies:The Maya Way to Heal Your Body and Replenish Your Soul.*

We arrived at Rosita's office, a modest cinder-block building on the outskirts of the village, a little before lunch. Rosita, a focused and intelligent woman, welcomed us in and after introductions and an explanation of our work and why we had come, the three of us settled around her kitchen table. Her kitchen was small, clean and rather barren as she was in the midst of a move to other quarters. We told her about our travels, especially about our recent journeys with the Hopi.

"There is one of the Mayan dialects that is so similar to the Hopi language that they can understand each other," she said. "There are twenty-five Mayan dialects. It was the dialect of the Mopan from this area and in Petén. It is clearly a root language of the Hopi. They were invited to a Hopi ceremony in Arizona and found out that they could understand each other."

"Rosita, let me ask you about the Mayan healing practices," I said, after I told her more of our Hopi connection. "What is the limit of your holistic healing? Are there things that can't be healed? Is it a matter of the patient's beliefs or faith?"

"Well, I think it depends on whether it's a healer that works specifically in spiritual healing or physical healing," she said. "If you don't get results within a reasonable amount of time, either they don't understand the illness or they're not treating it properly. Maybe you think it's just a cough but it may actually be a lung infection. I put it in three categories. If it's an acute problem, like a bad backache, I expect it to be better in three treatments. If it's a stomach problem, I expect it to get better in three days using herbal remedies. If it's a spiritual problem, I expect it to get better after the first treatment but if I don't get any results by the third treatment, I would have to refer. This is not universal but it's how I work."

"Have you found that you can help most people that come to you?" I asked.

"I would say most people but not everybody," she answered.

"Our brother-in-law, Alan, has been battling cancer for years. Could that be healed with your techniques?" I asked. Alan, a kind and gentle soul, was in a 15-year struggle with cancer, a struggle he and my sister, Susan, handled with grace and equanimity. In the months shortly before our trip, things had become critical and Julia and I were spending weeks living with them near their home in Washington, D.C. Far from morose or anxious, this was a peaceful, loving time as all of us put our lives on hold and just spent time enjoying each other and the many family and friends that flowed through their home.

"I don't treat cancer," she quickly answered. "It scares me, to be perfectly honest. I used to treat it but I had three patients die in three months. There was too much grief so I prefer not to go there. I usually don't treat terminal illnesses. My specialty is household remedies for common ailments. That's really where I shine. And I also focus on all things having to do with women's health. I tend to treat women and children, using especially what Don Elijio taught me about uterine massage. I've also added a great deal to it. I've studied and researched it for about thirty-five years."

15

"This uterine massage, is this something that the Mayans were doing hundreds of years ago?" I asked, "or is this something developed recently?"

"This is specific to all Native Americans," she answered. "I don't think it's specific to just the Mayans. I've talked to people from Native American tribes who say that their aunts or their grandmothers used to do it. Most native people all over the world know about uterine massage. I met a 99-year old Moroccan native healer and I showed her my massage. Then, she showed me her massage and it was 90 percent the same. This is something in the universal consciousness. It's something that people have always had because it's so necessary."

"The uterus moves around?" I asked.

"Yes. We call it the 'wandering womb.' We have come to believe that it's unusual to find a woman that has a womb in the proper position and we have a list of about thirty-six ailments that it can cause, all of which are correctable and preventable with the massage. We add other things to it like steams or castor oil packs for fibroids or a uterine meditation to get in contact with the consciousness of the uterus so it can talk to the woman and tell how it got to this stage and what it needs. The emotional history of the uterus can also be discovered through this guided meditation."

"Emotional history? Like trauma, abortion, things like that?" I asked.

"Or incest or shame and guilt that are related to the genitals," she said. "This is something that everybody shares. A common thing that moves the uterus is lifting heavy burdens during menstruation or too soon after childbirth. Even severe falls from doing gymnastics or pushing too long or hard during childbirth or even wearing high heels or back problems or repressed emotions, can also lead to that."

"If people cannot come here, where else can they go to get a uterine massage?" I asked.

"I've trained about five hundred people and you can find them on the web under arvigomassage.com. They're all over the world—doctors, nurses, acupuncturists, physical therapists. I've been training people to do Mayan abdominal massage, which is not just for the uterus. It addresses the prostate and all the digestive organs. If you think about all the problems people can have from the rib cage to the pelvis, that's most of our problems other than skeletal and joint problems—all the things that can happen with stomach problems—indigestion, irritable bowel syndrome, acid reflux, colitis, gastritis, liver problems. We even have good results with Type 2 diabetes, which turns out to be linked to pretty strong emotional trauma that settles into a person's solar plexus. The diaphragm contracts and cuts off the blood supply to the pancreas and then the liver. We've been able to reverse Type 2 diabetes with this abdominal massage."

"What kinds of problems do uterine massages clear up for women?" I asked.

"Ovarian cysts, frequent urination, uterine bleeding, painful periods, too much or too little flow of blood, late or early periods, inability to conceive or chronic miscarriages or early or painful delivery."

"What percentage of the women treated by you gets relief?" I asked. "I know you don't know about the people you trained."

"I do know because everybody has to hand in fifty case studies. By now I've read fifteen thousand case studies. The easiest thing to alleviate is painful periods, backache, frequent urination, swelling prostates with men. We have a 90 percent success rate, maybe higher, even with the very elderly. This is all with external massage. And as far as fertility problems are concerned, we have a 50 percent success rate. Eating chicken is a problem for couples that are having trouble conceiving. Chicken is laced with estrogen to get them fat fast. It used to be twenty-four weeks from egg to market as a full-grown chicken. Now because most chicken-feed is laced with an estrogen compound, it's six weeks.

"In my point of view, it's the primary cause of fibroids, polyps, infertility, PMS. It's in the eggs, the dairy, even some of the beef. It is even sprayed on some vegetables to stop the bugs from reproducing. Many couples in their twenties can't get pregnant. Either the male has too low of a sperm count because he's estrogen-dominant or the female can't ovulate because she's estrogen-dominant. And if people are eating meat, they should try to get estrogen-free meat and only eat it two or three times a week. If you eat beef, it's the same because the body needs three days to rid itself of the uric acid after you eat meat. I believe some people need to eat meat. It depends on your blood type. But it should be organically grown."

17

"In which situations is it best to rely on modern Western medicine techniques?" I asked.

"Emergency medicine, stitching, repairing," she quickly answered, probably having heard this question many times before. "Sometimes people need surgery. Often I've recommended surgery, especially for women with fibroids. What I find is what is very difficult for Western medicine is easy for alternative physicians and what is easy for them is difficult for us."

"Could you give me some examples?" I asked.

"Well, like gastritis or backache. Doctors don't know what they are doing there. It should be against the law for medical doctors to treat people with backaches. They mess them up with painkillers and muscle relaxers or surgery when what people need is some really good body treatments. They need to get their hips and shoulders in proper alignment, the spinal column aligned and then the muscles soften and let go of their spasms. The muscle relaxers doctors prescribe often cause constipation because they also relax the muscles of the intestines. The painkillers can be devastating to the nervous system, the mind, and you can't stay on them for very long. When you stop using them, you have a backache that's actually worse. The painkillers made you think you were out of danger, and so you've been doing things that you shouldn't be doing. Pain is a message. The brain is telling the body to stop, rest, relax and give it time to heal." (The Journal of the American Medical Association reported in February of 2008 that though spending by Americans on spine and back treatments had risen 65% from 1997 to 2005, their backs were not getting any better.)

"We've seen the problems with painkillers recently," I said. "A few weeks ago, we went to Washington to be with my sister and brother-in-law. When we got there, nobody thought Alan would live through the week. He was taking morphine for the pain. It took two of us thirty minutes to walk him to the bathroom and that's all he did all day except sleep. He couldn't eat because of the chemotherapy and morphine. He was mentally, physically and emotionally out of it. But then, on his oncologist's discreet advice, we switched him from morphine to marijuana and by the time we left three weeks later, he was walking a mile to the restaurant to eat a full meal. That was about a month ago and he's still much better."

"Those prescription drugs might have killed him," Rosita

18

said. "For what you've just described, marijuana is the treatment of choice. They say that the best use is with sesame oil in a capsule. It hits the blood stream much more quickly and effectively. You get a quart of sesame oil and a half a quart of dried marijuana. Mix them together and put the mixture in the oven overnight with just the pilot light on, for ten or twelve hours, at about one hundred degrees. The next day, strain it and put it into capsules or take it in half teaspoon doses or put it in dropper bottles. You should take it on an empty stomach. The marijuana should be squeezed through a muslin cloth to get all the nectar out. It can be used for people with severe dental problems and for those who can't take pain relievers or have backaches that prevent them from being able to move."

(In February of 2008, one of the largest and most prestigious physician organizations, the 124,000-member American College of Physicians, endorsed the use of medical marijuana, calling for full legal protection for medical marijuana patients and increased funding for marijuana research.)

"And by the way, you said you were going to tour Tikal tomorrow. If you do, try to find a guide named Luis Arturo Gonzalez. He's a very spiritual guide. He does a spiritual tour with a beautiful, heart-felt presentation. There were once many Mayan spirits in Tikal, but most have left."

"Have you experienced these spirits?" I asked.

"I work with them in the sense of prayers and offerings and they bring me dream-visions," she answered. "I have lots of dream-visions that come from the Mayan spirits by way of guidance and explanation—about healing, about life, about a certain plant, or it might just be time to make contact."

"What are your thoughts about 2012?" I asked.

"I don't believe that it's the physical end to life as we know it. Five hundred years from 1519, the day that Cortes landed in the new world, ends in 2019. That's seven years from 2012 to 2019. I feel this period is a transition between the final end of hell on earth that we are now experiencing. I think the major transition is going to be all for the best. We will be coming out of the underworld and going into the upperworld. We are in the crossroads between the old world and the new world and of course there's going to be tremendous disruptions of energetic forces, which is what we are seeing. What doesn't serve us will fade. What serves us, what teaches love, will come to fruition."

"Before we head out, is there anything else you'd like to say through our book?" I asked.

"Yes. I think the most important aspect of Mayan medicine is the spiritual healing and the spiritual healing is based on love—the transference of love of the human being that comes as a channel from the Mayan spirits and the Great Creator God. It comes in the manifestation of prayer, of burning copal incense and of spiritual paths. This is how love is transferred through spiritual healing that can also affect physical manifestations. It's not just about herbal remedies. It's not just about massage. A great deal of my healing has to do with my spiritual healing. It's about a person opening up to themselves, of forgiving themselves, forgiving others and trying not to judge any human being. We all make mistakes. The lack of forgiveness is what would prevent love from channeling through from the Mayan spirits."

After lunch together, we headed back to Flores feeling the bumpy journey had been well worth the effort.

"Willie, do you know a Tikal guide named Luis Arturo Gonzalez?" Julia asked as we drove back to Flores. "We're going there in the morning and Rosita recommended him."

The possibility of having not just a physical tour of the Tikal but a spiritually-oriented one as well was right up our alley.

"Yes," he answered. "I know Luis. Do you want me to find him for you?"

"Yes, please," we answered.

Willie stopped at several houses and a cantina in El Remate. Everyone knew Luis but nobody knew where he was. Willie finally got his cell number and reached him by phone. He arranged for us to pick Luis up on our way to Tikal in the morning. Luis later told us if our call had come a few minutes later, he would have committed to another group and we would have missed going out with him.

Chapter 3

Tikal

Human consciousness is rapidly transitioning to a new state, a new intensity of awareness that will manifest as a different understanding, a transformed realization, of time and space and self. By this thesis, the transition is already under way—though largely subliminally—and will become increasingly evident as we approach the year 2012.
- Daniel Pinchbeck, *2012: The Return of Quetzalcoatl*

That night, after returning from Rosita's, we wandered around Flores with our daughters. All of us were excited to visit the ancient Mayan city we had heard so much about and to meet Luis. We left early the next morning. Halfway to Tikal from Flores, we picked up Luis where he was waiting in El Remate at the pre-arranged spot. He hopped in the van with Julia, Julie, Alicia and me and instantly the tour began—and continued for the next six hours.

Luis is a vibrant, intense man who looks to be in his forties, though he may be older. Trim and fit, his features are more African than Mayan or Spanish. He talks rapidly but clearly, pulling his thoughts and information together from a vast storehouse of scientific and archaeological information and spiritual understanding. You quickly realize that this is a very intelligent, very devoted, and yet very humble, man. We all liked him immediately.

After a half-hour drive, we arrived in Tikal, stopping first at the visitors' center—complete with its shops, restaurant and miniature model of the site—before taking the 30-minute walk to the ancient city. Though words can never do Tikal justice, here are a few facts. It is the largest, most impressive and magnificent of the ancient cities of the Mayan civilization. It is now part of Guatemala's 222-square-mile Parque Nacional Tikal. It is a UNESCO World Heritage spot frequented by thousands of tourists every year from around the world. This vast Mayan ceremonial city sits on lowlands and is ringed by virgin rainforest. Here there are thousands of plant species, including the conspicuous gigantic ceiba tree (the sacred tree of the Maya, from which they make their sacred copal incense), as well as spider and howler monkeys, toucans, green parrots, macaws, coatimundis, ocellated turkeys, and perhaps at night, even an occasional jaguar.

Tikal, which in Itzá Maya means "Place of Voices" or "Place of Whispers," was one of the major cultural and population centers of the Maya civilization. Discovered by the outside world in 1848, monumental architecture was built here as early as the 4th century BC. It was here, where a fusion of the Toltecs from the great ceremonial city of Teotihuacan in Mexico and the Mayan tribes of the Petén area, that began the true rise of the Mayan civilization that quickly spread throughout the area to Copan, Quirigua and Palenque.

The main structures of Tikal cover over two-and-a-half square miles. The city was at its height in the Mayan Classic Period from approximately 200-830AD, reaching a peak population of between 100,000 to 200,000 in a total environ of over 23 square miles—at a time when London was a muddy village of a few hundred. At its peak, it grew to a vast commercial and military power that ruled the area to a degree never before seen in Mesoamerica.

Tikal is only one of a huge network of massive Mayan ceremonial cities scattered throughout the region. Recent satellite imagery has revealed yet many more structures under the dense and remote Central American jungles. Almost all of them rival the grandeur of the ancient Egyptian archaeological sites, which were constructed three thousand years earlier. Most of the major Mayan sites include towering stepped pyramids, astronomically-aligned plazas and ceremonial buildings, all covered with hieroglyphs that have only recently been deciphered.

Many sites also included an astronomical domed-shaped observatory very similar to modern observatories. In the Pyramid of Kukulcan in the ancient Mayan city of Chichen Itza in the Yucatan, a natural phenomenon occurs every year at the spring equinox: the sunlight creates a shadow of a plumed serpent undulating and descending down the pyramid's stairs. Equally amazing, *National Geographic Today* reported in 2002 that if you clap your hands in front of the 1100-year-old pyramid, it will echo back an *exact* imitation of the voice of the quetzal bird, long held sacred by the Maya and thought to represent Quetzalcoatl (also called Kukulcan), their revered teacher of love.

Even more puzzling is that this great city-state civilization seems to have sprung out of nowhere. From an earlier, much simpler and less-developed civilization that gave no indication it was soon to birth such a complex and highly-advanced offspring. In 200-400AD, when the Maya began building their great ceremonial centers in stone, their systems of hieroglyphs, astronomical calculations and mathematics came forth fully formed and flawless in every detail. As is the case with the Egyptian Great Pyramid at Giza (which was built to a greater exactness than the space shuttle), there seems to be no trial-and-error period, no formative stages. Indeed, the Mayas ascent is as enigmatic as their decline centuries later.

Though only a fraction of the buildings at Tikal have been excavated in decades of archaeological work, the city contains hundreds of significant ancient buildings. Built during the city's height from the late 7th to the early 9th century, six very large Mesoamerican stepped pyramids with temples on their tops are located in the large ceremonial area.

The largest, Temple-pyramid IV or The Bichepalous Serpent Temple, is 230 feet high and was dedicated in 720AD. Temple V is from around 750AD and is the only one where no tomb has been found. The ancient city also has the remnants of royal palaces, a number of smaller pyramids, residences, and inscribed stone monuments. If the hieroglyphs have been correctly interpreted, Tikal dominated the central Mayan lowlands by frequent warfare and either being in alliances, or in conflicts, with many other Mayan city-states, including Uaxactun, Caracol, Dos Pilos, Naranjo and Calakmul.

To the Maya, the pyramids represented the sacred mountains, home to the life-giving and all-pervasive *maize*—corn. (The staple of the Mayan, Hopi and other indigenous diet, maize was, and is, revered.) *Maize* is intertwined with the Mayan reality—physically, mystically and emotionally. Indeed, the ancient Maya believed that humans were created from corn dough after two failed attempts to create us from mud and then wood. Many indigenous people believe that corn was one of the greatest gifts from the Creator and revere it with an almost religious devotion. Given that scientists have never

23

been able to ascertain its wild ancestor and that corn will *not* grow without human intervention, the indigenous beliefs probably contains more truth than modern botanists could ever understand.

The grandeur of these and the thousands of other ancient Mayan cities is matched only by their simplicity. The temples are mainly constructed out of limestone which was very important for construction because it also provided lime for plaster and stucco used to cover the walls. Since they used only stone tools, archaeologists refer to the ancient Maya as "Stone Age" people. This label is semantic only. It can never do justice to the high level of civilization they reached—a level the scientific community has only recently acknowledged equals or surpasses that of the ancient Egyptian pyramid builders.

These ancient structures mapped out the Earth's revolution around the sun with the exactness of modern-day calculations; they recorded the orbital cycles of Mercury, Venus, Mars, Jupiter, and Saturn; recorded the 25,920-year Precession of the Equinoxes, kept calendars of both lunar and solar eclipses and predicted exactly when the earth and sun would align with the center of the Milky Way—an event that occurs every 28,500 years and *will* occur in 2012—all without our modern precision instruments.

Some researchers find comfort in considering the ancient Maya almost as cultural idiot savants who just happened upon this complex knowledge that they developed. After all, they reason, the Maya did not use the wheel, had no beasts of burden or metallurgy—all signs of advancing civilization. Also, they were obviously "heathens" who had to be brutally brought into the "one true Church." However, what they developed on so many levels—in their architecture, their astronomy, their mathematics, their calendars, their level of social civilization, and their worldview—can never be dismissed as just a developmental lucky fluke.

Around 830AD, the people of Tikal, along with those of many of Mayan city-states, mysteriously deserted their grand city, built no new major monuments, burned some of their palaces, and by the end of the 10th century, the site was abandoned. Though it has been speculated that these cities were abandoned after 500 to 600 years of intense activities because of internal revolution, environmental degradation, drought, etc., the riddle as to why the Mayans *consciously* and *deliberately* abandoned their great centers has never been solved. It is one of the most baffling archeological mysteries of all time.

They left behind architecture, artwork and scientific and astronomical achievements that rivaled the highest levels achieved by other ancient civilizations such as the Egyptians, the Greeks, the T'ang Dynasty of China and the Gupta Dynasty of India. However, as we will soon see, these achievements, as great as they are, are perhaps dwarfed by the awesome value—even to those of us living today—of their spiritual calendars. And because they were one of the last of the ancient civilizations to be crushed by the brutal European invaders, their footprints are some of the *freshest*.

The Toltecs, a Yucatan-Mexican branch of the Mayan civilization, appeared in the area at the end of the tenth century. All followed the teachings of a spiritual and secular leader called Quetzalcoatl or Kukulcan. This ended the Classic Mayan period (200-830AD) and began what is referred to as the post-Classic Mayan era (900-1520AD).

Though they continued to build grand ceremonial centers like Uxmal and Chichén Itzá for awhile, they no longer recorded dates and astronomical data in stone but rather on paper codices. All but four of the thousands of these books or codices—the *Popul Vuh, The Books of Chilam Balam, The Dresden Codex* and *The Annals of the Cachiquiles*—were destroyed by the Spanish clerics who arrived with the conquistadors in the 1500s and believed them to be works of the devil. However, none of these books that survived the invasion revealed any information of the earlier Maya from the Classic period that ended in 830AD.

Another change occurred from the Classic to post-Classic period. Warfare and human sacrifice became pervasive, as the people veered from their original spiritual teachings. By 1441, a hundred years *before* the Spanish conquistadors arrived, the Maya civilization was collapsing in chaos and disunity. By the time the Spanish arrived, these magnificent Mayan cities had been long abandoned and the Maya had left their urban life and retreated into rural villages in the jungle. It is almost as if, out of nowhere, this area of the world experienced a Golden Age during its Classic period—an age marked by high-minded teachings, the construction of magnificent ceremonial centers and the creation of sacred calendars that reveal the Creator's unfolding plan. Then their culture collapsed. No one has been able to really determine why.

By 1697, 170 years *after* Cortes arrived with brutal frenzy, disease and lust for gold, Maya as a political and economic society was at an end. Later, the Aztec would re-occupy these Mayan's ceremonial centers. However, as a culture, Maya remains vital to this day, and in places, they are still keeping alive their sacred calendar

The Tikal temples still sit majestically—but abandoned and decaying. Their black and gray mottled surfaces are only remnants of their long-faded beauty. They were once covered in bright red or pastel colors, patterns and artwork. Artists' renderings of what these temples once looked like are awe-inspiring. However, it is not just the sheer size and splendor of these architectural monuments that is impressive. Here, created in massive stone buildings, stelaes and glyphs, like an ancient calling card from a highly intelligent people, is a wealth of astronomical and astrological information, much of which is more accurate than that derived from modern-day telescopes and computer research. Indeed, as we shall see, these calendrics are not only a record of the celestial movements but may well be a roadmap of the future of humanity and the Universe.

Before our trip, I had started to do some reading on the ancient Maya and found all of this archaeological, architectural and astronomical information compelling. However, it was not really this information Julia and I were seeking. It would only be the backdrop to frame the story of our search for any wisdom the ancient or modern Maya might possess that would lead to an ever-increasing expansion of love on the planet. Great scientific and astrological knowledge and the ability to build impressive cities do not in and of themselves reflect true wisdom—as evidenced by our modern world. Our goal was to advance the healing of the planet through unconditional love, as it was the lack of love that we believe has created so many of our problems. This was the search that had brought us to Tikal.

∞∞∞∞∞∞∞∞∞∞∞∞∞∞∞∞∞∞∞∞∞∞∞∞∞∞∞∞∞∞∞∞∞∞∞∞

As Luis and our family headed up toward the ceremonial center, we passed the group from Activation Maya doing a ceremony around a massive ceiba tree. We waved, but continued on our journey with Luis not wanting to interrupt what we knew would be a very informative and inspiring tour with him. A couple of people from the group peeled off and joined us.

"This is the only high-canopy forest in Central America that has never been logged. There are many jaguars still here," Luis said as we approached the first structures, a series of low, squat mold-covered buildings. "This is not just an archaeological site, but primarily a spiritual center. It will activate your chakras. Send out positive energy with the mind and the heart and love will bounce back at you. You will bring the positive straight into you. Just as we have these chakras, the planet has them as well and just as we can do acupressure and acupuncture to heal our bodies, we can also do them for the planet. We are coming to a very crucial moment in the life of our planet. The entire planet is about to reincarnate."

"What does that mean?" I asked.

"That we are increasing our vibrational frequency from about eight percent to about twenty-five percent," Luis said as we passed through a short archway at the entrance. "That is happening about now. We will be able to work miracles again like we did in the past. The angel within humankind is starting to wake up. We will be getting help from other dimensions or we would not make it. We are now going to enter the energy part of Tikal."

We walked a short distance and Luis led us into a small stone chamber that was surprisingly cool in the tropical morning heat.

"Now hum from deep inside of you and hear the vibration, the echo," he said. We hummed and heard a melodious vibration return to us. "It's amazing, isn't it? It helps you vibrate. Once you find your vibration with the harmony of the Universe and with the energy of Mother Earth and nature; things just start falling into place. The Hebrews had a special mantra which they used to bring the energy of God directly into them when they left Egypt. It sounded like this [he hums a low chant]. The Maya had the same. This is where they did their initiations. Sometimes they used drums, too. The initiates would astral travel from here and the priest would sit over here and protect your body as you astral traveled. This is also where they would come in private and let out some of their blood and ask God to forgive them for their mistakes."

At this point, one of the groundskeepers joined us, a friend of Luis. They chatted in Spanish while motioning toward Julia.

"He says that you are a sister," Luis said after they finished.

"What does it mean that she's a sister?" Alicia asked.

"It means that she is pursuing a spiritual path. That's what he meant," Luis replied.

From the chamber we walked through the complex to an immense pyramid maybe 200 feet high with a temple on top and broad steps covering all the way up one face. There was a steep wooden staircase on the side for tourists to walk up. The girls headed up as I continued talking with Luis.

He spoke about Native American legends, of the return of the White Buffalo in 1996 and of the Eagle and the Condor, both signs of the beginning of a new age on the planet. He wove in the writings of Carlos Castaneda, Jose Arguellos, the Hopi migration north, the thirteen Mesoamerican crystal skulls (thought to house all human wisdom and knowledge), the alignment of the planets, and the sacred number thirteen, into a cohesive picture of major, positive earth changes soon to come.

I had brought a small medicine bag to give as a gift. In it, along with several other items, was some hair from the sacred White Buffalo that we were given when we visited the farm in Arizona where she lives. I got leather bag out of my backpack and gave it to Luis. He looked at me and tears swelled in his eyes.

"There were several teachers of love here. Quetzalcoatl, the Maya called him Kukulcan, and others," Luis said. "These are people who survived the great flood of Atlantis and they spread Atlantis' heart all around the planet. They are the ones that encoded all the information into these buildings. All of a sudden, after the glaciations in 7500BC, humankind started to build architecture on the planet, but with the mathematics of how the Universe functions built into it.

"The Atlanteans were re-mapping the whole planet. Before 2012, the thirteen crystal skulls will come together. When that happens, the vibrational frequency will change and we will feel like we put our finger into an electrical socket and the jolt will wake us into reality and out of this dream that we are now in. We will shift from the masculine to the feminine. The legends say that when the thirteen skulls come together, all human knowledge and wisdom of the past, present and future will be available to all who open up their awareness. In a time of great crisis for humanity, these skulls will all come together again and we will be able to access their sacred knowledge.

"Even the Dalai Lama came to Mayan city of Chichén Itzá last year, to reactivate the energy there," Luis said without missing a beat. "He had a crystal skull with him. Only four are now available, but it doesn't matter who finds it. It doesn't matter who buys it. They will all come together when the time comes. We are not ready yet. First we have to clean up ourselves, forget about evil and greed and pay for the mistakes we have made. Then we will change into the next round. The information in the crystal skulls came in from the elohim—the angels—for humankind in general. They can be used by everyone, everywhere. Science has tried every kind of analysis with technology and they have never been able to determine how they were carved."

I had read about the thirteen crystal skulls, the first of which was found in 1927 by Anna Mitchell-Hedges, the seventeen-year old daughter of English adventurer, traveler, and writer, F.A. Mitchell-Hedges. She had found it as they excavated a temple at the ancient Mayan city of Lubaantum, located in British Honduras, now Belize. It is approximately the size of a normal human skull and included a detachable and moveable jaw. Since then, several other crystal skulls have been discovered and various mystical qualities have been associated with them, including the ability to heal physical problems.

If the person interacting with them is spiritually intuned enough, it is said that the skulls will talk or sing to them, either out loud or through thought transference and can create visions and expand intuitive abilities. The skull was eventually given to Norbu Chen, a powerful healer of the Tibetan sect of Red Hat Lamas, who had studied with Mayan priests in Guatemala. The Mitchell-Hedges skull is now on tour around the globe.

Just as a silicon crystal computer chip holds vast amounts of information that lies inert unless hooked into the proper computer hardware, so it is thought that the crystal skulls lie seemingly inert unless hooked into its proper hardware—which in this case is the human mind and consciousness. It is possible that they may act more as a battery charging up parts of our brains where the knowledge is actually stored.

Crystals are sacred to many indigenous people across the planet. Many consider them "solidified light" with healing powers.

Several North American Native tribes also have legends of the crystal skulls. I recently talked with one Native American elder who is in possession 13 skulls (but wishes to remain anonymous and does not wish to be sought out). He said until we have begun to clean up the environment the skulls will still be "dirty" and unable to reveal all their full wisdom and knowledge—information that will fill us with a sense of "identity, belonging and hope." He also said that we do not need to seek out the skulls but just reach out to them in our minds and hearts to contact them and access their wisdom.

Modern-day scientists are still baffled as to how the Mitchell-Hedges skull was crafted by an ancient society using basic tools. In 1970, the skull was brought for testing to the laboratories of Hewlett-Packard, one of the world's leading manufacturers of computers and other electronic equipment. The scientists there were well acquainted with all techniques of working with crystals.

They first tested to be sure it was indeed natural quartz crystal and their tests showed that it was the most pure quartz crystal known. This test also proved that the detachable jaw was from the same original large piece of crystal. The team was astonished that so large and complex a skull could come from one large pure crystal.

As described in *The Mystery of the Crystal Skulls:Unlocking the Secrets of the Past, Present, and Future* by Chris Morton and Ceri Louise Thomas,

> Whoever made the skull would had to have started with a huge chunk of angular quartz crystal around three times the size of the finished skull, and when they first started carving they would have no way of knowing whether the inside was pure or full of fractures and holes. They would have to carefully grade the sand by the size of each of its grains . . . right down to a microscopically fine grain size, like powder, to finish off the final smooth polish. What is more, if they had made a mistake at any point, they would have to start all over again from scratch.

Since quartz crystal is almost as hard as diamonds, the scientists at Hewlett Packard knew it would have been impossible for a stone-age culture to carve such a perfect specimen so they suspected it must be a forgery done with modern tools. However,

30

they determined that even modern precision carvers with electric diamond-tipped equipment would have taken over a year to create such an incredible object—especially since they determined that using such tools would probably have caused the crystal to shatter.

Upon further investigation using extreme magnification of the surface of the skull they found no evidence of modern tool markings or markings of any kind. In the magazine *Measure*, the Hewlett-Packard team reported the skull had to be made by hand and they estimated that a team of ancient carvers would have made a "300-man-year effort" to complete the skull. One team member commented, "This skull shouldn't even exist!" Since unlike most materials, quartz crystal does not corrode, erode, decay or change over time, they had no way of determining its age.

The scientists further determined that the skull was made from piezo-electric silicon dioxide crystal—the same type of naturally occurring quartz used in modern electronic equipment. This type of crystal has a negative and positive polarity just like a battery and if pressure is applied it generates electricity and can actually hold electrical energy under control. These are the qualities that make this substance so vital to the electronics industry where it is used in computers, electronic devices, radios, television systems and telecommunication satellites—where it has literally changed human life on planet earth in its modern-day applications, allowing us to communicate instantly with people around the globe. Could another ancient crystal-based technology soon usher in another life-altering change for humanity?

In January of 2008, author and Mayan Elder Hunbatz Men was sent a crystal skull from an art collector in China. The collector told him it was found in the Tibetan Himalayas near the border of China along with twelve similar skulls. All the skulls were being distributed to countries around the world. Men was told that these skulls belonged to an ancient people called the Dropas, who were said to be less than four feet tall. In the cave, skeletons of very short people were found neatly and peculiarly arranged along with stone discs that revealed a strange and unknown language. Men believes their origins may be extraterrestrial.

Respected Mayan elder Don Alejandro Cirilio Oxlaj Peres, head of the Mayan Council of Elders in Guatemala, agrees that the crystal skulls have a part to play in the coming changes on earth. In a recent article, he explained they were not made by humans, but by beings from another dimension, another planet. Don Alejandro believes the skulls are gathering together to help us with our "new world" which begins on December 21, 2012.

∞∞∞∞∞∞∞∞∞∞∞∞∞∞∞∞∞∞∞∞∞∞∞∞∞∞∞∞∞∞∞∞∞∞∞∞∞∞

"What do you think people need to know to prepare for these coming changes?" I asked Luis as we continued wandering through the once-magnificent city.

"There is a book, *Autobiography of a Yogi*, by Paramahansa Yogananda that is like a roadmap to follow into this next cycle, but before then, we will bring a lot of disaster on ourselves planet-wise. Try to go into yoga and take care of the temple," he answered, pointing toward his body. "Take care of yourself. Be very careful about what you eat and what you expose yourself to so you can keep healthy. Develop good habits and keep the laws—the laws of God. Give love and love will bounce back to you. As Christ Himself said regardless of whatever happens, as soon as you get faithful and in the right vibe, nothing will happen to you. In that time, we will master the world of matter and you can walk between two armies and nothing will happen to you. Don't bind yourself to terrestrial things that you cannot take with you when you go. Try to go to old ceremonial cities, like here, or old forests where the energy is old and sacred."

"Is Bob Marley popular here?" I asked, as we strolled further into the vast complex.

"Certainly he is. There is not one home out here that does not have Bob Marley's music," Luis said with a big, impish grin on his face. "The African-Caribbean people have to have someone. That's where Bob Marley comes in. He brings back the old African magic ways, the spiritual structure again."

Bob Marleys's music is considered by millions worldwide as a spiritual path leading us, as Dennis Forsythe, author of *Rastafari: The Healing of the Nations*, says, "from one state of consciousness called Babylon to a higher state called Zion." The New York Times called him "the most influential artist of the second half of the twentieth century." From 1976 until his tragic death at 36 from brain cancer in 1981, his concerts were sold out, especially in Third World countries where he was seen as a symbol of hope for eventual liberation from oppression and poverty. He could draw 180,000 in Milan one night and 100,000 in Dublin the next. In one twelve-city tour, he performed for more than a million fans. Jack Healey of Amnesty International claims that Marley, more than any other world figure, remains "the symbol of freedom throughout the world."

Conscious reggae music, often called "roots reggae," was birthed in Jamaica by Marley in the 1970s and early 1980s. There are now many conscious reggae artists continuing his legacy, mostly Rastafarians from Jamaica. Reggae is perhaps the only music popular in *every* country in the world and in every socio-economic bracket. It has become a tribal drumbeat of One Love. To many of the world's illiterate masses it is a lyrical form of social, political and spiritual communication and understanding. Reggae's "one drop" beat matches that of the human heartbeat and its message is a cry for justice and an end to oppression—both by individuals and by governments. It also carries a message of love, forgiveness, healing and spiritual freedom. As Bob sings, "Emancipate yourself from mental slavery. None but ourselves can free our minds."

By now we had wandered into one of the main ceremonial courtyards, about the size of a football field, with several low pyramids, uncovered and in various stages reconstruction. The crowd was light. Maybe ten or twenty other people were exploring this area. The plaza felt comforting, almost familiar. I thought I wouldn't mind spending all day under the shade of one of those large trees in the courtyard. Built at a human scale, it was not overwhelming. A family of coatimundis, a South American rodent that looks like it jumped out of a Dr. Seuss book, wandered playfully around the tourists, brazenly seeking a handout of food, which Alicia, a great lover of children and animals, gave them.

"Tikal is on one of the thirteen most powerful energy vortexes on the planet," Luis continued. "That's why they built a city here even though there was no natural water source and everything was built on raised terraces with the foundations on bedrock. The structures are earthquake-resistant and we get 520 earth tremors a year, more than one a day. There are several main temples here. Temple One and Two were built in relationship to the sun's zenith passage in this latitude on the 29th of April.

"Temple One was to open the chakras. Temple Two was to cheat death. According to the Indian way, before you are born, you choose where you want to be born. But when you are born, you do not remember this. You have to find the purpose while you are alive and when you achieve the purpose, you are a hero. If you haven't found the purpose until late, because the days of life are counted, then you could come to this temple and fast, stay awake and pray to be given more time in your life. They called it 'cheating death.' "

"What was Temple Three?" I asked.

"Temple Three was to open the third eye, to see the future. It is in relationship to Mars and Mercury. Temple Four is for flowing with the harmony of the Universe, finding the balance. That's why the lintel above the door had two heads, for the duality. It is aligned with Venus and Jupiter. You should climb up there. You can see the other temples."

We all climbed up to the top of the Temple IV, maybe two hundred feet high. From there, we looked over what appeared to be virgin jungle with the upper parts of several pyramids and their combed tops poking through and one fully uncovered pyramid visible. It was ancient, powerful, mystical. I was glad our family could share this place together and with this man.

After we climbed down, we walked to the most dramatic area—the Great Plaza—a large courtyard with two huge, tall pyramids at either end, both fully uncovered and in excellent stages of preservation. Seventy stelaes—large stone monoliths six to eight feet tall and originally painted red—have been located around this area. These stelaes, each of which once had an altar beside it, commemorate the rulers of Tikal. Their faces can still be seen today carved on one side of these large stone monuments. One could almost picture what it must have been like to be here a thousand years earlier for a ceremony or initiation.

"Here the Mayans encoded all of the buildings," Luis said as we sat between the two pyramids. "Here is the mathematics of the moon and the sun and, like in the Pyramid of the Cheops in Egypt and the pyramid in Teotouchan, is the speed of light. Where did they get it from? It's not clear yet. The distance between these two pyramids is a mathematical constant that ended up with the most accurate calculation in the history of mankind of the earth going around the sun. The Mayan recorded this as 365.2422 days, which is six seconds more accurate than the Gregorian calendar we use and this was not confirmed until very recently. How could they calculate this? If you look at the comb on that pyramid, you can see the head of an American Indian carved in relief."

"Why do you think Tikal was abandoned?" I asked, as we looked up at the Indian relief.

"Around 830AD, four volcanoes in Asia erupted covering the whole planet with a layer of ash reflecting out the light and the heat so there was less production on the planet. Here there were many people, 325 people per square mile. That was the straw that broke the camel's back. Some left to head up north to join the Toltecs and some who didn't like the system moved further north and became the Anasazi."

"And the Hopi believe they were once the Anasazi, too" I said.

"Yes. At one time, there were seventy million Mayan people," Luis said, "but the greed for gold and silver wiped them out. The Spanish destroyed many temples looking for gold and silver but the Mayans never used gold and silver. That was introduced from the Incas. Within one century, there were only three million left so they had to pretend they converted into Christians to survive. So today, Mayans in my country, seven million of them, are Christians on Saturdays and Sundays but the rest of their life, they're Mayan."

"What do you think of the Hopi's concept that the reason this area was abandoned is that the signs came for them to continue their migration?" I asked.

"Just like the assemblage spot in the human body changes," Luis said, "the energy in a place changes as well. It was the time, then, for a big shift so they had to go up north and the volcanoes were one of the signs of this shift."

"What's your take on 2012?" I asked.

"On the morning of December 21, 2012, we shall see the Milky Way rise once again like the morning of Creation. The sun will rise right through the rift—the center of the Milky Way. Scientists have now confirmed that on that day, the sun, when viewed from earth, will align *exactly* with a huge black hole located between the constellations of Scorpio and Sagittarius. That is the center of the Milky Way. The entire Milky Way rotates around this "galactic core" like a cosmic wheel with a black hole hub. That's what the Mayans re-created every time with their sacred ball game when they kicked a ball through a ring protruding from the courtyard wall. In the evening of that day, December 21, 2012, if you are in Temple One, you shall see, after the sun sets, through the north side holes of Temple Four, Venus and Jupiter.

"It's like telling mankind, 'This is the moment you are rising out of the old age to the new one.' It's the meaning of Thirteen Heavens. We will step out of the Age of Pisces and into the Age of Aquarius, a higher awakening. That's what is encoded in these buildings and far more than that. They encode every little detail—yesterday, today and tomorrow—every little detail of mankind.

"This was the story that was given to the American Indians to keep when the Spanish arrived. This was the story they revealed on the fifth of May 2000. On page seventy-four of one of the surviving Mayan books, the Dresden Codex, it tells that when there was a conjunction of five planets—Mars, Venus, Mercury, Jupiter, Earth—and the crocodile would open up and the earth would start flooding again. The beginning of this change is right now. After the birth of the White Buffalo in Wisconsin in 1996, American Indians met here in Tikal and revealed this story that was given to the Mayans and that story is exactly what was encoded in the mathematics of the buildings. The American Indians kept the knowledge secret."

We continued our walk in silence, considering the vast potential of the reality he had just revealed. For a while, Alicia walked ahead of us on the path with Luis, discussing her plans for her future with him as if he was a close friend and mentor.

"I'm thinking about going into accounting," I overheard her say. "I really do well with math."

"That would be good. I'm an accountant," he said, to all our amazement. "I worked for years for a big oil company. But now I do this healing work, this spiritual guiding. You, too, are a powerful healer. I can sense it."

"That was the other work I was interested in," Alicia said thoughtfully. We all laughed.

By now, it was mid-afternoon and over ninety degrees and very humid. We had been wandering the city for almost five hours, and we were all cooked. I could not absorb any more data if I wanted to, so we all agreed it was time to head to the restaurant at the

36

welcome center. As we waited for our lunch, we asked Luis if local Mayan healers might help my brother-in-law.

"I know this medicine man in the Highlands," Luis said as we waited for our food. "His name is Roberto Pauz. He travels in the astral and he heals people in the astral, psychic healing. There are a couple of things you have to do to get him to help you. You have to get candles of the five Mayan colors for the cardinal points—red toward the east, black toward the west, yellow toward the south, white toward the north and blue in the center. You have to light these candles in a room where the sick person sleeps. You put a picture of the sick person under the blue one in the middle, upside down with his name written on the backside, all on a piece of black velvet cloth. Then, Roberto will find him in the astral and see what he can do. I know a woman he healed of breast cancer and a gentleman of prostate cancer."

"We will do this," Julia said.

"It may work," Luis said. "My heart was about to give out and I asked him to help me and he asked me to put these candles out like I told you. I put them out in my room and about midnight I was half-awake, half-asleep when I heard what I thought was a frog jumping on my door and all of a sudden I saw this dark figure moving into my room. He grabbed my hands to my sides and drove like a knife into my chest. That was on a Friday. Monday I was running around playing soccer. I've never had any problems since then."

After lunch, we headed out feeling grateful that Rosita had led us to Luis.

"Here are some books and DVDs about our work," I said to Luis as we dropped him back in El Remate, feeling as if we had made a new lifetime friend. "We signed one for you. I think you'll enjoy it."

"And would you try to get this copy to a man named Danny Diaz?" Julia said. "We met him at the Activation Maya event and we had hoped to see him today. He's a young, thin man who looks like a Native American with a long black ponytail."

"I will find him and give him your book," Luis said smiling as he closed the van door.

Chapter 4

The Mayan Teachings
&
Their Sacred Calendars

The next Pachakuti [World Age] has already begun, and the upheaval and chaos characteristic of this period will last until the year 2012. At that time the world will be turned right side up again. The pillars of European civilization will collapse and the ways of the Earth Peoples will return. The Conquistador will perish by his own hand and his own blade. For the Inka this next Pachakuti holds the possibility of chaos and the end of the world as we know it. But it also promises the emergence of a new kind of human at the end of this period of turmoil.
- Inca Prophecy as told to author Alberto Villoldo by Inca Elder don Humberto

When we returned home from Tikal, I started to read several books on the Maya. Many were about the ancient Maya—their beliefs, their culture and their sacred calendars. I also read a series of books written by Martín Prechtel, a Native American raised on a Pueblo Indian reservation in New Mexico, who lived in the ancient village of Santiago Atitlan on Lake Atitlan in southern Guatemala from the 1970s to the 1990s. While there, he was trained as a shaman and eventually served the local Tzutujil Mayan population as a full village member, becoming a part of the village leadership. His portrayal of modern Mayan life in Santiago Atitlan, before the escalation of the brutal Guatemalan conflict in the 1990s, showed that a certain level of wisdom still existed with modern-day Mayans—at least in this place at that time. We decided that our next trip would be to Santiago Atitlan to see if this ancient Mayan wisdom was still vital there.

During this same time, we got an email from Danny Diaz,

the man we had met briefly in El Remate at Activation Maya. Our Tikal guide, Luis, had found Danny and gave him our book and Danny had sought us out. We called him at his home in Los Angeles, glad to have made the connection.

"We were sorry Tata Pedro left Activation Maya before we could connect with him," I told him after catching up on each other's lives. "In April we're heading to Lake Atitlan to seek out the wisdom-keepers in that area. Do you know any elders in the Atitlan area?"

"Yes. Tata Pedro lives in San Pedro, one of the villages on the lake next to Santiago Atitlan," he answered enthusiastically.

"We had no idea that Tata Pedro lived there," I said, joyously realizing that the elder we had traveled so far to meet months earlier was being brought so easily to us.

"And Chus Landa is there too and he can be your interpreter," Danny continued. "They are both friends of mine and I can link you up. They are very loving souls. I can't go, but I look forward to getting together with you and Julia soon."

"We're on our way to Arizona next week and we're going to be in Southern California for one night next week to have dinner with Julia's mom and step-dad. You want to join us after dinner? We leave early the next morning for Prescott, Arizona. We're involved in a One Love Concert for Leonard Peltier."

"Yes. That would be great!" Danny said.

"I got a better idea," I said. "Why don't you fly to Prescott with us from California for the Peltier weekend? The Hopi elder, Radford and his wife, Lorna, will be there. They're in our book, *The Beauty Path.* You could travel with us to Prescott and you could fly back to L.A. when we fly back to North Carolina.

"Oh, man! That sounds great!" he said.

A week later the three of us flew from Los Angeles to Phoenix and drove two hours to Prescott for the concert. Leonard Peltier is a Native American Activist that has been falsely imprisoned for over thirty years. He has been nominated four times for a Nobel Peace Prize. The LPDC (Leonard Peltier Defense Committee) had asked me to organize a concert to kick off a two-month exhibition of Leonard's beautiful artwork at the Smoki Museum in Prescott. We invited Radford to speak and asked three Native American recording artists to perform—Native American flute player, Travis Terry, and two reggae groups, Native Roots and Casper and The 602 Band. All immediately agreed to appear.

As Julia, Danny and I drove toward Prescott from the Phoenix airport, the three of us felt as if we had known each other forever. Danny is a handsome man with classic Native features and a long black ponytail. He is quiet and humble but his aura and his heart are big. Danny told us a little about his life in Guatemala. He was raised in a large extended family that farmed a tract of family land. When he was a college student, fearing for his life, as did many Guatemalan student activists during that country's vicious war, he fled to the United States and lived penniless until finally arriving in Southern California. He now lives with his wife and her nephew in L.A., where he makes and plays beautiful Native American flutes. He also owns 50 acres near Tikal that he wants to use as a spiritual retreat to host gatherings.

After checking into our hotel, Danny, Julia and I went to the Smoki Museum for a symposium of speakers scheduled for the first night of the weekend. Across the street from the museum, there was a public skateboard park crowded with teenagers on a Friday afternoon. As we watched their grace, energy and joy of life, we all understood that much of our work was for this generation. For the most part, it is the youth in their teens and twenties, when idealism is often at its peak, who come to our events and read our books.

That night at the museum, Radford opened the weekend with a beautiful prayer and talk.

"Greetings. I am glad to be here," he began in his calm, melodious cadence, as much like a chant as a prayer. "I am a Hopi. I am Sun Clan and also Eagle Clan. I am a religious leader and a spokesperson for our highest priest who is also our village chief. I also speak for the council of the village and provide help to a lot of the elders we have in the village. I was told by my uncle that when the Hopi tribe accepted the education of Western people, that we were to be their ears and eyes; we were to be their tongue. When we learned the Western ways and language, we would be the ones to help our people, the Hopi people. Whatever is being dealt with relating to the Hopi, we would be the ones to interpret and speak for them and so with that in mind, my uncles sent me to school. I have gone through the Bureau of Indian Affairs schools, went to college, and became a teacher. Currently I am the librarian at the Hopi schools and I am working on my doctorate.

"What we do in our ceremonies is pray for peace for all people but not only the people but as well for the animal kingdom and the plant life. We also refer to ourselves as plants and plants need care. Where do we get the care from? Our belief is we get it from the Great Spirit that provides us life and so, in all of our prayers, that's who we pray to for help. I believe the event we have here, today, is a good reason. Our prayers we put together into one, to make it stronger—one strong prayer for Leonard, for his wellness, for his strength, for his spiritual wellness. All of this has been taken away from him. I pray, we all pray, that he gets all of what he has lost. He is an individual and he, like all of us, has a responsibility on this Earth. To take that responsibility away from a person is not the way.

"We have to be united. We have to be one. We have to love one another. That's why peace is what we, as Hopi people, try to relate to other people. We believe in no wars. That's why what is happening in other countries is what we feel, as Hopi people, is not the way. We *must* talk to one another. We *must* respect one another. We *must* respect what we do as a culture. Each culture has its own way. Each culture has its own language. Each culture has its own spirituality. But they are the same. Every human being's needs are the same and as Hopi, we believe that we are one. We originate from one and we consider *every* person as our brother or sister. And that's how I look at you right now. You are all brothers and sisters to me.

"To make this prayer strong, we need to pray together. We know we have different beliefs. Whatever you believe in, you pray to that and that is fine. So I pray for Leonard Peltier to be strong. Give him his strength. Give him the love. Give him the health that he lost. We pray that he returns home now and be among his family, among his tribe. I pray that he be with his spiritual elders. I pray that he returns and continues his spiritual duties. I pray that he also makes people understand what has happened to him, understand what he believes in and makes people see that he needs help. We all need help."

As the evening continued, several speakers spoke with anger, not just toward the government's actions in regards to Leonard, but toward the present administration and the war in Iraq. Given the situation, such feelings are understandable. However, the more they

41

spoke and railed against the government, the more it created a very negative vibe in the room. They were not leading the audience into any positive action except writing their government representatives about Leonard and the Iraq War. One speaker scolded the younger generation for not protesting in the streets as his generation had against the Vietnam War. This triggered a heated interchange from several youths in the audience.

Since I was also one of those that took to the streets in protest during the Vietnam War, I knew these times were very different. During Vietnam, we were being drafted straight out of college. We had no say in whether we agreed to kill and die for a war that made no sense. We took to the streets not only to object to an immoral war but also to object to *our* being sent to fight it without our consent. The Iraq War is very different. It is being fought only with people who have *voluntarily* joined the armed services. Also, during our college days, there were no cellphones, Internet, video games, and hundreds of TV channels all pumping at max-speed 24 hours a day. At 11:30 at night, the TV went off and in dorm rooms, apartments, and communes, young people everywhere—under various states of consciousness—reasoned until the dawn on creating a better world.

As I listened to several speakers, including Leonard's lawyers and a well-known white Native American activist, I was becoming more uncomfortable with their angry message, which was in such a contrast to ours. I later learned that Julia, Radford, Lorna and Danny were equally ill at ease with the vibe. We had designed our One Love Concert, scheduled for the next evening, to encourage the audience to claim themselves as teachers of love—and you can't teach love coming from anger.

Everyone in our concert, including Radford, Travis Terry, Native Roots, and Casper and The 602 Band, would emphasize this message of universal love. This was the same message we had carried forward in all our events. This was the first one that we had participated in that was not totally our creation. Just as this night's message was creating anger and alienation in the audience, our message the next night was designed to create peace and unity.

We had encountered this angry vibration many times during our journey—high-minded, well-intentioned people embittered by the unconsciousness of the world. Some had been personally hurt by this unconsciousness; others were frustrated as they viewed the pain

42

it caused others. Often, as you bring forward a message of love, you grapple with this energy, sometimes engaging it and at other times blessing it on its way. Given the problems of the world—past and present—it is understandable that anger, disillusionment and discouragement will come up for many people who sincerely want to help heal the pain of the planet. I have watched this anger come up in myself many times. It still does.

The Mayan calendar, as we shall soon see, reveals that this awareness of the power of love to heal past and present wrongs will become the foundation of the coming *World Age*—the initial vibration of which began about the time of Gandhi's experiment with non-violence.

This use of the vast healing power of love applies to both individuals and to struggles among societies and nations. Though it is not *yet* possible to end all wars, all injustice, all exploitation, all deceit or the pain they cause, we can, however, understand that no matter what a person's life situation, no matter how poor they are, no matter how oppressed they are, no matter what they have done or what was done to them, they can, in every minute of their life choose love—in their next thought, their next feeling, their next action. When they do, they are claiming the assignment that the Creator gave each of us—to learn and teach love as much as we can while we walk our own individual paths on this planet. This is the most powerful path we can ever walk. When we do this, we are free and no oppressive system, no matter how powerful it may seem, can stop us on our journey Home to the Creator.

The concert the next night, attended mostly by high school and college youths, was uplifting and heart-opening. Radford opened with a prayer for all humanity followed by a moving performance by Travis Terry playing his flute accompanied by a young woman playing a huge, five-foot wide Native American drum.

"That's the way it was. It was the harmony and rhythm of Mother Earth, the drums," Travis said, his powerful, rhythmic voice joining with the drum, a blend of song and poetry—his voice rising with passion, his eyes seeing a vision of the past, of the future. "We were *free* and we danced and we danced and we danced! This is who we were—Native People—Pima, Apache, Kiowa, Navajo, many nations!"

"These symbolize the best of the best in song," he continued after more of his beautiful flute playing, "because as the mother drum and the father flute combines that energy, that balance of being Native, the heartbeat, the song is what we listen to when we are born into this world. I'd like to leave this with you. Despite the fact that we have all this turmoil, doesn't mean nothing to us. The fact that you had depression back in the days, doesn't mean nothing to me. Back in the days that you had racism and discouragement, doesn't mean nothing to me. All we were, was who we are and what we will always be—Indian, Comanche, Sioux, Zuni, Iroquois, Seminole and the list goes on to my brothers and sisters and children. This is who we are. This is for you, from my heart. [He touches his heart and waves it toward the audience and holds up a huge handmade Native American flute and starts to play gently, peacefully. The crowd is quiet, reverent—transfixed by the power of the vision he has just shared with us.] This goes to every nationality—to the Irish, to the German, to the French, to the Spanish, to the Polish and every manner of tribes in the world. This is how it began."

After his performance, Native Roots and Casper and the 602 Band performed—all Native Americans, all conscious of the healing message of love. They were incredible, as they always are, merging this message of love with powerful reggae music. The next day, we all headed our separate ways feeling we had all learned something and had helped Leonard on his path toward freedom.

∞∞

After returning from Prescott, I made arrangements to go with Julia and Alicia to Santiago Atitlan later that month. Meanwhile, I continued to research the Maya. I was vigorously searching for a message of One Love from either the ancient or modern-day Mayans. The more I researched, the more discouraged I became. I was even considering abandoning the search and this book. After our first trip to the Guatemalan Highlands, a spiritual tour of the ancient Mayan city of Tikal, meeting with a few people actively involved with workshops and books about the Mayans, and after reading many books on the subject, I was impressed with the Mayan's high level of civilization, their magnificent ceremonial cities, their calendars and their vast and accurate knowledge of astronomy.

However, amazing as all this was, I was having trouble determining if their teachings emphasized unconditional love for all humanity—the basis of all truly evolved teachings. I was also troubled that toward the end of their reign, the Mayans were involved in war, corrupted politics and, as some believed, perhaps even human sacrifice. If all the Mayans had to offer was their ability to build grand structures and determine the course of the celestial bodies, they could offer little help to heal the world than our present-day modern societies, who are equally accomplished in these areas.

Maybe there was no Mayan message of One Love, I was beginning to think. Then I read two books that have revealed to me the true core of love coming from these people—past and present. One had to do with their direct spiritual teachings and the other had to do with their sacred and prophetic calendars. Between the two books, an incredible message of love and a vision of an orderly and Divinely-guided Universe were unfolding.

The Mayan Teacher of Love

The first of the two keystone books was *The Gospel of the Toltecs: The Life and Teachings of Quetzalcoatl* by Frank Diaz. The Toltecs were the inhabitants of the region before the Mayans and were probably their ancestors. According to Diaz, the Mesoamerican prophet, called Quetzalcoatl by the Toltecs and the Aztecs, Kukulcan or Kukulmach by the Mayans and Wiraccocha by the Incas, brought his teachings to this region. He has been compared to Christ, Buddha, Mohammed, and Krishna, as well as Deganawidah—the Huron peacemaker who founded the Iroquois Confederacy. When Quetzalcoatl appeared among the Mayans, it was then that their rapid expansion of consciousness began during their Classic period (250-830AD).

Just as Christ gave the core teachings to much of the Western world, the ancient Jewish prophets to the Jewish world, Buddha, Mohammed and Krishna to much of the Eastern world, Quetzalcoatl—often depicted as pale, tall, long-robed, bearded, with an elongated skull and having no facial features similar to those of the indigenous tribes—gave the core teachings to much of the Mesoamerican world. The people of this region, like their

45

counterparts in the Christian, Islamic, Jewish and Hindu world, have struggled to implement this loving guidance. Quetzacoatl's promise is one of continuing future enlightenment. He is represented as the "plumed or feathered serpent"—merging the Earth (serpent or body) with the heavens (feathered birds or spirit) and the unifying of *all* duality—heaven and Earth, spirit and matter, light and dark, good and bad, right and wrong, science and myth. (Sculptures of plumed serpents have been found in Anasazi ruins in Arizona, thought to be left by the migrating Hopi.)

Some believe that there have been many people who held the title of Quetzalcoatl and some researchers believe he was not a human at all but rather a Mayan deity or a representation of a certain consciousness. Diaz, however, focused on the writings of Quetzalcoatl Ce Acatl (947-999AD), and by interpreting and researching ancient accounts of his life, has brought forward his clear teachings of love.

Born of a virgin birth, he lived an intense and often painful life, was tempted and fell and then after reaching spiritual enlightenment (like Buddha), brought forward his clear teachings. Here are just a few of Quetzalcoatl's words as interpreted through Diaz's book—words as clear and loving as Jesus' Sermon on the Mount:

> God is One. He does not demand anything; He does not need anything.

> Know the honorable condition, and that it is good. Do not commit adultery; do not become drunk; do not deliver yourself immoderately to gambling nor subjugate yourself to chance; do not mention your lineage nor your virile condition; do not be indiscreet or cowardly; do not strive for first place.

> How good if by your side the positive word is spoken, the word that causes no harm. If you transmit it, do not enhance or diminish it; say only the exact word. Be aware of the empty and distracted words. For those only provoke perversion. They are not serene and straight words.

46

You will not forget the elders, the poor, the suffering, the unhappy ones; the ones that have not found home and are living in confusion; the ones who are shedding tears and biting their fingernails; the ones with their hands tied behind their backs.

Do not search excessively for a good appearance. For silently He will take you as you are, in any place, at any moment . . . Love one another; help one another. Help those in need with a blanket, a truss, a jewel, a salary, food. For it is false to reject those around you. Give alms to the hungry, even if you have to give your own food. Clothe the ones in rags, even if you have to go naked. Help the one who needs you, even if you have to risk your life. See that you share both one flesh and one humanity.

Do not go into someone else's coffer. Do not support yourself from someone else's plate . . . do not take the lead. If you are given that what you need in the end, do not be mad. And if you are given nothing, be grateful anyway. Heaven wanted it that way. It is deserved.

Do not be sad for human pain and misery; do not be sick or tormented because of it. Is it that only compassion and blandness should be our faith? Be a warrior.

For one shining moment in Central America, Quetzalcoatl ushered in a Golden Age—an age whose reverberations can still be felt. Many have attributed him with revitalizing not only the long-lost spiritual teachings and initiation ceremonies of Mesoamerica but the revitalization of the long-abandoned ceremonial and initiation centers such as Teotihuacan and Chichén Itzá. Indeed, Mayan culture collapsed and was revitalized several times in its history. Quetzalcoatl provided a much-needed spiritual impulse to a people gone astray. He returned to his followers four years after his death (some legends say he sailed away), promising to return again at a distant time. "I only came to prepare a way," he told his people before his departure. "A new day is coming, the magnificent day of radiant beauty when I must return to myself."

In the Aztec mythology, Quetzalcoatl's prophesied return date was April 21, 1519, the *exact* date to the day they encountered the Spanish Conquistador Hernando Cortes near present-day Cozumel, Mexico. Quetzalcoatl was to "come like a butterfly," which the Aztecs believed to be the sails of Cortes ships. Given these "coincidences," it is easy to see how Cortes was greeted as a returning deity—an understandable mistake that cost the Aztecs their empire. Cortes with a group of 600 men went on to conquer the Aztec empire of several million.

In another place and time, a 950-year old Hopi prophecy predicted the exact date when their *bahanna* (white) brother would return (1540). However, their prophecy warned them that if the good *bahanna* brother returned, he would complete their spiritual understanding. However, if the wrong *bahanna* brother returned there would be much suffering. As prophesied, in 1540, a small band of Spanish explorers arrived in Hopiland. Soon, there was soon no doubt which of the two—the good or the bad white brother—had arrived.

However, this common myth of a returning white brother may represent a deeper archetypal longing. As Frank Waters writes in his *Book of the Hopi*, "The coming of the Hopi's lost white brother, the return of the Maya's bearded white god Kukulcan, the Toltecan and Aztecan Quetzalcoatl, is a myth of deep significance to all Americas. It is an unconscious projection of an entire race's dream of brotherhood with the races of all continents. It is the unfulfilled longing of all humanity."

Mayans, like Christians, Jews and Muslims, had their teachers of love and were also monotheistic, believing in one God, whom they call *AHAU*. In many ways, the Mayans may have represented a greater level of spiritual awareness in regards to their understanding of humanity's relationship to their Creator. As Mayan Daykeeper Hunbatz Men writes in his book, *The Secrets of the Mayan Science/Religion*:

> Despite their marvelous knowledge, the Maya did not
> repudiate their sense of spirituality and fall into

48

materialism. On the contrary, their ethics and esthetics were highly spiritual, establishing a binding truth based on the conviction that each individual was one with every other being—the very same entity. Hence, 'you' was declared non-existent, leaving the notion that 'you are me' and 'I am you.' This conjunction of human with human is the *human being.* Thus, ethics was based on the law of mutual respect elevated to the category of religion . . . The Maya conceived that God was in us and we are in God . . . We would like you to realize that we are all Quetzalcoatl or Kukulcan. We need only to develop our faculties of consciousness to fully realize that status.

Finally, here was what I had been seeking—a Mayan message of unconditional love. Though after Quetzalcoatl Ce Acatl's death, the post-classic Mayans did struggle with living his words, even relishing in war and corruption. However, the "original instructions," the same as had emerged through other great teachers of love, were there—embedded in their consciousness. That the Mayans had not followed them perfectly, I could live with as no other people had yet been able to either. Now, if I could only determine what all these calendars were about. Were they, too, part of their teachings of love?

The Mayan Calendars

Author's note: There are many theories about the Mayan calendars that have been brought forward in the last few years by well-known researchers such as Jose Arguellos, John Major Jenkins, Terence McKenna, Daniel Pinchbeck and Dr. Carl Calleman. Most agree on the main point that the Mayans did develop sophisticated calendars that serve as a timetable to the unfolding of events and consciousness not only on this planet, but in the entire Universe. They are in essence "galactic clocks."

There are some disagreements among these authors as to what the exact timetable and events are, but their agreements are greater than their disagreements. Most of the researchers are non-Mayans and many are recording their personal revelations in addition to hard evidence revealed through ancient Mayan hieroglyphs, codices and sacred buildings. The Mayan elders themselves have not offered a definitive conclusion and indeed, this might be difficult as even their strand of understanding may have been broken in the last thousand years. I have chosen to present the conclusions of Carl Calleman as his information has been confirmed by Don Alejandro Cirilo Perez Oxlaj, the head of the National Mayan Council of Elders of Guatemala.

Calleman's conclusions align with my long-held belief that the planet and humanity are unfolding according to Divine will and are heading toward greater levels of love and enlightenment, no matter how it might appear otherwise. Also, this perspective offers us some peace of mind as we comprehend that the Creator has revealed this timetable and plan at *this* particular time in history—a time when the threats to humanity's survival are real and many—because it can be brought into fruition. And if enough of us hold this vision, its chances of coming to fruition are greatly increased.

∞∞∞∞∞∞∞∞∞∞∞∞∞∞∞∞∞∞∞∞∞∞∞∞∞∞∞∞∞∞∞∞∞∞∞

Shortly after reading Diaz's book, I read *The Mayan Calendar and the Transformation of Consciousness* by Dr. Carl Calleman, Ph.D. Unlike so many other books on the Mayan calendars which focus only on the mathematics and prophecies, what he revealed was that their calendars, of which there are several dating back 2500 years, were instruments to awaken people to the reality of the Creator's unfolding plan for us. However, for over a thousand years, this message has been hidden within their codices, glyphs, ceremonial cities and buildings.

Only recently has the code of the Mayan glyph writings been decoded and since then, a wealth of information about their lives, history and beliefs have been revealed. These calendars not only incorporate their accurate mapping of the movement of planetary bodies but also their sacred and prophetic calendars, especially the *Tzolkin* and the *Tun*, incorporate within them an incredibly accurate understanding of universal, galactic, planetary, and human evolution.

Let me briefly explain what has been revealed. This is an overview—the whole calendrical system is very complex—but it will suffice to help us understand about the coming changes and how to prepare for them.

The Mayans—the first people to make use of the number zero—and created calendars that have amazed modern-day astronomers. Without even the wheel, much less telescopes and computers, they somehow managed to create these amazing calendars and inscribe them in stone. Among other things, their calendars tracked the exact orbits and stellar conjunctions of Mercury, Venus, Mars and Saturn; calculated the length of the Earth's orbit around the sun and the Moon's around the Earth and kept track of both lunar and solar eclipses, as well as the 25,920-year precession of the equinoxes. Only in modern times have astronomers matched their feats. Even to this day their yearly calendar is 1/10,000 of a day more accurate than our current calendars.

The Mayans were obsessed with time but their view of time was quite different than ours. Rather than seeing time as *linear*—beginning at one point and continuing into infinity—the Mayans saw time as *cyclical*. Like the graceful rhythms in nature, they perceived rhythmic cycles within time. Rather than a straight line, to them time was more like a wheel with predictable and ever-repeating cycles or patterns.

However, unlike modern calendars, which only relate to the *physical* Universe, and therefore keep people wedded to the world of illusion, the Mayan calendars, believed to be created by Quetzalcoatl (Kukulcan), are designed to reveal the inherent *spiritual* nature of the Universe. They are not about *time* but rather are incredible tools to measure the *flow of Creation*. The time they keep is *Holy Time*, revealing God's purpose—for the planet, for the species and for each of us individually.

The Tun Calendar

This section will reveal the shear enormity of what we are looking at—a cosmic blueprint which enables us to understand and predict all human behavior, *past, present and future*. As this system has been revealed to me over the last few months, it has definitely increased my peace of mind—and I know it will do the same for you. It is proof that a loving, non-punitive, all-knowing God has given us the knowledge and wisdom we need to usher in an age of love and unity.

There are three main Mayan calendars, the *Haab*, the *Tun* and the *Tzolkin*. The workings of the *Haab* and *Tzolkin* have been passed down from generation to generation and both have remained in use to the present day. However, the understanding of the details of the *Tun*, or *Long Count*, as it is also called, seems to have been lost to the people and is only recently coming to light- -mostly by non-Mayan researchers interpreting their glyphs, stelaes and codices. All the calendars are considered to be the most sophisticated calendars ever devised.

The *Haab*, their yearly calendar similar to ours, mapped the 365-day solar year. It consists of eighteen months of twenty days each (360 days) plus five days that are for giving thanks. This calendar was very practical and aided them in planting, understanding weather patterns, and in planning rituals and celebrations. However, it is their two main sacred calendars, the *Tun* and the *Tzolkin*, on which we will be focusing.

According to Calleman, their prophetic *Tun* calendar is divided into many sacred periods. It outlined and prophesied the different stages *all* creation—the Universe, our galaxy, our planet and humanity—would be going through at any given period of time. Sometimes these periods were vast, incorporating billions of years. However, as we approach 2012, these periods consist of shorter and shorter periods: first of millions of years, then thousands, then hundreds, then tens, then months, then weeks and finally periods lasting only days. Each designated and named period was affected by a different energy from which you could predict what character that period would take on. For instance, some periods would be conducive to positive change, others prone to strife and suffering; some periods might encourage art or literature or free expression; other periods would suppress it. Just as the full moon is now often recognized in affecting our individual behavior, so was the energy of these cycles thought to affect planetary behavior.

The *Tun* begins 16.4 *billion* years ago and ends on December 21, 2012. (Though most other Mayan calendar researchers agree with this date, Calleman believes the date to be October 28, 2011.

52

Time will tell.) Within this 16.4 billion year timeframe, the cycles are those divisible by either 13 or 20, their sacred numbers (thirteen and twenty are also key numbers in our DNA molecules and there are twenty digits and thirteen main joints in the human body). According to Carl Calleman's calculation presented in his book *The Mayan Calendar and the Transformation of Consciousness*, there are many key dates representing the beginning of nine major eras called "Underworlds" or "World Ages." If this subdividing time into predictable periods that manifest various vibrations is accurate, then these periods themselves, as well as their start and end dates, should reflect significant events. Do they? As they are studied, it is revealed that these key dates *do* indeed correspond with key events in the Universe, on the planet and within the evolution of humanity.

The Nine World Ages

First, let's look at the *big* picture—the nine World Ages—including key dates and what "vibration" influenced each main cycle. These World Ages or Underworlds also incorporate the sacred numbers of 13 and 20. (The following is based on Calleman's *The Mayan Calendar and the Transformation of Consciousness*):

1. **Cellular Cycle - 16.4 billion years ago** (thirteen *hablatuns*—1.26 billion-year cycles—ago), marks the beginning of the *Tun* calendar and the physical Universe. This date is now believed to be *approximately* the time of the Big Bang, the birth of the physical Universe. The Hubble Telescope approximates the Big Bang at 14.5 billion years and counting as it probes deeper. In essence, their calendar begins when our physical Universe begins. This cycle is governed by physical laws of action-reaction.

2. **Mammalian Cycle - 820,000,000 years ago** (16.4 billion divided by 20 or thirteen *alautuns*—63.1 million-year cycles—ago), animal life evolved from cells. This cycle is governed by stimulus-response.

3. **Familial Cycle - 41,000,000 years ago** (820 million divided by 20 or thirteen *kinchiltuns*—3.2 million-year cycles—ago), monkeys appeared and began forming families. This cycle is governed by stimulus-individual response.

4. **Tribal Cycle - 2,000,000 years ago** (41 million divided by 20 or thirteen *kalabtuns*—153.846-year cycle—ago), the first tail-less apes appeared and the tribal organization began among the ancestors of *Homo sapiens*. This cycle is governed by similarity-difference.

5. **Cultural Cycle - 102,000 years ago** (approximately 2 million divided by 20 or thirteen *piktuns*—7900-year cycles—ago), *Homo sapiens* appeared and developed language and agriculture. This cycle is governed by shared reason—the foundation of culture.

6. **National Cycle - 5125 years ago** in 3113BC - (approximately 102,000 years divided by 20 or thirteen *baktuns*—394.26-year cycles—ago), the development of patriarchal nation-states, law, writing, and exploitive economic, religious, social, and political systems. This cycle is governed by law and punishment.

7. **Planetary Cycle - 252 years ago** in 1755 - (approximately 5125 years divided by 20 or thirteen *katuns*—19.7-year cycles—ago), the introduction of industrialization leading to electricity, technology, democracy, genetics, atomic energy, etc. This tied the entire planet together in the Planetary cycle governed by power.

8. **Galactic Cycle - January 5, 1999 to February 10, 2011** ushers in the completion of a global communications network—the Internet, satellite TV, etc.—creating a global consciousness. This cycle is governed by ethics consciousness.

9. **Universal Cycle - February 10, 2011 to December 21, 2012** (a 260-day *Tzolkin* day count) governed by our conscious co-creation.

With their *Tun* calendar beginning approximately at the origin of the Universe, it means their calendar is operating within a *universal* framework—not just recording events on our planet and in our solar system and galaxy, but in the *entire* Universe. It appears that their calendar begins when the physical Universe—the world of duality—begins with the Big Bang, the explosion that created the physical Universe from pure energy.

Scientists believe our Universe all started with this Big Bang. However, it is now clear the "physical" Universe is just an *illusion*. There is *no* physical Universe. It only appears so to us. Modern-day quantum physicists have now proven that the physical world is in reality *congealed* energy. They have yet to find any physical "matter." As they were able to peer deeper into the atom, through the nucleus, the protons, the neutrons, etc., they found they were all energy. There was *no* matter.

As world-renown physicist Niels Bohr once said, "Those who are not shocked when they first come across quantum theory cannot possibly have understood it." As spiritual teachers have been saying through the ages, quantum physics has proved that the "physical" Universe is an illusion. The sacred Hindu scriptures have a word for this world of illusion. It is *maya* (which was also the name of Buddha's mother).

In addition to the main World Ages above, the *Tun* reveals that we are now in the last of five *Great Cycles* or *Long Counts*—5125-year cycles consisting of thirteen 394.26-year *baktuns* (13 x 394.26=5125) or 260 *katuns* of 19.71 years each. Each of the thirteen 394.26-year *baktuns* (each *baktun* is also 144,000 days) of a 5125-year *Great Cycle* carries its own predictable vibration that affects what will happen during that period, during that particular 394.26-year *baktun*. Each of these *baktuns* are further divided into twenty *katuns* of 19.7 years (20 x 19.7 = 394.26 years), again each with their own predictable vibration for that *katun*.

Four 5125-year *Great Cycles* have ended and 2012 marks the close of the fifth and last of that cycle. Not only are we presently

55

now in the *last* of the five 5125-year *Great Cycles,* but we are also now in the thirteenth—and last—394.26-year *baktun* (1618-2012) of this *Great Cycle*. We are also in the *last* 19.7-year *katun* (1993-2012) of this *last baktun*. To add to the excitement, not only are we in the last *baktun* and the last *katun* of this present *Great Cycle*, but we are also in the closing days of a 25,652-year cycle of five *Great Cycles* (5 x 5125= 25,652). The closing date for all of these is December 21, 2012 (written as 13.0.0.0.0 in the Mayan Long Count notation). As *all* these ages simultaneously reach their fruition, the dominant vibration for the *end* of this present 19.4-year *katun* (1992-2012) is the "return of the Deity heralding the start of a new age." And *all* previous *Great Cycles* have ended with a transformation of humanity.

As you get deeper into their *Tun* calendar, significant dates marking the beginning or end of these key time periods are designated. These dates do indeed align with major events, as they must, if this calendar is truly prophetic. There are key *Tun* marker dates for first life on land, the first use of fire, the first art in caves, the extinction of the Neanderthal Man, the beginning of Christianity, the fall of the Roman Empire, the rise of capitalism and Protestantism, the beginnings of science, the American and French Revolutions, the Industrial Revolution, Einstein's discovery of the Theory of Relativity, the Hubble Telescope discovering an infinite Universe, WWII, the first nuclear bomb explosion, even for the present-day IT revolution, the collapse of the World Trade Centers and the invasion of Iraq.

If all this is accurate, the beginning and end of the present *Great Cycle* should also exhibit major planetary changes, as well as major changes in humanity. Has that happened for this 5125-year *Great Cycle*, the one we are now in and is about to close? We do not yet know about the end of the present Great Cycle in 2012 but let's look at what happened at its beginning.

This present 5125-year *Great Cycle* began in 3113 BC and, as expected, many major changes began at this time. In essence, "civilization," as we know it, began. Around 3100, was the founding by Pharaoh Menes of Egypt—the first true nation-state. Soon after, Sumer was founded and writing first appeared; then Babylon was founded near present-day Baghdad. Hindu scriptures point to 3102 BC as the start of the *Kali Yuga* (Age of Masters and Slaves) and the end of this *Kali Yuga* means a return to the Golden Age.

In other words, at the beginning of the *Great Cycle*, humanity began a 5125-year World Age that saw the decline of the cooperative, harmonious, unity-oriented tribal cultures and the worldwide development and spread of exploitive, warring, duality-oriented nation-states. In essence, the first nations and "advanced civilizations" began at the beginning of this *Great Cycle* and they will soon reach their culmination in 2012.

Humanity's spiritual evolution has also advanced during this *Great Cycle*. Spiritually, the *Great Cycle* marked the beginning of the monotheistic belief in a Creator God, who had created *all* people. This date—3113 BC—also coincides with the cultivation of corn in North America, the building of Stonehenge in England and, shortly thereafter, in 2975 BC, the construction of one of the first pyramids in Egypt (Djoser's Pyramid), the first Sumerian writing, the first use of metal ushering in the close of the Stone Age—all heralding a *sudden* emergence of the first more technologically advanced human civilizations. All this began very close to the 3113 BC beginning date of the *Great Cycle*. At the cycle's midpoint, around 550 BC, another spiritual renaissance appeared with the advent of Buddhism, Confucianism and Taoism.

As this *Great Cycle* or *National* period (3113 BC-2012) progressed, there emerged human rulers who claimed to be divine, societies divided by class, economics and hierarchical ranking, brutal, exploitive and dehumanizing political and economic systems. Humanity left the small-scale, sustainable, cooperative, often-matriarchal tribal agrarian cultures and entered into an era of ever-expanding, patriarchal, national societies of competitive industrialized nation-states, all addicted to organized warfare. Where humanity was once 100% tribal, today it is believed that it is now less than one percent of humanity is living tribally.

During this *Great Cycle*, people began to think judgmentally and with condemnation, evaluating what was good or bad, which people were enemies and which friends, which religion was right and which was wrong. This dualism manifested in greed, exploitation, domination, and wars for power and the perception of limited resources. The beginning of this period may have been the "fall from grace," a concept found universally throughout the history of humanity. This was, and still is, a 5125-year detour into fear created by perceiving ourselves as separate—separate from God, separate from our Mother Earth, separate from each other. It is a period where the *love of power* has reigned.

Within each of the thirteen 394.26-year *baktuns* of this *Great Cycle*, each of the twenty 19.7-year *katuns* (which are called *Katun 1, Katun 2, Katun 3*, etc.) are cyclical and repeat every 260 years (13 x 20). If you know which of the twenty *katuns* you are in at any given time, you would understand what that period would be like, what vibration will be affecting us during those 19.7 years. Whenever we are in a *Katun 5*, the dominant vibration is "rulers and subjects separate, rulers badly treated, even killed." The American Civil War (1860-65) was during a *Katun 5*. *Katun 8*'s vibration is "culture is in disarray." The tumultuous 1960s was a *Katun 8*. World War II was during a *katun* calling for "a bleak time—drought, famine, occupation, change."

More recently, the *Tun* calendar has been equally as accurate in its predictions. In 1992, the year the Internet went worldwide, was the predicted time of "global consciousness," which the Internet has given us. The period just prior to this was depicted by the Mayan calendar as one of relative peace. Indeed, 1992-1999 was one of the most peaceful periods in the history of humanity.

The Mayan calendar indicates 1999 as the beginning of the *Planetary* period and the close of the *National* period. It was predicted that one effect of this change would be that the power structure would start to think about planetary control rather than warring among their individual nations for control of certain areas. It was during this period that a series of protests began against the World Trade Organization (WTO), the International Monetary Fund (IMF), the World Bank, the Group of Eight (G8), the European Union, NATO and multinational corporations—all of which have replaced individual countries as the power-players in the global political and economic fields.

The vibration that was ruling at the beginning of the present Iraq War (2003) was one of "collapse of international law." With the United States declaring a preemptive war on a country it only *believed* to be a potential threat, the United States has effectively undermined international law and our moral authority to enforce it. Now every country can demand the same right to take these actions.

The 2003 Iraq war, which took place under a different *katun* than the 1991 Iraq war, was launched in spite of the protests of many Eastern and Western countries and in defiance of the UN Security Council resolutions. This represented the de facto collapse of the power of the United Nations and even of NATO—in essence the "collapse of international law." Of further note, the war is being fought in Iraq, home to ancient Babylon—one of the birthplaces of the nationalism of the *Great Cycle*. As we pass through the *Galactic* cycle (1999-2012), the centuries old Western dominance will come to an end.

As we have seen, the *Tun* calendar is divided into periods that come under certain "galactic beams," certain vibrations—certain *aspects* and *intentions*—that supported or undermined certain activities and behaviors. These vibrations define each particular period. The Dark Ages was under one vibration, the Renaissance under another, the Industrial Revolution, the Nuclear Age, and the IT Revolution, under yet others. These "galactic beams" are the winds and waves of history. These aspects and intentions affect not only large periods of time, but as we get closer to the end date and continue dividing by 13 and 20, it maps out shorter periods of time, some of only a few years and, toward the end, of a few months. And, as we are about to see with the *Tzolkin*, the vibration of *each* day is also predictable.

Perhaps the Maya were *consciously* responding to one of these waves when, around 830AD, they decided to abandon their ceremonial cities throughout the region. They left these ceremonial cities and retreated into rural villages in the jungle. Perhaps they understood that a truly spiritual life is more easily followed living close to the land rather than in urban centers. This date, 830AD, also marked the end of the 394.26-year Baktun 9 and the beginning of Baktun 10—a *baktun* of decline. Maybe they saw their decline coming. Their calendars were predicting this coming age of decline and perhaps they sensed it was time to leave their cities, knowing they had completed their Divinely-guided task of codifying and recording in stone certain knowledge and wisdom—a coded *matrix* that would be of great value to future generations.

The key thing to understand within their *Tun* calendar is that for 5125 years, from 3113BC to 2012, duality has had the winds in its sails. We have been passing through a 5,125-year "galactic beam of duality" and we are soon to emerge from it. By "duality" I mean all perceptions of seeing ourselves separated from our Creator, Mother Earth and each other. These mistaken perceptions inevitably lead to warfare (both personal and organized), greed, selfishness, win/lose thinking, exploitation (of both people and the environment) and domination in all forms (from marital to national). Throughout history, duality has usually manifested in three areas of human life—sex, money and power—where its misguided expression has led to much suffering.

That is why even high-minded endeavors and movements aimed at alleviating suffering and establishing a more just and equitable world, have never grown to full fruition under the winds of duality. Democracies have become corrupted by money and continue to wage wars. The United Nations has become compromised and is often ineffective. The end of physical slavery was replaced by economic slavery. Civil rights were granted to many but prejudice within the heart and mind remains. The granting of full rights to women coincided with their being depicted as sexual objects.

Those people wedded to duality thinking—from political, social and religious leaders to ordinary people—have prospered under this vibration. After all, they had the "wind at their backs." That will all soon change.

It has been a journey into duality, into right/wrong, good/evil, win/lose thinking that has offered humanity much pain and little peace—emotionally, spiritually or physically. This age of duality is marked by delusion and deception, exploitation of the weaker, seeking happiness outside ourselves, and the two ever-present unconscious manifestations of the mistaken belief in separation—the ego and the desire for dominance over others in all their various and twisted forms.

This cycle ends on December 21, 2012. It *is* the "end of life as we have known it for the last 5125 years" and good riddance to it! As it ends, the age of duality awakens to oneness and a new age of unity unfolds. In the past, so often people's answer to their problems was power. Now it will be love. This will be a planetary event and, like a rising tide raises *all* boats, it will touch everyone as the love of power is supplanted by *the power of love*. As always, every living being will be offered the opportunity to change.

As the new World Age of Unity dawns, we have the free will to choose. As Mayanist John Major Jenkins writes in *The Mystery of*

> . . . What we actually experience depends on our choices—whether we cling in fear to familiar illusions or open to love and trust to the great mystery that seeks to transform and elevate us. . . And here's the nub of the sacrifice doctrine: our goal is not the sacrifice of literal hearts, bodies, or even our egos, but the sacrifice of our illusions. In that surrender, we lose nothing real but gain everything worth having: our true selves . . . the galactic alignment of the era-2012 [is] a great opportunity for spiritual seekers to reconnect with the source of perennial wisdom. But we shouldn't wait until 2012, for we are in the alignment zone now [1980-2016]. The time, as always, is now.

When duality started to express itself starting in 3113BC with the founding of the first city-states in Babylon, Sumer and Egypt, it spread across the globe. As it did, because of its exploitive and domination-driven worldview, as well as its advanced weaponry, it quickly conquered and then absorbed into itself all the unity-based indigenous cultures it encountered. It was the same in Asia, Europe, Australia, Africa, and then finally in North and South America. Now it is time to re-invigorate this ancient holistic worldview.

Basically, for thousands of years visionaries and unity thinkers have been swimming *against* the prevailing current of duality. On December 21, 2012, the current changes direction. Unity will be going *with* the prevailing current. How exactly this shift will manifest on the planet is still unknown but what is clear is that the more our "sails of love" are extended, the more wind we will catch as this age transforms from the love of power to the power of love.

The Tzolkin Calendar

Just as the Mayans' *Tun* calendar maps out the 16.4 billion year flow of Creation, their *Tzolkin* ("count of days" or "pieces of the sun") details the vibration for *each and every* day. With their *Tzolkin* calendar, you can determine each day's "day sign." This is the vibration created by the combined influence of one of the 20 *aspects* and one of the 13 *intentions* assigned to each day. It outlines that particular day's ethics and wisdom. You can determine which days are auspicious for some activities and which are inauspicious. For example, the *Tzolkin* tells us which days favor beginning a new enterprise, a wedding or planting in the garden.

Each day was designated by the aspect *and* intention that, combined together, affected that day. Each of the 20 aspects has a name (Ik, Manik, Imix, Kan, Akbal, etc.) and the 13 intentions are represented by numbers 1 thru 13. Each day has a special meaning designated by the combination of their aspect and intention (10-Kan, 7-Akbal, 6-Imix, etc.). The *Tzolkin* consists of 260 days (13 x 20) representing 260 possible combinations of aspects and intentions. Every 260 days the cycle repeats itself. They would often depict this as two interlocking cogged wheels—one for the 13 numbers and one for the 20 signs (see wheels in photo section). This 260-day period, not nine months, has been found to be the *natural* gestation period of a woman (when not influenced by modern drugs, chemicals and other disruptive factors) and is the time from the planting to the harvesting of corn in the highlands of Guatemala. When the third wheel, the 365-day *Haab*, was added, each cycle would repeat itself every 52 years. They called this 52-year cycle a *Calendar Round*, which was approximately the expected lifetime of an ancient Mayan.

The *Tzolkin*, like the *Tun*, is not so much a time calendar as a pattern or decipherable *code* of Divine light and creative energy, revealing the unfolding of the Creator's will on Earth. Each day was like a different melodious, beautiful song. It was, and is, a key to understanding the human experience. Just as the *Tun* reveals the vibration of various *ages*, the *Tzolkin* reveals the key vibration of each *day*. For instance, September 11, 2001, (a 6-Imix day in the *Tzolkin*) was a "day of change and new beginnings." October 7, 2001, the day the U.S. invaded Afghanistan, was a day "to balance or settle."

The *Tzolkin* is considered to be a personal calendar For instance, it gave everyone a way to determine the spiritual intention and aspect of each day so you could be guided by it and attempt to live according to its aspects and intentions. Also, by knowing the day one was born, everyone would know that day's particular intention and aspect. In fact, every pre-conquest Mayan was named after the day on which they were born. Everyone in the tribe, by knowing one of your names, would know your purpose and role within the whole tribe. For instance, if a person was born under *Cib* (wisdom), they would have the wisdom of the Ancients. People born under *Muluc* (offering), gladly gave more than they asked for themselves. If born under *Ik* (wind), they would be a good orator and spread spiritual inspiration as if by the wind.

Before the conquest by the Spanish, the sacred Mayan calendar was shared by all people in the entire Mesoamerican region, reaching even into the present-day United States. On each and every day, people in the entire area, involving many tribes and millions of people, were "spiritually synchronized" through the use of the same 260-day *Tzolkin* calendar. In the remote areas of Guatemala, Mayans have been following the *Tzolkin* without interruption for over 2500 years. Their timekeepers still offer their wisdom in many of the traditional villages. In recent times, the revolutionary *Zapatistas*, based in the Mayan areas of Chiapas, Mexico, choose auspicious dates from this sacred calendar to organize their protests—many of which have been successful.

Unlike our present-day calendar that reinforces our worldview that we live in a purely *mechanical* Universe, the Mayan sacred calendars reinforced a worldview that we live in a purely *spiritual* Universe. This key difference represents two different world views, two different stories, two different realities.

Focusing on the 2012 end-date diminishes the real value the Mayan calendars hold for humanity. As we can see, the Mayan calendars were never a countdown to doomsday or judgment day. They were, and are, timetables to the unfolding of human spirituality and enlightenment. The Mayan calendars are not solely about time. They are about the flow of Creation and keeping humans conscious of it *day by day*. Their calendars are an accurate schedule for the evolution of the Universe, the galaxy, the planet, and humanity. As Calleman writes, the Mayan calendar is "fundamentally a time schedule for the evolution of consciousness." It is the cosmic schedule for our own enlightenment.

The Mayan Calendars
The Timetable to Enlightenment

The Mayan calendars reveal that humanity has a history and a future charted by a Divine plan. It reveals that the Earth passes through certain major "galactic synchronization beams," as José Arguelles calls them, the present one taking 5125 years to completely pass through with its end date of December 21, 2012. This beam can be sub-divided into other energies taking ever shorter periods of time to complete. Each period is dominated by a certain vibration or mindset.

We are in the last few years of this 5125-year *Great Cycle* of the evolution of our species. We are also now in the briefer period that began in 2007 of the "tearing down of everything the power structure stands for." Unable to understand this shift, it will be met with resistance from strongly-entrenched power players. *All* dominance—whether it be physical, military, religious, economic, or political or dominance of men over women—will be breaking down.

As it does, we can expect to see fewer threats of major wars between national superpowers and more resistance of disenfranchised groups against the *global* power structure. However, this energy will be offset by the rising evolution of human consciousness toward love and our awareness that we are co-creators of our reality. As Calleman recently wrote, "All hierarchies will have crumbled. With the end of duality, the dominance of one soul over any other will naturally come to end.' "

Things will be moving very quickly during the *Galactic* period (January 5, 1999 - February 10, 2011) and even more so during the *Universal* period (February 10, 2011 - December 21, 2012). During the *Universal* period, there will be a twenty-fold *acceleration* of spiritual time where we will see as much consciousness change in a 260-day *tun* as we saw in a 19.7-year *katun* during the *Planetary* period (1755-2012) and in a 394.26-year *baktun* during the *National* period (3113 BC-2012). In essence, consciousness will be evolving at mach speed.

Mayanist John Major Jenkins explains that the Mayan end-date of December 21, 2012 is determined because that is the *exact* date that the Winter Solstice sun conjuncts the center of our galaxy, the crossing point of the Milky Way in Sagittarius. On that day, an area in the Milky Way the Mayans called the "dark rift," *Xibalba bi*, the "Hole in the Sky," points directly to this crossing point. This conjunction—this *Galactic Alignment*—occurs every 25,800 years. On that day in 2012, the Winter Solstice sun will *eclipse* the center of our galaxy—the Milky Way—when viewed from Earth.

The Mayans believed this galactic center, like a powerful radio transmitter, is constantly sending out spiritual energy and on that day it would be received on Earth as an open door—*complete and unobstructed*—with no negative filters to impede its power. On that day, a powerful shift in consciousness will occur. Mythologically, it is also the day associated with the return of their teacher of love—the Plumed Serpent, Quetzalcoatl (Kukulcan). Or as Jenkins states, "The world is reborn when the December solstice sun aligns with the dark rift in the galactic center."

Thousands of years ago, without the aid of telescopes or computers, the Mayans exactly predicted this rare astronomical event—the sun aligned with the center of the Milky Way. In September 2000, centuries after the Mayans noted this as their place of origin and rebirth, scientists, using the Hubble Telescope, determined that there was indeed a "dark rift" *exactly* where the ancient Mayans noted—an supermassive "black hole" with a mass four million times that of our sun. Over 30 million stars gravitate towards it. It is the "hub" around which our Milky Way rotates. It is the *center* of our Galaxy, the origin point of the Big Bang around which all the stars in our galaxy revolve. It is the cosmic womb of our galaxy from which new stars are born and from which everything, including us and our planet, originates.

This means, as we look at the sun on December 21, 2012, we will be looking directly toward the core or the galactic center of our Milky Way—an event that occurs exactly thirteen *baktuns* (5125 years) from the beginning of this World Age in 3113 BC. This will be the first time in recorded history that this "star gate" will be open and witnessed. At that moment, we cross the "Galactic Equator" and usher in a transformation to the power of love. We are really already in the initial period of being aligned with the galactic center.

As further evidence that December 21, 2012 was not just

chosen by the Mayans arbitrarily, is the fact that it is also the *exact* day the Earth completes its 25,920-year wobble on its axis, a process that creates the precession of the equinoxes—a major astronomical event. Also, it was 25,920 years ago, in 24,000BC that the last set of five Great Cycles began. This was the peak of the last Ice Age and the emergence of what we call "modern humanity."

When this cosmic event occurs, a spiritual gateway will open, catalyzing a new leap in human consciousness, a great collective awakening, a new World Age, symbolizing a rebirth of humanity. It is also interesting to note that astrologically, 2012 is the close of the Age of Pisces and the dawning of the Age of Aquarius. Of further interest astrologically, one year before this end-date, on December 24, 2011, all the planets in our solar system will be spaced 30 degrees apart—something that occurs only once every 45,200 years.

As we approach 2012, it is not to be feared but welcomed. It becomes clear that the Creator has left within the calendars, codices and buildings of an ancient civilization in Central America the entire passage of time and history with predictable, understandable and verifiable patterns. We are, as Mayanist Ian Lungold says, "either experiencing a 16.4 billion-year chain of incredible coincidences or we are right on schedule." This reality can serve to remind us of a benevolent Creator—an all-pervading Intelligence—whose Universe is unfolding in perfect order and who has revealed this order to us at *this* time for a *specific* reason.

Calleman further explains in his book, *The Mayan Calendar and the Transformation of Consciousness*:

> As a result of this change in consciousness, holistic, female perspectives will become increasingly dominant toward the later days of the cycle . . . The second prediction we may make is that the Galactic [cycle] will be a cycle when the belief in God, and maybe even more so in a higher spiritual ethics, will return. In the time to come, a new spirituality and a new belief in God and His/Her goodness will find much more evident manifestations . . . This is the much heralded pole shift, which is really a pole shift in consciousness and has nothing to do with the Earth's axis or any other geophysical phenomenon.

The Mayan calendar also explains how there will be enough evolution within the hearts and minds of humanity to bring about much-needed change to once again live in a symbiotic relationship with each other and the Earth, something that many have begun to doubt is possible. Their calendar reveals that we have passed through many planetary cycles controlled first by action-reaction, then stimulus-herd response, then stimulus-individual response, then mind-reason, then law and punishment, then power, and then ethics. We are now entering the final *Universal* cycle—conscious co-creation with the Creator. People all over the planet are learning (remembering) that we create our reality with our consciousness—with our intentions, thoughts and emotions. We are moving from being at the *effect* (victims) to understanding we are the *cause* (creators) of our realities. It is the Age of Conscious Creation.

We exercise our abilities as co-creators by coming to rely more and more on our *intuition*—our own personal knowing and wisdom—as opposed to relying solely on the knowledge we have accumulated with our minds. As we follow this intuition, our own personal path of service to the planet, our place within the cosmic plan, will be revealed to us. Our *willingness* to find our path is all that is needed. The Creator will do the rest. From this awareness of ourselves as co-creators, vast possibilities are available as we are tapping into the energy of the Universe. It is through this energy, that the 5125-year cycle of duality will be transformed.

These Mayan calendars define the path toward enlightenment and therefore they are calendars of our progression toward peace and unity. They are tools that can unify humanity with all its varying religions, traditions and world-views and reveal to all that we are part of a much larger plan—one that *finally* leads toward world peace. We do not need to abandon civilization and all its useful technological tools but transform it into a more enlightened stage.

During this final period, there will be a joining of the wisdom of the East and West, intuition and logic, spirit and matter. This began during the period from 1947-49, when the independence of the Eastern societies of India, Indonesia and China freed about half the world's population from direct Western control. This was also the time of the birth of many in the West who would later welcome into their Western cultures such revered Eastern spiritual paths as meditation, yoga, tai-chi, chanting, and holistic healing.

Some will choose to integrate these East-West polarities; others will resist. When this is resisted, there will be conflict, such as that created by the Iraq War and manifested in Islamic terrorists' attacks of Western targets. However, to offset these conflicts, there will be an ever-increasing number of people worldwide aspiring to—and reaching—a more enlightened state. We do this by understanding and integrating within ourselves the driving force of the dualistic worldview—the ego. We begin to remember our oneness with all or as the Mayan greeting says, *Lak'ech,* "I am another you."

As Calleman writes in *The Mystery of 2012: Predictions, Prophecies & Possibilities*:

> The Ninth Underworld [the *Universal* period] may be seen as a gift from God, since it is not only about creating balance, but also about the enlightenment given to humankind as an expression of divine grace. This is when we will fully understand why the cosmic plan was designed the way it was, and we will overflow with gratitude to the Creator. At the same time, we will recognize our own divinity, for there will be no separation between the divinity of the Creator and our own . . . The ego that was established to serve the dualist mind . . . simply cannot survive the high frequency of the Universal Underworld. . . In the dualist frame of consciousness, the ego was an important tool for survival; in the unitary frame of consciousness, it will jeopardize the survival of the individual . . . the mind has to be disengaged if it is not to lead the individual to complete heartbreak and personal collapse.

With this clearer perspective, we will begin to realize that our temporary separation from our Divine source, created by our dualistic worldview—the cause of almost *all* human suffering—is finally ending and we are awakening in the same place where we fell asleep—in the Oneness of the Creator. We will realize we never really left Home—only in our dreams, only in *maya*. This might seem overly idealistic, even naïve, however, from this expanded awareness, *all* is possible as we complete the 16.4 billion-year journey through the world of matter.

So the big question is: *What exactly is going to happen on December 21, 2012*? There is no certain answer. Actually, according to the Mayan calendars, everything and every age is predictable from the creation of the Universe *until* 2012. Then it's a blank slate. Many researchers, writers and TV programs present a fearful message of doomsday. This is understandable since we have all been interpreting this sacred information while still under the present *World Age* of duality—where *everything* is viewed fearfully. Through the eyes of fear, 2012 would appear as a global *emergency*. However, through the eyes of love, 2012 would appear as a global *emergence*. It is now time to view it through the eyes of love.

This Golden Age will *not* occur by itself. It will manifest through the vision, commitment and work of people awakening to the power of love worldwide. We will manifest this in our everyday lives by embracing our roles as co-creators. As we approach the end of the *Great Cycle*, more and more people will be seeking greater harmony and freeing themselves from the illusion of duality and separateness. As Dr. Calleman says in his book:

> The reason humanity has lost faith in the idea of a millennium of peace is that it has become blind to the existence of a cosmic plan, according to which our minds change . . . the Mayan calendar tells us that at the end of creation we will be ruled by the unitary mind, or, as the Hopi say: one world, one nation, under the Creator. Thus the road to peace is largely one of transforming our minds to a unitary enlightened frame of consciousness, and by taking such a path, deepening our realization that we are all one.
>
> The Mayan calendar shares many of its messages with other spiritual traditions: "We are all One," "Life has a purpose," and "God is Love." Yet it should not be overlooked that it also conveys a unique message: There is a deadline for the creation of the enlightened golden age at "the end of time," and we all need to participate as co-creators in that process. This

is the crucial message of the Mayan calendar that needs to be assimilated today.

At this point, after so many millennia, we are finally no longer *puppets* of the Divine process of creation but its *creators*. Even powerful leaders who believe they form their world to their wishes do not yet understand that even they are operating robot-like, driven by the energies of the prevailing age. As each individual strives for this remembrance, they help all of humanity. When we wonder why we lingered so long in the forgetting, the answer will be: *We didn't*. We just temporarily fell asleep and dreamed it.

What is clear from this emerging information is that something strange and wonderful happened in Central America centuries ago and there are many theories as to what it was. Unlike anything the world had ever seen, local indigenous tribes seemed to rapidly grow into advanced civilizations that were *both* spiritually enlightened *and* materially prosperous and stable. This growth spurt defies all anthropological understanding for the otherwise orderly advancement of civilizations. However, similar dynamic accelerations are observed in various civilizations worldwide, some occurring at the same time that they occurred in Mesoamerica.

Who is responsible for creating this repository of wisdom encoded in the hieroglyphs, buildings and calendars of these ancient people? Some, like Jose Arguelles, believe that enlightened beings came from other planets—perhaps Pleiades, Arcturus, Venus or Orion. Others believe they were descendants from the collapsing fabled island of Atlantis. In fact, almost all ancient Mesoamerican cultures have myths of their ancestors arriving by boats from the east after a massive flood. Some believe the Mayan priest/kings were Ascended Masters—fully God-realized beings—sent by the Creator to assist the planet. Yet others believe they were highly evolved humans closely in touch with the Divine. Whoever they were, they have left us, through the Mayan calendars, an astounding cosmic calling card. They have left us the sheet music of the Universe—and we each have our part to play in this grand cosmic symphony—by our willingness to be an instrument of peace played by the Creator. In time, the answer as to who they were may be revealed, but for now, perhaps the more important questions are: *What was their mission? What was their message?*

70

Chapter 5

Santiago Atitlan
Then & Now

Around the year 2012, a large chapter in human history will be coming to an end. All the values and assumptions of the previous World Age will expire, and a new phase of human growth will commence.

- John Major Jenkins, *Maya Cosmogenesis 2012*

Finding that indeed the core Mayan message and all their prophetic information was leading us to the remembrance of our being conscious co-creators and that we are unconditional love just like our Creator, I re-committed to this book. In *Memoirs of an Ex-Hippie,* I had found this message in the counterculture of the sixties and seventies. In *Rasta Heart*, we found it in the Rastafarian community, Bob Marley and conscious reggae music. In *The Beauty Path* it was revealed within the Native American culture. And now here it was again in Maya. I was now looking forward to our upcoming trip to Santiago Atitlan in southern Guatemala to see if this ancient information was still vibrating in the modern day. We emailed Danny's friend, Chus Landa, and made arrangements to meet with him and Tata Pedro soon after we arrived at Lake Atitlan.

In late February of 2007, Julia, Alicia and I returned to Guatemala, this time to visit Lake Atitlan. I had been reading books by Martín Prechtel, the writer, artist and musician who had lived in the Mayan village of Santiago Atitlan from the early-1970s to the mid-1990s. Martín, a half-blood Pueblo Indian from New Mexico, became part of the village's spiritual hierarchy and had recorded their wisdom and initiations in several books including, *Stealing Benefacio's Roses, The Disobedience of the Daughter of the Sun, Long Life, Honey in the Heart,* and *Secrets of the Talking Jaguar.* I thought that this quiet Tzutujil Mayan village might be a good place to seek out a present-day Mayan message of love.

We flew into Guatemala City, several hours east of Lake Atitlan and south of Tikal and Flores. The flight over the city was a study in contrast. From the air, the downtown area looked rather modern, with a few gleaming skyscrapers and luxury apartment buildings. We passed over wealthy residential neighborhoods, full of grass, trees and swimming pools. Then, off to our left, was a huge swath of slums that went on for acres and acres—with no parks, no trees, no grass, no playing fields—just acre after acre of small shacks with their ubiquitous tin roofs. Throughout this part of the world the effects of the 5125-year progression of civilization—the spread of the exploitive and competitive political and economic systems—can be seen everywhere.

We encountered our first translation problem by taking a wrong turn from the car rental agency and immediately getting caught in the rush-hour traffic of the capital. Guatemala City seemed to be a rather nondescript and, at times, decrepit city, known for violence in some areas. However, we never went into the Old City— its historic district. The city has lost much of its colonial charm from the past when it was called the "Jewel of Central America." After over an hour of being stuck in traffic, we headed out toward the old capital, Antigua. There we planned to spend the night before heading the next morning to Santiago Atitlan, three hours further down the road.

Once we were out of the city area, I was pleased to see the roads were well-maintained, one of the bonuses of the end of the civil war when foreign capital flooded in. There were few cars. For the most part, the people drove with a modicum of sanity. There were few pedestrians in the rural areas. Most people took the beautifully decorated converted school buses, known as "chicken buses," that often traveled at dangerous, break-neck speeds. This was all a welcome relief from our many trips in Jamaica, with its pot-holed roads, abundance of foot and car traffic and most drivers driving like teenagers with absolutely no sense of their own mortality.

Late afternoon we arrived in Antigua, about 28 miles from Guatemala City. For over two centuries, Antigua, built in the 1500s, was the country's original capital. It was abandoned as the capital after a devastating earthquake in 1773, one of a string of such earthquakes. It is a charming city—actually more like a town. It is perhaps one of the best-preserved colonial cities in Spanish America—its ambiance fiercely protected by The National Council for the Protection of Antigua Guatemala.

The Spanish Colonial style permeates every part of the town: its houses, churches, squares, parks and ruins, as well as its traditions and folklore. It has a historic town square area, full of cobblestone streets, distinctive hotels, shops, and restaurants. Antigua, now a tourist Mecca, sits in a highland valley overlooked by the spectacular 10,000-foot high Agua Volcano. A little further away are two other volcanoes, Acatenango, and the always smoking, sometimes erupting, Fuego.

The city is a celebration of Guatemala's Spanish and European roots—roots that began in the 1500s. Only about twenty percent of the country's population—the ethnic Europeans (whites) and the mixed blood *Ladinos*—celebrate this legacy. This 20 percent, which controls Guatemala's political, social and economic power, are very proud of their old capital and its Spanish roots. However, this beautiful city also stands as a testament to the European colonizers' assault on the indigenous Maya—a native people who have survived and today account for almost eighty percent of the country's eleven million people.

Entering the town, we immediately got lost looking for our hotel, a small ten-room former convent on the edge of the historic district. Luckily, there were many policemen and uniformed private guards on the streets to ask for directions—all were armed with large shotguns, reminding us of the threat of violence built into this country's fabric. As recently as August, 2007, *The New York Times* reported that even though the 36-year violent conflict ended in the mid-1990s, "the bloodshed and rampant impunity have not. More than 5,000 murders are reported each year. Many are committed by the same groups—both left and right—that terrorized the country during the war."

We made the mistake of asking the locals where our hotel was in Spanish, which neither Julia, Alicia or I speak, but we can say, "Por favor, donde esta Hotel Dona Beatriz?" ("Please, where is the Dona Beatriz Hotel?") Of course, now they figured we were fluent in Spanish and off they would go, wildly gesticulating and giving us absolutely incoherent (to us) directions, always finishing with a warm, satisfied smile, to which we would say equally enthusiastically, "Gracias, mi amigo!" and head off in more or less the direction they initially pointed, having no idea what they said or where our hotel was.

For over an hour, we rode around this little 20 square-block area, often passing our newfound friends several times and waving as if we had followed their directions exactly, found our hotel and were now sightseeing. Finally, after Alicia remembered from her high school Spanish class that "izquierda" means "left" and "derecho" means "right," we located our hotel and checked in, all feeling that if you had to get lost for an hour, Antigua sure was a beautiful place to be lost.

After dinner and a stroll around the city, the next morning we left for Santiago Atitlan, one of 12 Mayan villages on the shores of Lake Atitlan. We drove through a few small villages, broad valleys and over mountain passes—all beautiful, all seemingly peaceful— with no hint of the ongoing violence. Occasionally, we passed an architecturally-designed restaurant or gift shop, a sign that with this relative peace, tourism was beginning to flourish.

After driving up a long mountain to the village of Solola, we began our eight-mile descent into the tourist village of Panajachel. From there, small ferries would take you to the other villages, including Santiago Atitlan (called "Santiago" by the locals). The road down was steep, curving and narrow, demanding all my attention, but then we came around a bend. There it was, thousands of feet below us—Lake Atitlan—its blue, clear water sparkling in the afternoon sun.

Lake Atitlan has to be one of the most beautiful places on earth. The lake, 18 miles long by 12 miles wide, was formed by a collapsed volcano and is now ringed by three volcanoes—Toliman, Atitlan and San Pedro—that, at a height of 10,000 feet, tower above the lake and the villages. They serve as a constant reminder of our frailty and the possibility of life changing in an instant, which it does often in this area.

We drove through Panajachel looking for the hotel where we had arranged to leave our rental car and take a small foot ferry over to Santiago. We would be returning to stay at the hotel for a few days later in our trip. A few decades earlier, Pana (as the locals call it) was a quiet Cakchiquel Mayan village on the northern shore. Now it's a conclave for adventurers, eco-tourists, backpackers, hippies

74

and folks like us hoping to get a little enlightenment and life direction from the quarter million indigenous Mayans living in the lakeside villages. Pana has attracted so many international tourists, some of whom never leave, that it is often referred to as "Gringotenango." The waterfront area is full of hotels, quaint restaurants, craft stores and stalls, and the usual street vendors. Hard drugs, especially cocaine, have also moved in with their sordid legacy that has had somewhat of a corrupting influence on a few locals, as it always does.

We headed across the lake in a 12-seater open ferry. Immediately out on our 30-minute trip to Santiago, we hit some rough water, which is common when the winds—the xocomil, "the wind that carries away sin"—pickup in the afternoon. The rough ride, which can become dangerous on very windy days, was just a minor distraction to actually being on the lake, where everywhere your eyes rest, it is inspiring. The air was cool and clean, the views not dimmed by pollution, the water crystalline.

Arriving at the dock at our hotel, the Posada Santiago, we all fell in love with the place instantly. When we travel, we always seek out the quaint, smaller hotels that are someone's labor of love. Posada Santiago, one of only three small hotels in Santiago, was just that, a vision of owners Dave and Suzie—a vision that was interrupted for ten years, from 1980 to 1990, as the hotel sat abandoned because of local violence from the war.

Walking up from the boat dock, we passed the small pool and adjoining wood-fired hot-tub—both looking out over the majestic lake and volcano. Above the pool, and across the small road, is the hotel. Its adjoining restaurant, with its high ceilings, friendly bar, Internet area, conversation pits and front porch, makes you instantly feel at home and makes you want to hangout there even when you're not eating the restaurant's delicious food. We quickly settled in to our stone cottage, complete with fireplace and porch overlooking the lake.

After a swim, hot-tub soak and dinner, we called Danny's friend, Chus, and made arrangements to meet him at our hotel the next afternoon. He said he had talked to Tata Pedro and we would meet with him later in the week.

"You know, I decided we would come here after reading Martín Prechtel's books," I said to Julia and Alicia over dinner.

"When he lived here before the civil war, he found much wisdom within the local Tzutujil Mayan people, especially within their initiation ceremonies. I want to see if this wisdom is still here like it is with the Hopis and other tribes who still retain much of their ancient wisdom. But I have no idea how I'll find this out. Most everyone here speaks Tzutujil, not even Spanish, and we don't speak either."

"Well, Dad," Alicia said, "remember before we came, you said you didn't have everything arranged, but you had a strong feeling that everything was going to fall into place? You weren't even sure if we were going to get up with Tata Pedro and now that's arranged, so let's just see what happens in the morning."

"You're right, sweetheart. Thanks for the reminder," I said, glad to have Julia and Alicia around when my doubts come up.

The next morning, we were talking with Lia and Claire, two women Julia had met the previous day by the pool. Lia had just started The Children's Village in California, a group home for foster children that also included rental housing for senior citizens who mentored the children. David, the hotel owner, passed by our table and I asked him if he knew of a guide that could take us through the village and give us an understanding of how things were there.

"Dolores Ratzan is coming in a half-hour to take Lia and Claire and another couple on a village tour. She speaks Tzutujil, Spanish and English. You can join them," he said, as I got a knowing smile from Alicia.

Soon Dolores showed up, a handsome, proud, intelligent woman with classic Mayan features and dressed in her traditional Tzutujil dress. (The Tzutujils, pronounced "two-two-heel," are one of twenty-two Mayan groups. The Tzutujils live in Santiago and in San Pedro, Tata Pedro's village nearby on the lake.) As we assembled for the tour, I told her of my interest after reading Martín's books.

"I know he fled the civil war in the 1990s with his wife and children," I said, as we started walking the short distance to the village. "Did you know him?"

"Yes, I did," she said with a sly smile. "I am that wife. Martín is my ex-husband."

Martín Prechtel was raised in New Mexico and experienced the humiliation, self-loathing and anger that so many Native Americans have. In his early twenties, he hit the road with only an acoustic guitar and his mother's painting supplies. After several rather raucous years kicking around Mexico and Central America, he landed in Santiago Atitlan in 1979, where he soon met Nicolas Chiviliu Tacaxoy, who, until his death in 1980, was the most legendary and powerful shaman in southwestern Guatemala. Chiv, a member of the Tzutujil spiritual hierarchy, immediately asked Martín why he had taken so long to get there as Chiv had been psychically calling him to Santiago for years through his dreams, vivid dreams that Martín immediately remembered having years earlier for eleven nights during a legendary New Mexico blizzard.

Martín soon became Chiv's student, living in his family compound along with the many members of Chiv's extended family. Over many years, Martín learned their language and customs and was embraced by the Tzutujils of Santiago. Eventually he became a village leader, ceremonial flute player and well-known artist. He married Dolores and they had two children. All four of them were forced into hiding in Guatemala when Martín's name was added to the government's death squad's list of possible guerilla sympathizers, which he was not. Ironically, since he took no stand in the fight, he was also suspected by the guerrillas.

Chiv had told Martín that his purpose was to one day leave the Santiago Atitlan—the "Umbilicus of the World"—and return to his former home in the U.S. He was to take with him the "Village Heart," the complex knowledge of the chief and the vision of the shaman he had become, and try to plant it in Martín's native country—which he is presently doing.

After a year in hiding in Guatemala with several near arrests, Dolores, Martín and their two young children fled, almost penniless, to the U.S. After a rather homeless, nomadic life living in cars and on the streets, they settled in New Mexico, where Martín pursued his art and became a well-known healer. Dolores returned to Santiago when the violence ebbed. Martín, still well-known for his beautiful transcendental art, lives near Taos and operates his international school, Bolad's Kitchen, and travels and speaks of his experiences.

Through his books and his vivid description of the Tzutujil people and their customs, I felt I was able to discern much of the ancient wisdom of Quetzalcoatl's teachings—wisdom embodied by the Tzutujils' initiations—had survived all the assaults of the last thousand years, at least until Martín left in the mid-1990s. I was curious to see how things were after the years of war, the loss of their initiation ceremonies and the introduction of the zealous evangelical churches.

Martín described life during his time in Santiago as a study in contrasts—at times loving and kind, at other times, brutal and harsh. As the civil war intensified in the 1980s and 1990s, Santiago Atitlan, always known for its fiercely independent villagers, became one of the many remote Mayan villages that the government decided to brutalize to be sure they did not join or support the local guerrillas, who were fighting for better treatment of the people. By then, the government's power was unraveling and the military leaders who ruled the country, encouraged and supported by the American Central Intelligence Agency (CIA), reasserted themselves with a vengeance.

Between 1982 and 1987, there were two presidential elections, two military coups, two states of alert, two constitutions, an eleven-month state of siege, four amnesty periods, and four heads of state, three of them army generals. Similar events were unfolding in countries throughout the region as American-backed governments, in the name of halting the growth of communism and protecting corporate interests, attempted to crush the people's movements.

Though it is commonly referred to as a "civil war," the 36-year long bloody Guatemalan conflict defies simple terms. The "guerrillas" were not trying to take over the government but rather to get it to end its exploitive and brutal policies. For 500 years, when the Vatican decreed that the indigenous Mayans were not human and therefore had no souls, the masses of Guatemala—Mayans, *Ladinos* and *mestizos* (mixed blood)—have been exploited, mistreated and brutalized by the government, the wealthy oligarchy and the large coffee plantation owners. For centuries and up to the present day, several wealthy families and landowners, most with their own para-military forces, have divided the country up into their personal

78

kingdoms, viewing the poverty-ridden and powerless locals as their private slave force. The details of the Mayan holocaust are intense but similar to what happened to the Native Americans after Columbus.

In Guatemala, the issue has always been about land—the country's only natural resource, a resource that is of little value without a large indigenous population to work it, preferably at slave wages and conditions. In 1952, under the enlightened leadership of the democratically-elected President Jacobo Arbenz Guzman, an Agrarian Reform was launched to humanely redistribute land to the people. Much of this land had been seized from the locals in the late 1800s and much was seized in the 1900s including land stolen in the decades leading up to the Agrarian Reform.

The CIA feared the communists were taking over the land and, eventually, control of the country. Arbenz's government was overthrown in 1954 with the full support of the United States and the CIA. The U.S ambassador directed bombing raids from the roof of the U.S. Embassy and soon after, directed the formation of the military regime from his office.

This was not an isolated incident. The U.S. government was influential in overthrowing other democracies in the region and/or supporting brutal dictators when they felt it was in their "national interest," just as it continues to do to this day. The Guatemalan military replaced a decade of democratically-elected administrations and within weeks dismantled a decade of just reforms. With the support of the wealthy landowners, they ruled the country until the mid-1990s. The Agrarian Reforms—the only viable and just solution to the country's problems—were dead.

Arbenz's overthrow convinced many that only an armed struggle could free the masses from their government's tyranny and the U.S. aggression. Revolutionaries transformed the people's fear into hope and hope into action. Things began to reach a boiling point in the 1960s when tens of thousands of peasant farmers rose up and said "Nunca Mas!" (Never Again!) The resistance fighters were receiving aid from Communist Cuba under Fidel Castro and the United States, fearful of any advance in Communism in its backyard, backed the Guatemalan government. The government struck back with a vengeance. By the time it was spent, over 200,000 had been killed, including entire villages of men, women and children. Many more had fled in exile in what was one of the most brutal conflicts in the hemisphere in the twentieth century—a conflict barely covered by the American press.

The intensity of this senseless violence was described in the Guatemalan newspaper *El Grafico* in 1982:

> Massacres have become commonplace, massacres in which no respect or mercy is shown for grandparents, children, or grandchildren. Shortly before the coup we published an editorial entitled "At Least Spare the Children." The cases discussed in that article are very similar to the current one: excessive use of force, unrestrained sadism, psychotic mercilessness. It would be difficult for any person in their right mind to imagine this kind of extermination. . . How is it possible for a human adult to murder, in cold blood, a baby of less than a year-and-a-half? . . . Nor is it acceptable to kill pregnant women, for these acts of bestiality only serves to sink the nation deeper into the most degenerate immorality.

However, *before* the war hit Santiago full-force, overall, Martín depicted a society that was like a flower growing in rocky soil, constantly encouraging kindness, wisdom and concern for one's neighbors to burst through an extreme and demanding, though beautiful, environment. When he arrived in 1979, there were 25,000 people living in extended family compounds of several structures made of wood with thatched roofs that peaked in a huge pottery bowl. Almost all of Santiago's citizens were Tzutujil Mayan, though the *Ladinos* still controlled the local economy and politics.

Life for the Tzutujil was difficult, as they practiced subsistence farming on small plots and often made dangerous canoe rides across the inlet. Drownings, poverty, malnutrition, and sickness were everyday realities. Parents would expect to lose several young children in a lifetime. It took total dedication to grow enough to feed one's family and even then many villagers died from malnutrition, parasites and diseases.

However, to them, their simple village life was the beautiful, harmonious way of keeping all creation—past, present and future—

alive. Every activity—walking down the street, farming the volcanic soil, grinding their precious corn, washing their traditional clothes at the lakeshore, praying to Maximon, their local deity, even arguing—was sacred and necessary to keep the Earth and the entire Universe alive and balanced.

For instance, it is still common in Atitlan everyday to see men carrying one hundred pounds of small limbs for firewood on their backs with a pack carried with a "burden strap," a sling across their forehead. This *ruq'a ejqan*—the hand of burden—is much more than a simple device to ease his load. It is a symbol of his life, of carrying the food and fuel on which his family and village depended. It is worn with honor, not regret.

The Tzutujils are tenacious, holding fast to the only place their people have every known. The conquering Spaniards call this place Santiago Atitlan, but to the Tzutujils it is *Rumuxux Ruchiuleu*, the "Umbilicus of the Universe."

As Martín describes in *Long Life, Honey in the Heart*:

> The people of Santiago had no concept of their town being part of somebody else's country. As far as they were concerned, everything real in the world was part of their territory. Their land was the world to them. Guatemala as a country was a mythological spirit realm . . . These strange spirit realms could be visited, but you had to return "Home" to the real Tzutujil land to be truly alive. There was no possible way of saying "leaving home" in the Tzutujil language. . . The village itself was known to all Tzutujil as *Ch'jay*, meaning literally "At Home."

They are Tzutujils—*Atitecos*—and everyone considered themselves and every other villager royalty—no matter how raggedly or ignoble they may appear to strangers. Every child was a prince or princess, every adult a king or queen. Anyone not from their village was a *turista* from Tourist Land, even if it's only Antigua, coming to visit the Center of the World. These *turistas* were to be viewed compassionately—uninitiated people doing the best they could, considering they were not Tzutujils.

They called themselves *Vinaaq*, "Named Being," the term used by all Guatemalan Mayans when referring to themselves. Sometimes they call themselves *Nim Vinaaq*—"Big People" or "Magnificent Adults." To be Tzutujil was not a matter of race but rather of memory. They believed that all people forget their original "spirit language" at birth and would spend a lifetime longing and searching to remember. To be Tzutujil, was to remember.

Every rock formation, every tree, every stream, is part of their stories, their history, their realty. According to one legend, a certain rock was where a Goddess who, grief-stricken and longing for her beloved, could go no further. A ridge might be the backbone of a dead giant form another legend.

It was Martín's experience with the young men's initiation that revealed a level of wisdom that I thought was worth exploring and explaining. The Tzutujil had five stages and initiations in their passage to become a Magnificent Adult—birth to adolescence, adolescence to childrearing, childrearing to grandchild rearing, grandchild rearing to adult, and adult to death. This meant that at any time, everyone in the village was going through some stage of their life's initiations. They did this not for themselves but to save the Earth—to keep it alive.

As you passed through each stage, you did not discard that stage, but rather they were cumulative. The Magnificent Adult was still the child and adolescent they had once been—and would always be. They were also the village mentors with the ability to see the world through the lenses of five sections of vision. Their view was clearer than the young's because their worldview was through a longer five-initiation telescope, where a youth's vision included only two sections. If fully initiated, the person would become an Echo Person, someone whose inspiration echoed on long after they were physically gone.

After Martín moved into the village, he was asked to join the ceremonies as a flute player. In time, he established himself as a member of the village hierarchy, the *Scat Mulaj*. He describes this group as a "mystical group of village sacred leaders who formed a large theocracy of men and women dedicated to the making of ritual and public decisions for the village welfare." This devoted group listened much more than they spoke as they mentored villagers with their myriad of problems. Their group wisdom reflects a complete and compassionate understanding of human nature and the human condition. As Martín noted:

> The *Scat Mulaj* in their initiated calm knew that there was no cure for the unfairness and hardship in any human's life. To the Tzutujil, people were not put into this world to have a good time: they were put here to be beautiful . . . whatever they came up with was masterfully engineered to keep suffering from escalating into mass depression and violence by making sure the village grieved for any person's difficulty . . . Being heard by the elders and the village at large didn't fix anything, but it made life bearable because we were together, in love with the adventure of our tiny collective . . .

In time, Martín was asked to be in charge of the young men's initiation, which lasted for a year. Initiation chiefs were not allowed to argue during their year tenure, thereby exemplifying the behavior they were attempting to teach. (When we were in Hopiland, we met a man whose position in the tribe included him expressing a positive vibe for a complete year.) These initiations had been going on in Atitlan for centuries. What kept the initiations viable in spite of the encroachment of the modern world was the fact that the Guatemalan government had made it mandatory for all young men to join the army or the police force for a year. The village had negotiated with the government to allow the young men to work off this service with their one-year tribal initiation. Since this initiation included the men acting as protectors of the village just as a local policeman might, the government agreed.

The year-long initiation was a serious life-or-death issue to the village. The core of the initiations were centuries-old stories, many taking place in the immediate or surrounding areas, that have never been written down or told outside the ritual. There was a wise story offering guidance for every stage and circumstance of life. Often the initiates would journey on a vision quest to the places where the stories took place and by doing so would become their own ancestors. Wisdom and challenges were transmitted through the initiate's dreams, dreams that were guided by the elders. The rituals were elaborate and the description goes way beyond the scope of this book.

However, the men's initiation (and there was one for young women as well) is described in detail in Martín's book, *Long Life, Honey in the Heart:A Story of Initiation and Eloquence from the Shores of a Mayan Lake*. My goal here is to reveal the kernel of wisdom that I found at the core of these traditional practices. It seems to reflect that the clear and ancient teachings of Quetzalcoatl, and perhaps other Mayan teachers of love, were eventually incorporated into a brilliant system of stories, rituals and perceptions that survived many centuries.

Basically, the men's initiation taught the young men how to maturely and spiritually re-channel the two strongest desires that all young men confront—sex and the warrior spirit. If the boys were not properly initiated, the elders knew that their vision would be spiritually shortened. Like youths everywhere, they thought they knew everything and had to be pushed by the adults into the next stage. The initiations were designed to spiritualize a young man's desire to be a brave warrior by making "war against warfare." They knew the great suffering the *uninitiated* warriors could cause to all people. The instinct for battle, heroism and protection was used to fight not an enemy, but rather death itself, to assist in the villagers' struggle for life.

As Martín writes *in Long Life, Honey in the Heart*:

> . . . the widows explained that justice in the hands of humans was impossible and irrelevant to the mission of being human. They explained that the Canyon Village did not want to make young men into hateful makers of war sent to exact revenge on some human enemy in return for the maddening death of the people we'd lost to violence, accidents, or life. It didn't take much talent to do that, and it only created ghosts who made more war.

The same wisdom was applied to sexual feelings. As soon as a young man or woman began courting, they were removed from their family's compound and their initiation would begin. This was the beginning of feeling "the physical presence of the divine in their longing for each other." This approach hopefully would save them from having children before they had become "truly human and eloquent." Their energetic, but volatile, adolescence was called the "great swelling of the earth," or the "pollination of the cornfield," or the "holy illness."

During this time of their year-long initiation, they were not allowed to continue courtship. For the next year, they would live in a compound with other young initiates and several village elders. However, the youths felt honored and valuable to be carried off by the village's sacred hierarchy. They felt loved when they saw the pain their absence caused their families.

In addition to serving as a village policing force, the male initiates were led by the elders in ceremonies, vision quests and the transference of ancient knowledge and wisdom—the goal of which was to refine their natural desires to be beneficial to both the tribe and themselves. The initiation would help them shake off their spiritual amnesia and remember so they could become adults and eventually Magnificent Adults. The family ties were temporarily severed so that the youth could mature and become an adult. They learned the destructiveness of disrespect and the value of honor and truthfulness. Only after they successfully completed the difficult year of initiation, during which the men initiates were exposed to the spiritual aspects of the Female for the first time, could they marry. Otherwise, they might be forever unhappy in their union always seeking something from the other person that could only be found within.

Knowing how the young men's desire to prove themselves to be a brave warrior can result in individual acts of senseless violence or the youths being duped by corrupted leaders to fight in national or tribal wars, the Tzutujils' ancient initiation directed the youths in a positive direction. Their role models were not violent, revenge-driven warriors but rather mature family men who had added to the beauty of the village by their wisdom and peacekeeping.

The young men's initiation was demanding and dangerous, involving great feats of strength, bravery and discipline—mental, emotional and spiritual. Some dropped out and a few even died. However, this danger was not taken cavalierly. For the Mayans, a major theme in the youth initiations was the confronting of death in a controlled way *before* they were married. Only then could they be totally independent adults rather than dependent children throughout their lives. For those who completed it, they had become adults in the truest sense—and everyone in the village knew it and honored them. As full adults, they realized that "every human being's goal in the village was the eventual admission into the pursuit and maintenance of the sacred."

Given that the Tzutujils knew that few societies still honored such initiations, they felt that most uninitiated people outside their world were spiritually immature and not fully adults. To leave Santiago Atitlan was to venture into the dark, confused realm of the uninitiated, the tribeless, the unstoried. It was the Land of the Dead, the Land of Forgetting.

The role of the elders, their Magnificent Adults, their spiritual leaders, also revealed tremendous wisdom. The role was not an easy one. They were the village's peacemakers. As Martín writes, "A life dedicated to the spirit was more strenuous than most outsiders could ever know . . . The masters of the making of these offerings and the remembering of complex ritual language was this hierarchy of men and women." It took tremendous dedication and discipline as well as time, energy and money. Members of the *Scat Mulaj*, who spoke in an esoteric and archaic form of their dialect and used kinship terms among themselves that were not used by other villagers, did not seek the position, as leaders do in most modern societies, but rather the active chiefs would have similar dreams endorsing that new person for membership. They considered these dreams "calls to service from the spirits, not messages from the dreamer."

In marked contrast to modern-day politicians who usually use their offices for self-enrichment, spiritual service in the *Scat Mulaj* was not financially compensated. Since members were responsible for sponsoring the ceremonies and initiations with their numerous feasts and offerings, it put a tremendous economic strain on each member, especially those in charge of major initiation ceremonies, where they would seldom serve more than one year. Often the member could be reduced to poverty. It would often take months to recover from the physical demands of the position and up to five years to recover from the financial demands. However, even the poorest villager could become part of the village "royalty" and earn the right to serve their people by becoming initiators. One of the three top chiefs of the *Scat Mulaj* was always an ordinary person.

Like the Hopi elders, and again *unlike* modern leaders, these elders never separated themselves from the people. They lived the same hardworking, humble lives as their neighbors, in constant contact with the everyday happenings of the village and the world. Each headman or headwoman in the *Scat Mulaj* had an ordinary villager assigned to assist in their decision-making. In this way, the leaders never lost touch with the everydayness of the village and the needs of the people.

Aside from the structure of the leadership and their intricate and enlightened initiations, other Mayan customs reflect a great degree of wisdom. When a Tzutujil couple wanted to marry, the "bride price" would take the boy several years to pay off, during which time he was deeply indebted to his relatives or friends. This assured he did not take his vows lightly and was fully committed to his new family, as he would still be indebted if he or his wife terminated the marriage.

After the marriage, anticipating the usual problems from in-laws which can often destroy a union, the couple was adopted by "word warriors," two mature, non-related couples that would serve as lifelong advocates and advisors to the couple, often against the combined forces of the families. As Martín writes:

> Like love lawyers who worked for the young people's mutual affection, they realized that what made most couples hate each other was their trying to be what the world wanted them to be. The Tzutujil were smart, but they never let their intelligence get in the way of their natural emotions. One did not need to kill or repress every stupidity, because there was a village device waiting to deal with the inevitable shortcomings of us all . . .

Even birth—which Guatemalans refer to as to "Give Light"—was an opportunity to deepen tribal and village ties. Every newborn infant, who Tzutujil mothers referred to as "my First Dawn, my First Sun," might be breastfed by every lactating mother in the village so that they would never feel as a stranger in any family compound. The child was now related to everyone. This often served as a peacemaking tool during arguments when someone might remind the arguing parties that they were both suckled by the same women or that one person was once suckled by the other's mother or grandmother or sister. If the argument was not resolved, revenge and reprisal was discouraged. As Martín noted, ". . . any action of bad intent I'd take against another villager, whether spiritual or literal, justified or not, would only make the village a worse place for us all to live."

When the bellybutton stumps fell off after birth, they were saved in a family bag, hundreds of years old, with those of all their ancestors to remind everyone of their deep roots. Each new arrival was given a baby feast with villagers bringing in corn, the life-giving staple of the tribe, from which a ritual drink, called *maatz*, was made and drunk by the villagers to celebrate the birth. Twenty ears of this corn were set aside in the rafters of the family home. When that person died, whether it was a week or a century later, this same corn was once again planted and made into *maatz* and drunk in remembrance of their life. In other Mayan villages, a baby's hands were temporarily tied at birth to symbolize that no one should accumulate things the rest of the village does not have and to remind the child to be generous.

Another aspect of their traditions that Martín felt reflected great wisdom was the mutual indebtedness between the elders. This is what they called *kas-limaal*. Given the demands on the spiritual leaders, they would often have to ask for help or borrow money from each other to complete their assigned ceremonies and feasts. The goal was to be indebted to as many ex-chiefs as possible during your time as chief. They were always willing to do this as they understood mutual indebtedness between the elders served to tie them all together in their leadership. It created closeness between the elders that surpassed that of blood relatives. It kept them *interdependent* rather than isolated. In this way, elders were perfectly comfortable to call on other elders in the future to serve the Village Heart.

Suffering, sacrifice and even poverty went with the chiefs' territory. It was the price they paid and the expected side effects of their spiritual position—a sacrifice consciously made in serving their people. They were not the "sucklings at the village breast but the breast itself." Even they were going through their own initiations by being challenged to give so much of their meager worldly possessions to bring the youths into adulthood. As the young chiefs accepted the help from the older chiefs, they swallowed their pride and learned humility.

"The idea is to get so entangled in debt," Martín writes, "that no normal human being can possibly remember who owes whom what, and how much . . . in sacred dealings we think just like nature, where all is entangled and deliciously confused, dedicated to making the Earth flower in a bigger plan of spirit beyond our minds and understandings."

On yet a deeper level, this sacrifice reminded the leaders to trust totally in the Divine to provide for their needs. The ex-chiefs would share their many stories of their own personal needs being met miraculously by mysterious good luck. However, this happened only *after* they had completed their assigned tasks with honor and a willingness to give to all—even to the point of poverty and indebtedness. To complete the circle, these new ex-chiefs were now expected to share some of these newfound, Divinely-granted gains with the upcoming new chiefs, continuing this eloquent and compassionate cycle of mutual obligation. To the Tzutujil, the "honey in our heart comes from the tears of the village indebtedness."

As the elders told Martín in *Long Life, Honey in the Heart*, his debts to them should never be repaid and they must accept the generosity from the ex-chiefs:

> The young chiefs, in the interests of the village heart, must swallow their pride and accept this wealth. That is why in our language we call our wealth "our poverty." True wealth lies in being loved enough for giving, being humble enough to be filled by the older people in the village, and being smart enough to know it must all go to the youths' fruition . . . Always the Spirits, the Gods, the Saints, the Many and the One will come through the people to help you. When you learn to trust in this, you realize how all true survival relies on mutual indebtedness, and then you have become an adult.

I began to think back on the many conscious recording artists and speakers who had appeared for free at our One Love events and books and realized how indebted I felt to them and would always respond to their requests for books, contacts, support, etc. Recently, a friend had given us many beautiful "One World" peace flags she had designed and we had given her our books—all to give to the youths and elders. I warmly realized that this concept of mutual indebtedness of the elders had become part of our journey—of our "village"—as well. I also realized that our book, *In the Spirit of Marriage*, had carried the same key message as the young men's and women's initiation—be careful making another person or your relationship your "god." In the end, it will only disappoint you. Instead, see your union, and every relationship, as a context to learn and teach unconditional love. It was comforting to know that this remote Mayan tribe had reached the same conclusion hundreds, if not thousands, of years ago.

As I looked upon the hundreds of individuals that we passed in our stroll through Santiago Atitlan with Dolores, I could only guess, *Is that a spiritual elder? A member of the Scat Malaj? Are there any left after the civil war, the missionaries and the loss of their initiations?* The answer eluded me, but I remembered I had once asked a Havasupai tribal member how I could identify their spiritual elders as I walked their village at the bottom of the Grand Canyon. "You should treat everyone as an elder," he said, "no matter who they are. They are whether they remember it yet or not."

Martín summed up the situation well when he wrote:

> The tourists were completely unaware that what to them was just a pile of poor wrinkled Indians was, in fact, a whole magnificent gathering of queens and kings, a knowledgeable royalty who actually knew holiness and God personally as one knew a neighbor.

This reflected a comment I once heard from a friend in Jamaica who had just returned from exploring her pre-slavery roots in Ghana, Africa. "You see people emerging from mud and thatched huts," she said wistfully, respectfully, "and they look like kings and queens."

Finally, the government's need for more and more soldiers in the escalating civil war led to the end of the initiations since the young men could no longer defer their military service by their one-year initiations. At a meeting after this was announced, Martín suggested that they make the initiation voluntary but the elders knew that would not work. Initiation was not a desired thing they explained to him, but rather something mandatory and imposed. Few would voluntarily accept its hardships and dangers. Many would pull out in the middle, endangering the individual and the village.

However, the slide toward the end of traditional Tzutujil life had begun several decades earlier in the 1960s and 1970s when this tranquil village was invaded by civilian thugs who brutally forced the young men into covered trucks to be recruited into the army. If the parents could, they would ransom their sons back by giving the thugs their ancestral land—their only means of sustenance. This practice was illegal, but common, and no one was ever punished.

In fact, the government even banned *voluntary* initiation rituals, much like when the U.S. government banned Native American ceremonies until 1976. This ban was also supported by the missionaries who knew they could never fully convert the local Tzutujils until their ancient traditions were crushed.

When the proclamation banning the initiation rituals was read on the temple staircase, the crowd of over two thousand people exploded in anger, shaking their fists in the air. Martín describes the heart-wrenching feelings of the leaders:

> We knew full well that the whole culture was beginning to crumble before our eyes. By the time we wandered to our homes in the dark, some of us took along a friend because we didn't want to go alone toward the end of our world. . . The leaders felt alone and the last of their kind . . . This year's particular time of sadness was worse; the village as a whole was apathetic, depressed, and without direction, resigned to sinking into an uninspired future of ritualless subsistence.

Within a year or two, the initiations fell apart—another casualty of the modern world's encroachment into ancient realities. With the increasing influence of the churches, which declared the Tzutujil ancient customs and beliefs "devil worshiping," many of the youths turned against their centuries-old traditions. It was many of these youths and their parents who petitioned the government to end the initiations. However, these youths could not be blamed because they could not value something they to which they had never been exposed.

Santiago Atitlan
Now

We had come all this way, to this ancient village on Lake Atitlan, to see how much of this wisdom had survived and I hoped that our tour with Dolores would reveal this to us. Dolores, a Tzutujil Mayan born in Santiago Atitlan, had known the village during its earlier peaceful years, the tumultuous years of the civil war and now during its post-war incarnation. She had known the village when its traditional religion, customs and initiations were almost intact and she knew the village now that they were almost lost.

There were eight in our tour group from our hotel—Dolores, our family, Lia and Claire and a young couple from the States. As we turned the first bend in the short walk from our hotel, the village was laid out on a hill in front of us. Beginning about a hundred feet above the water, the village spread out over the steep hills in a haphazard fashion—a large cluster of small cinder-block houses with tin-roofs. Several landmarks stood out—the ancient Catholic church, a modern evangelical church and a new cellphone tower. A massive volcano rose above and framed the village. The only thing that seemed to tie the village to its roots was a brightly-colored knot of thirty or so women below us, knee-deep at the water's edge washing their clothes on large flat stones, their beautiful tribal skirts floating gently in the water around their legs.

For centuries, Mayan women have been weaving these brightly-colored, embroidered garments. The markings on their clothes in each village are distinctive to that particular village and include certain embroidered patterns indicating the person's marital status and position in the spiritual hierarchy, as well as elements of personal creativity of the weaver. These garments can take months to weave on a small backstrap or foot loom. Their clothing, called

92

traje, consist of a *huilpil*, or multi-colored blouse, a *corte*, an ankle-length wraparound skirt, and a *faja*, or waist sash. At times, they also wear a headdress called a *panuelo* or a *cintas*, four- or five-foot-long colorful ribbons that are braided into their shiny, long, black hair. Some also wear a colorful shawl or *rebozo* and a decorated apron or *delantal* as part of their *traje*.

"Everything looks like it's been recently built with cinder-blocks," I said to Dolores as we approached the village. "Are any of the traditional family compounds still here?"

"That doesn't happen any more. People now have their own home. When Martín was living here, we didn't have the kind of house you see now. The old time Mayans used to live there," she said pointing to a much smaller hill below the massive volcano. "It's a Mayan temple. It was buried by the Spanish when they came 500 years ago and they moved everyone into Santiago. In our old village, they use to call it 'The Birdhouse.' That's why we wear lot of birds in our clothing [she points to her beautiful blouse, elaborately embroidered with several multi-colored storks]. They moved everyone here because that way it was easier for the Spanish to control everyone. Nothing is left in the old village but some Mayan glyphs and sculptures. You can still see it. Some archaeologists from France wanted to dig it up but the local people said 'No,' even though they were going to get paid for it. My ex-husband, Martín, lived there [pointing to a modest cinder-block home looking out across the lake]. That was his studio. I live there now."

"Today is market day and they are having a mass," Dolores said, noting that the road was busier than usual. Open pickups dangerously overloaded with men, women and children standing in the bed, kept driving by. "This is for the massacre that happened in 1990 on December 2nd. So every month on the second they have a mass because a lot of people died."

"They've been doing this every month for sixteen years?" I asked. "What happened in 1990? Was that when the army was posted here?"

I had read about the atrocities in Santiago Atitlan in Martín's books. The Tzutujils, for the most part, were non-aligned, viewing both sides—the government and the rebels—as uninitiated and therefore both were incapable of truly "seeing."

"Yes. When the local men would go to work, they would

93

never return home because the military would grab the men. The men would bring their lunch to work but the military thought they were bringing food to the guerilla people. When they go to the mountains to work in their fields, they never returned and the ladies would go to the military camps to ask, 'Have you seen my husband?' and they would say, 'No. We didn't see your husband. The guerilla people are taking your husbands away.' "

"And this village of twenty-five thousand lost eighteen hundred people?" I asked. (There is no way to determine the definite number as many simply disappeared, never to be found. Everyone lost someone, leaving the entire village traumatized.)

"That's what they say. And then one night in 1990, they started killing women. The military started going to homes asking for food and the women said, 'We don't have food. We barely have enough for our families.' And they pointed the machine guns at the families. When some people saw this, they ran in front of the Catholic Church and started ringing the bell. A couple of thousand people gathered. They said that the military are starting to kill the families. They are the ones killing all of the people here. They decided to get the mayor and go back to them. So a couple of thousand people marched into their army camps. When the military saw that group of people coming they said, 'Here are the guerilla people coming.' They wanted to fight us. They started shooting machine guns up in the air. And the mayor arrived to speak to them, but they didn't want to hear. They just opened fire with everyone standing there. When that happened, the people did not want the military to be living here. They called the president to come see what they did to the people."

"How many people did they kill that day?" I asked, still amazed that such a peaceful village could have known such senseless violence for so long.

"Thirteen people died. It was at night, at eleven-thirty at night. And the people said, 'We don't need the military here. We can take care of our own village.' And then the army left."

"How are things now in the village after the civil war," I asked. "Is the government still mistreating you?"

"No, not anymore," she replied. "Things are much better. People are happy. They can work in the fields. There are still a lot of poor people, but it's better. After the war, we had some projects here

94

from different countries. Some people from Oklahoma helped six or seven thousand children. They gave them food, clothing, whatever they needed. They even built homes for some."

"How much of the old ways are gone?" I asked. "Has the village become totally Christianized?"

"A lot of the people are Evangelica or Catholic, but around thirty percent of the Mayans are traditional. Even some of the people who go to the church, then they go see a medicine person and they go back to the old ways doing healing ceremonies."

"So there are still shamans here?" I asked.

"Oh, yes. Lots of shamans."

"Are the year-long initiations that Martín described in his book still going on?" I asked.

"That stopped thirty years ago," she said, as we passed a small, dark store, a loud mechanical noise coming from inside. Several women in traditional dress were walking in with large bowls carried on their heads. "This is where the women can come to get their corn ground with an electric grinder," Dolores said.

Now we were entering the village, with its narrow cobblestone streets and small houses and shops—*tiendas*—with their doors opening immediately onto the street. Stepping in the abundance of dog droppings seemed a much greater threat as we walked the streets than being hit by the occasional car or three-wheeled taxi. Children ran everywhere, seemingly happy and healthy. No one seemed overweight. Almost all of the females wore their traditional *traje*, though some of the younger girls had adopted Western clothing. Only a few of the men, and almost none of the boys, wore the traditional white pants that came to mid-calf with the decoratively embroidered waist sash and shirt. The women carried themselves proud and erect from years of carrying loads on their heads. Many of the men carried themselves proud and bent from years of carrying loads on their backs. Everyone had beautiful, straight, shiny black hair. Most people were short—five feet or under—making petite Alicia feel right at home.

"I see some of the men and the youths are wearing Western clothing," I said.

"A pair of traditional pants for a boy can cost fifty dollars," she said. "For a man, it's two hundred dollars, whereas jeans are only twelve. So, if your relatives are not doing the weaving

95

anymore, it is too expensive. On Sundays, they will wear their traditional clothes."

"It must have been very frightening when you and Martín and the children had to go into hiding," I said, feeling more comfortable now to talk of her personal history. Dolores seemed like a kind, open person.

"Oh, yes!" she replied. "We went to live in Antigua. I didn't tell anyone where I was going. After six months, they gave me a visa to go to the States."

"What was it like for you in the States?" I asked.

"It was frightening because I didn't speak the language, but I was happy to be there because it was not safe living in Guatemala anymore."

"If the army had found you guys here, would they have killed you?"

"Oh, yes!"

"When did it become safe here again?"

"In 1990."

"What made it safe then?" I asked.

"The president took the army away," she said.

"That was all it took, complaining to the president?" I asked, "Was that the end of the civil war in the country?"

"No. That was in 1996 when the government signed the peace treaty with the rebels. That's when it became peaceful. The military and the ex-guerrillas didn't have to fight anymore. The ex-guerrillas delivered their guns to the government."

"Was that because you had a good president in 1996?" I asked.

"Yes. It was Alvaro Arzu," she said.

With pressure mounting from the international political and financial powers against the government's brutal and repressive practices and its growing inability to suppress the guerrillas, the government settled with the guerrillas in the peace agreement called for by the Human Rights Accord of 1994. This agreement mentioned the underlying problems that had created the conflict, but provided for no definite remedies. It was hoped that Arzu would do that, but instead, he spent his term getting the country ready for globalization—another powerful form of the exploitation of the masses. By 1999, the UN Human Development Survey that

96

examined social conditions in Central America ranked Guatemala last—a position lower than it had at the end of the war three years earlier.

After the end of the war, under UN supervision, a Commission for Historical Clarification was formed to attempt to bring healing, justice and compensation to the atrocities of the war. Similar to the Truth and Reconciliation Commission instituted in South Africa at the end of apartheid, its success was limited. Though life has settled much since the peace treaty, inequality, exploitation and, at times, government-sanctioned brutality, still stalks the land.

"I hear that Rigoberta Menchu is going to run for president next year? Do you think she will get elected?" I asked.

"You never know who can get elected," Dolores said, her voice resigned to the realities of modern politics. "A lot of her family was killed by the government. She lives in Mexico. A lot of women now work in the government. When they had this war, they didn't respect the Mayan culture but now, like in this village, we have a Mayan lady that is the second mayor of the village."

Rigoberta Menchu, daughter of Vicente Menchu, a farmer who became a national hero as a resistance leader, is an indigenous Mayan woman who was the recipient of the 1992 Nobel Peace Prize. Her family lived a poverty-stricken life as farmers in the highlands and, after their community's land was seized by large coffee growers, they labored as plantation workers at the coast. Pushed to their limit, her father and brother joined the resistance and her brother was tortured and killed in front of her family by the army during the civil war. Her father was burned alive in the Spanish Embassy in Guatemala City where he and other Indian leaders, who were protesting against the violent government repression, had taken refuge. The government burned down the embassy with the leaders inside.

In all, seven of fifteen Menchu family members were killed during the course of the war. Rigoberta's mother, an active member in the local resistance, urged Rigoberta to join reminding her that, "I don't want to make you stop feeling like a woman, but your participation in the struggle must be equal to that of your brothers. Any evolution, any change, in which women have not participated, would not be a change, and there would be no victory."

Rigoberta became a village organizer for the resistance,

joining a group named Comite Unidad Campesina that demanded a fair wage from the plantation owners, respect for indigenous communities, decent treatment as humans, and respect for their religion, customs and culture. Her organizing work proved effective before she fled into exile in Mexico, where she still lives because of possible retaliation in Guatemala.

Her life is chronicled in her book, *I, Rigoberta Menchu:An Indian Woman in Guatemala*, where she writes, "We started thinking about the roots of the problem and came to the conclusion that everything stemmed from the ownership of land. The best land was not in our hands. It belonged to the big landowners. Every time they saw that we have new land, they throw us off of it or steal it from us in other ways . . . our enemies weren't the landowners but the whole system." (In the September 9, 2007 national elections, Rigoberta received only three percent of the votes.)

"Is the spiritual hierarchy still here?" I asked, curious as to how the war, tourism, TV, and churches had affected their traditional beliefs.

"Oh, yes!" Delores said, seeming to not want to explain further.

Now, we had all arrived at a small alleyway between two nondescript houses complete with barking dogs and large tubs filled with empty plastic one-gallon jugs. Dolores led us to the back of the alley and through a small door into a room about the size of a large living room. Except for a table and chairs, the room was empty of furniture, but at one end was a display of six or eight beautiful, intricately-carved wooden sculptures of various saints, three to four feet tall. A bowl for offerings sat nearby on a table alongside of some incense, corn, snacks and soft drinks. The room was dingy and dimly lit by one bare light bulb, but the statues gave it a kind of majesty and power. A radio buzzed annoyingly nearby until someone cut it off.

"The Mayan people five hundred years ago had their own sculptures made of rock," she said addressing our small group, reverently pointing to each saint, "and when the Spanish came, they threw away what was Mayan and brought in Catholic saints and the Mayan people adopted the saints like they were theirs. These were carved by Mayans four hundred years ago. Martín did his first ceremony here when he became a medicine man. This is St.

Anthony. He is the Lord of Corn. They bless the corn here. This saint is the Lord of Business. If someone is going to start a new business, they come here for a blessing. This female saint, they call her 'Mother Lake.' We have about two hundred and fifty thousand people around this lake that drink the water from the lake. That's why we call her 'Mother Lake.' She takes care of everyone. Her feast day is September 8. The fishermen give her big treats just to honor her. That's San Martin, Lord of Domestic Animals. This female saint is the 'Lord of the Midwives.' If someone becomes a midwife, before she starts to deliver babies, she has to make lots of offerings, many candles, flowers. She doesn't go to the school to study. She has to be going with the power of the medicine."

"Have you heard of any connection between the Maya and Hopi?" I asked.

"Well, when I was with the Hopis in the States, we did ceremonies together, very similar. We are brothers and sisters."

"Do the villagers still keep the Mayan calendar?" I asked.

"Only the medicine men, the shamans. They are the daykeepers. If someone wants to know about the future, they go to them."

"Has the village become very westernized?" I asked.

"Well, a lot of people have TVs, cellphones, but the roots don't change. They're still the same people. Some have become Catholic or Evangelica. What we do at home is still like the old days."

"Martín talks about how the elders drank a lot of alcohol in their ceremonies and meetings and many would pass out. Did your traditional alcohol have that effect?" I wondered whether the excessive use of alcohol by the elders, so detrimental on their spiritual path or any path for that matter, was introduced by the Europeans as it had been to Native Americans in the States or whether it had been part of their ancient culture. There may no longer be a way to really know.

"The alcohol was not as strong as it is now so now a lot of people use Coke or orange drink in the ceremony. The rum can make people drunk very fast."

"Is alcohol a problem here?" I asked. We had already passed several very inebriated men on our walk and it was still early morning.

"We have now about 45,000 people and maybe a couple of hundred men that drink. The medicine men used to take psychedelic mushrooms, but they do not do that since the Spanish came."

"Is diabetes a problem here?" Julia asked. "It is with so many Native Americans."

"Yes. Now you see some of that and black cancer," Dolores replied. "That wasn't a problem for our ancestors because they didn't use chemicals and fertilizers to grow vegetables or corn. Now some of the people die young, twenty or twenty-five."

"Is there still malnutrition like Martín talked about in the past?" I asked. In the sixties, malnutrition was almost universal in Santiago, with its staple of corn and beans. More than half the children died before six of not only malnutrition but flu, diarrhea and measles. In 1969 alone, 400 to 500 people died of measles in Santiago. Tuberculosis was common in adults and almost everyone had intestinal worms from drinking polluted water.

"There was a lot of malnutrition when I was growing up. When I was ten, I was losing my hair because of it, but now the children have enough to eat. The groups have been helping since after the war."

"How many villagers are Tzutujil?" I asked.

"All forty-five thousand. There are just twelve *Ladino* families here. Everyone speaks Tzutujil. Tzutujils also live in San Pedro, but they don't wear the traditional dress there."

Their dress has a deep cultural significance for the Mayans, linking them back to their ancestors. Many believe to give up this traditional dress, especially the women, was the road to ruin. It was fascinating to see an entire village free from the sexualization (at least in dress) of women that now is so pervasive in the Western world. It is a problem that causes so much pain through single parenting, loss of self-esteem, sexually transmitted diseases, and unwanted children.

This emphasis on sex also has a profound spiritual element. At a time when it is essential to awaken people to the awareness that they are *not* just a physical body but a spiritual being *in* a physical body, using another's body for pleasuring, only serves to solidify this painful and mistaken illusion. Or as Rigoberta Menchu's mother taught her, "My child, you don't need to paint your face because makeup abuses the wonders God has given us."

100

This perception of women as sex objects is also one of the foundations of *machismo*, with all its ugly and often brutal expressions. Rigoberta Menchu's mother also told her that, "The whole world is afflicted with this sickness. It's part of society. Part of it we can improve, and part of it we can wipe out . . . men weren't to blame for *machismo*, and women weren't to blame for *machismo*, but it was part of the whole society. To fight *machismo* you shouldn't attack men and you shouldn't attack women, because that is either the man being *machisto*, or it's the woman."

We were now approaching a very large cobblestone courtyard with a huge church on our right. The stairs leading up to the church were covered with villagers. A local man with a bright smile and a tie-dyed tee-shirt approached us.

"This is my husband," Dolores said introducing us. He was a sweet, kind man, short, as most Mayans are, and dressed in work clothes. He smiled shyly but proudly. I found myself glad that Dolores had remarried and had a child after the trauma and intensity of her earlier years. "This is the oldest church here. It was built in 1547. It's combined with Mayan and Catholic. The front part of the church belongs to the Mayan people. The middle part belongs to the Catholics. These old steps are left from the Mayan temple which was on this spot."

We entered the church. It was huge, clean, and well-lit, with a high ceiling and hand-carved colorful saints lining each wall. There were fifty or so parishioners spread around the many pews, mostly Mayan women in traditional dress.

"That's a picture of the priest, Stanley Rother," she said pointing to a large color portrait of a handsome bearded man wearing a priest collar and habit and a traditional Mayan scarf over his shoulders. "He died in 1981. He loved and participated in the Mayan ceremonies. He learned to speak the Tzutujil language. In that picture, he's wearing the same kind of scarf that the medicine men wear. He was killed by the government. His heart is buried here. The rest of his body is buried in Oklahoma."

Stanley Rother was a Catholic priest from Oklahoma who served at the Santiago church from 1968, at age thirty-three, until his violent death in 1981. A tall, quiet, easygoing man, he soon learned the Tzutujil language, which at that time had no written form. Since most villagers only spoke Tzutujil, they were therefore illiterate except for a few who spoke, wrote and read Spanish. He soon came to love the villagers, offering them comfort and advice during a very troubled time.

Though many in the Catholic Church hierarchy remained silent or sided with the government during the 36-year civil war, some priests and nuns, especially those in poor rural areas, supported the indigenous people's demands for better conditions. Unlike their superiors who taught that the oppressed must passively suffer on earth knowing that heaven awaited them beyond, these few, brave souls believed, as Rigoberta Menchu wrote, "The work of revolutionary Christians is above all to condemn and denounce the injustices committed against the people." For this, they incurred the wrath and violence of the government which soon announced tighter control over religion including searches and seizures in churches and convents. In all, twelve priests were assassinated and many fled the country. Others, disillusioned, quit their religious orders.

"This is what they call the Umbilicus of the Earth," Dolores said, pointing to a 2-foot by 4-foot section of the floor tiles up front near the altar that was ungrouted. A candle in a small vase was burning in the center of the tile. I had read in Martín's books that this was considered by the Tzutujils as the hole left when the Original Tree and Vine died back long ago. The *Scat Mulaj* fed the world there and began and ended all their rituals at this hole.

A small Mayan temple had been raised around it and when the Spanish came, as an act of dominance, they built their church directly over it. The hole was now in the middle of the church but had miraculously survived almost five hundred years. At one time, the Catholic priests, trying to suppress the villagers' traditional worship, had filled the hole with concrete. The elders chiseled it open again and again as the priests continued to fill it.

As the headman Ma Xcai told Martín, "Those Catholics are uninitiated; what can you expect of people who don't have their eyes opened? They're little children trying to help their mother's cooking by dropping dust and gravel into the corn dough. You have to be primitive to think you can destroy spirits by burning their images and stopping up the other world with a little mud! Anyway, it's a hole that needs to be dug again and we have chisels and sledge hammers. So, Brothers and Mothers, let's get to work!"

The hole still remains open and ironically on Good Friday,

the Catholics use it to brace a two-story tall cross. The Mayans, who across the region have adapted Christianity to fit their ancient beliefs, see this God's-gift-son Christ as the fruit of the cross, the Original Tree, so they cover him with beautiful flowers on Easter so that he is entirely hidden. His blood runs down the cross to feed the roots of creation through the hole—the Umbilicus of the Earth.

"Before Holy Weekend," Dolores continued, "they do a special ceremony here with a Mayan medicine man before they hang Jesus Christ on a big cross. Jesus Christ, to the Mayan people, is a descendant from a Mayan king."

"So when they pray to Jesus," I asked, "they're praying to the Jesus who came to them here centuries ago who they called Quetzalcoatl or Kulkucan?"

"Yes. That's right," she replied. "On the Thursday before Good Friday, they have a big ceremony here. They move all the pews to the back of the church and the Mayan medicine man puts mats and flowers and incense around the hole. People have a big procession and they sing. On Good Friday, they hang up Christ and Maximon, the Mayan god. He comes, but the Jesus Christ procession goes out to the steps and the Maximon comes behind Jesus Christ. The ceremony is combined Mayan and Catholic. Then the Catholic priest will do the mass for the Mayan ritual and they put Maximon on the altar with the saints. We'll go see Maximon's shrine next.

"One of the priests tried to stop the ceremonies and he moved one of the sacred skulls into the cemetery and he got sick. He had a dream and the skull said to move him back to the church and he did and then he got better. You can't move any of these sacred things. It's dangerous to move it. It was nothing to the priests, but then they started to have these dreams, they better listen to them. They have to respect the dreams. This priest almost died because he removed that skull."

"What's going on in that chapel?" I asked, pointing to a small chapel off to one side of the altar. It was packed full of people in devout prayer.

"The people at the main altar are all Catholic," Dolores replied. "The people in that chapel practice the Mayan ceremonies, too."

"The Catholic church allows all this?" I asked. "They don't try to get everyone to believe like them?"

"Well, this new priest, that's what he's trying to do but they went to the court and the court said, 'Let the Mayan people do what they want to do because this was their temple before it was a church.' Now the priest is better. He just has to do what the Mayan people tell him."

This customizing of Christianity to fit their ancient traditional beliefs is prevalent with Mayans throughout the country. As Rigoberta Menchu writes, "Our people have taken Catholicism as just another channel of expression, not our one and only belief. Our people do the same with other religions."

We left the main sanctuary and walked through a courtyard into a room that was now a small, quiet chapel. It was the room where Father Rother was sleeping when he was shot to death by the army. His picture was on the wall plus a framed piece of cloth with his blood stains still on it. An altar had been set up below his picture and the cloth. Some candles were burning as they had since 1981. There was a painting of Jesus in the back. He was dark-skinned. A sculpture of him hung nearby with huge hands and feet, representing the people that work the land and carry the wood for a lifetime.

"Stanley loved and was loved by the villagers," Dolores told us, her voice earnest and pained. "He built a clinic, fed many children, including me, so that my hair grew back. Stanley was trying to help and he supported our culture. That is why they killed him. Martín and I were on a death list with him. That is why we fled. Stanley left and returned. When things got bad, a couple of thousand tried to sleep in the church for safety. At a meeting, Stanley told the government that we did not need bombs and guns, but food and medicine."

"He could have left," she said, the pain still fresh. "He knew he was going to be killed, but he really loved the people here and he was helping and the people were doing better with his help. When he died, the people were crying, sad and angry with the military for killing him and they told his family that they wanted his heart to be buried inside the church. They have better lives because of him. They still remember him. They have built a Catholic elementary school and a high school to honor him because he loved the Mayan children. He was a really good friend of ours. Martín and I would have dinner with him upstairs. I was in Scottsdale, Arizona when I heard he died and I fainted because I couldn't believe they would

kill him because he never did anything wrong."

"I noticed there were mostly women in church," I said, as we left the chapel. "Are Mayan women respected?"

"Yes. Now they are, but it used to be the men told the women what to do, but now the women can do whatever they want. In the old days, women just stayed home. Now they can go out and work. We have women teachers and sometimes the men cook. My sister is the cook at your hotel. And we have medicine women."

We headed back to the square and then down a side street fifty yards or so until we came to another alleyway. This was Maximon's (pronounced "Mash-ee-mon") shrine. He is also called San Simon, much to the distress of the Catholics who disclaim him as a saint. A drum was slowly, methodically, beating inside the adjoining house, one of several he will inhabit during the year. We walked through the short alley into a small enclosed and covered courtyard, dark and dingy with several very inebriated men in the rear. It was packed full with high school youths waiting to get into Maximon's "chapel." Dressed in Western clothes with lots of makeup and baseball caps turned backwards, they looked like they might be from the city. They had clipboards, obviously on a school project. We waited near them as a stream of older American tourists came out of the chapel, all looking rather bewildered and stern—Maximon's magic having seemingly not touched their hearts.

After a fifteen minute wait, it was our turn to enter the small chamber. Immediately off to our right were three men dressed traditionally, one beating a three-foot diameter drum. They looked to be shamans. As soon as they saw Julia, they gave her a big welcoming smile, almost as if the knew her well.

"Hola, nuestra hermana!" one said. ("Hello, our sister!")

There in front of them sat Maximon—Guatemala's cigar-smoking, alcohol-drinking deity—a four-foot tall wooden carved statue wearing a fedora hat, sunglasses and several scarves draped over his shoulders. A lit cigar was in his mouth. His features and color were more white than indigenous. At his feet was a small table packed with beer, cigars, cigarettes, candles and incense. A stack of money was in the offering bowl.

We all stood around as reverently as we could taking it all in. It was surely a contrast to the enormous church we had just visited. However, there was no denying that there was a power to him and there was no denying that many Tzutujils attribute miracles in their lives to him. I said a silent prayer, willing to honor anyone's expression of the Divinity (and not wanting to lose heaven on a technicality). We took our pictures, left our offerings and emerged once again into the brightly-lit streets of Santiago.

As we headed back toward our hotel, I felt like I knew a lot more about the village than I had two hours earlier. And yet, I felt I did not really know it at all. It had gone through too many traumatic changes too quickly—the war, the missionaries, tourists, TVs, cellphones—to know itself in its ever-changing new incarnation. It would never again be the ancient, plodding, spiritual Tzutujil village it had been for centuries.

As Martín writes in *Long Life, Honey in the Heart*:

> . . . the tree had been cut down, its trunk and roots torn out, and the Hole filled. The village where I had become a human being had disappeared. The Canyon Village that understood how to initiate its people . . . no longer remembers how to reinvent a human being. This new town is now 100 percent missionized. It has been "liberated" from any accountability to its ancestors. It has become modern and forgetful. The culture of the initiated people has disappeared from view . . . Though the ancestral parent tree has been killed, there are still a few seeds of the old violated tree around . . . the day will come.

Julia at ancient Mayan city of Tikal

Tikal as viewed from the top of one of its pyramids

Touring Tikal

Tikal spiritual guide Luis Arturo Gonzalez

Burial vaults in the ancient city of Tikal

The island village of Flores in Lake Petén Itzá

Healer and herbalist Dr. Rosita Arvigo

The former capital city of Antigua, Guatemala

Lake Atitlan and its volcanoes

Santiago Atitlan with women washing clothes at the lakeside

Our tour of Santiago Atitlan with Dolores Ratzan

Maximon

Claire, Alicia, Lia and Julia at local orphanage

Panabaj after 2005 deadly mudslide that killed up to 2000

Our first reasoning with Tata Pedro in San Antonio

Woman in traditional dress uses a backstrap loom

Tata Pedro preparing his incense and candles for our ceremony

Our ceremony with Tata Pedro and Chus in sacred Mayan cave

Ajq'iij Pedro Cruz García (Tata Pedro) with his drum

Tata Pedro, Louise and Julia in San Pedro

Tata Pedro prepares for our lakeside ceremony

Like cogs on a wheel, the 13 numbers (intentions) and twenty aspects of the Tzolkin repeat every 260 days to create each day's ethics and wisdom

Ceremony at Mayan Grandfather Tree shrine

Tata Pedro in his ancestral cornfields

Belizean Flutist Pablo Collado at the Winter Solstice in Tikal

Julia and Danilo examine a stelae in the Grand Plaza in Tikal

Tata Pedro, Tata Mariano and Tata Nana (in shawl) preparing for Tikal ceremony on Winter Solstice in 2007
(© Bill Bevan at www.billbevanphotography@co.uk)

Danilo Rodriguez, Julia and Danny Diaz on the pier at our hotel

The Unificación Maya Ceremony on the 2007 Winter Solstice
(© Bill Bevan at www.billbevanphotography@co.uk)

Chapter 6

Tata Pedro Cruz

The nearby Andean spiritual leaders tell us that their prophecies call this time the Taqe Onkay—the great interweaving of tribes. Their prophecies call for pachacuti or "the Earth turned upside or set right." To them, this represents a new beginning and a "millennium of gold in the Earth." They refer to this as Taripay Pacha—the age of meeting ourselves again. They believe that when enough humans are free of fear and negativity, all humanity will reach a higher level of consciousness simultaneously. They speak of us "stepping outside of time." Perhaps this is why the Mayans ended their time-keeping at the close of this World Age.
- Joan Parisi Wilcox, *Masters of Living Energy:The Mystical World of the Q'ero of Peru*

The day after our tour of Santiago Atitlan with Dolores, Chus Landa, Danny Diaz's Guatemalan friend, who we met briefly at our Activation Maya presentation, came over to our hotel for lunch. On Danny's suggestion, we had contacted Chus a few weeks earlier to see if he could introduce us to Tata Pedro and act as our interpreter. He quickly agreed. Chus lives in nearby San Marcos, a twenty minute boat ride from Santiago Atitlan. San Marcos is the "New Age" village on the lake—complete with yoga retreats, pyramid-shaped meditation huts, holistic health centers, and several characteristic small hotels and restaurants, all clustered around the lakefront, interlaced with narrow cobblestone lanes allowing only foot traffic. The village has a whimsical, magical ambiance.

Chus, a vibrant, intelligent man whose intensity is tempered with his quick sense of humor and easy smile, operates a small backpacker's hotel, the Unicornio, made up of a peaceful garden courtyard with several small cottages and a shared bathhouse. Young tourists can get a clean bed for five dollars a night. It is well-known in these travelers' circuits and is usually full. Directly across the lane is a small outdoor cafe with tasty, inexpensive fare. You could stay a month for a couple of hundred dollars.

Chus, Julia, Alicia and I sat and talked around a table overlooking the lake at our hotel. We liked him immediately and quickly settled in together. He told us of his life as a constant traveler throughout South and Central America and Mexico, often playing Latin American music with his band, Sentimento Latino. He talked about the civil war which he said was not really a civil war, but a land grab by the military and the oligarchy at the expense of the indigenous people. Chus also spoke of the recent influx of the Evangelical churches that has resulted in the Mayans abandoning and forgetting their ancestral traditions and practices which are considered sinful and connected to witchcraft by the evangelical leaders of the Maya.

"But the civil war is now over," Chus said at lunch. "Now there is a new invasion here of spiritual seekers. This is much better, but getting very commercial. Some people always have a flag that says, 'I'm a shaman. I'm someone that walks in with light.' They do not have the truth because the people that have the truth don't say anything. They just express that through the peace inside of their soul—in the way they act, in the way they walk, in the way they breathe. And the people around them, they feel the same. They feel the peace. Because these people always say, 'I'm going to teach you. I'm going to teach all of you.' But just life teaches. The people that know, they share for free. They don't say, 'You cannot learn from me if you don't have a credit card. I know you are sick but you cannot come to my clinic without a credit card.' I don't believe in those things. I do treatments and share my knowledge for free. If you know how to heal people, heal the people. If they want to give you something after, that's fine. Share your knowledge for free. Doors open in that moment."

Soon Chus had to catch the last boat to San Marcos. Missing the last boat is about the only thing that creates any sense of rush around Lake Atitlan. Since most people move by foot or small ferry, there is an ambiance of quiet and relaxed calm. Few people wear watches. Most spend their days farming, cutting firewood, grinding corn, washing clothes, weaving, rearing children and other chores that create a serene feeling of simplicity. We made arrangements to meet Chus and Tata Pedro in two days in Panajachel where Julia,

Alicia and I were planning to stay for our last few days.

That night, at dinner in the hotel restaurant, a rather remarkable interchange occurred. As Julia, Alicia and I were eating dinner, we chatted a little with Lia and Claire, the two women who had joined us on the village tour with Dolores and who operate the foster children's home in California. They were eating at a nearby table. As our dinner was served and we returned to our table, another American woman about our age approached us.

"I hate to interrupt you," she said, "but David, the owner, said you were from North Carolina and I was wondering if you know my sister there."

"Where does she live?" I asked, thinking this was a wild goose chase as North Carolina is a huge state with millions of people.

"Well, she lives in a small town in the Blue Ridge Mountains called Blowing Rock. Do you know where that is?"

"As a matter of fact we do," I answered, astonished. "That's where we live! What's her name?"

"It's Lianne Mattar. Do you know her?"

"I don't think so," I answered.

"Does she have a son named Alex?" Alicia asked.

"Yes! He's my nephew!" she answered.

"I know him," Alicia said. "We went to high school together. They live around the corner from us."

"Oh, we know your sister," I said. "We walk by her house everyday and sometimes chat with her if she's out in her yard."

"That's her!" she said. "Next time you see her tell her Wendy ran into you. In fact, I'll be there in a few weeks. Maybe I'll see you there."

"That's amazing," I said. "What are you doing here?"

"I run an orphanage here in Santiago Atitlan," Wendy said. "I spend a lot of my time here."

"Then you must meet our new friends, Lia and Claire, eating over there," I said. "They run a foster care home in California and I know they'd love to meet you."

We all wandered over to their table and introduced Wendy to them. They, too, were amazed. After talking for awhile, Wendy invited all five of us to visit the orphanage the next morning, even though she would not be there. We all gladly accepted her invitation.

The next morning, we drove about thirty minutes around the lake to the orphanage. All along the drive were magnificent views of Lake Atitlan. Coffee plants were everywhere—in small patches and large fields. Large mounds of beans were drying in the sun by the roadside. Coffee had once been the economic mainstay in the Lake Atitlan region, as well as Guatemala in general, until globalization switched the coffee center to Vietnam, leaving many towns in the area scrambling to develop tourism to replace the income lost by coffee production.

Given the poverty of the area, I had no idea what to expect from a rural Guatemalan orphanage. What we found was quite surprising. The children's home included several modern glass and wood structures set on a hillside overlooking the lake. You would have taken it for someone's country home rather than an orphanage. As we approached, the three adult care-givers, two women and a man, came out to greet us, having been alerted by Wendy as to our arrival. They were kind, warm people.

Soon the children, who had all been involved in their assigned morning chores, started gathering around us, hugging our legs and looking up at us with longing, excited eyes. There were children from around three to twelve years old, all looking clean, well-dressed and well-cared for. Before long, each of us had our own small pack of beautiful, black-haired children following us around, each eagerly awaiting the next hug or pat on the back. They showed us their play area with a big sign outside on one of the buildings that said in big letters: "Dios Es Amor!" (God is Love!). Then they took us to the boys' and girls' dorms, clean buildings with large windows and orderly rows of well-made bunk beds.

We stayed about an hour, chatting with the staff and kids as best we could given our language barrier. We were all moved by such an innocent display of love and welcome. Alicia has always loved young children. I think she was near tears when we left.

"The children were so calm," Lia said as we drove back to the hotel. "Here they have no video games or Internet or TV that keep our kids so wired. The simplicity of everything really hit me. Caring for foster children in the United States is a bureaucratic and logistical nightmare. The regulations won't even allow our staff to stay overnight. We would never be allowed to take care of forty-five children with three people. We would be required to have many

125

more. By law, each child must be taken to the same school they used to go to so we are running the youths all around the Bay Area in the morning. Then in the afternoon, we have to pick them up again. After school, we have to take them to their therapists or their lawyers or their parents. Some of the parents are in prison so we have to take them there. The paperwork alone is overwhelming. Here it just seems like they take care of the children's everyday needs in a loving manner. That was really more what I thought I'd be doing when I left my career and started The Children's Village."

As she spoke, I thought about what a tremendous commitment of love people like Lia and Claire and Wendy were making. This was the vibration of unconditional love that one seldom hears or reads about. It is made in life-altering gestures by ordinary people who are doing extraordinary things everyday all around the planet. In their own unassuming way, these three American women represented the One Love we had traveled all these miles to find.

The next morning, Julia, Alicia, Lia, Claire and I took a boat back to Panajachel. Lia and Claire were heading back to the States and we were planning to spend our last three nights in Pana.

∞∞∞∞∞∞∞∞∞∞∞∞∞∞∞∞∞∞∞∞∞∞∞∞∞∞∞∞∞∞∞∞∞∞∞∞

After settling into our hotel, Julia, Alicia and I wandered the streets of Pana, stopping for dinner at a small outdoor cafe. Pana is much more developed as a tourist destination than any of the other villages around the lake. The village, even with a few modern hotels, retains its quaint charm with narrow lanes flanked by stalls of Mayan women selling crafts and weavings.

The next morning, Alicia stayed at the hotel to study for her upcoming final exams and Julia and I drove our rental car to the ferry landing to pick up Chus, Tata Pedro and Tata's friend, Tata Jose. As they walked toward us, Tata Pedro gave us a big smile and I felt like I had just made a lifetime friend. Tata Pedro, like all Mayans, is short, maybe five feet tall, but his presence is so strong you never think of him as small. He is humble and calm. He can be serious, almost brooding he has seen much suffering in his sixty-four years—but he is never far from a smile and a twinkle in his eye that makes him feel warm and approachable—like the wise grandfather you always wanted.

As we all climbed into the car, Tata Pedro asked if we could drive him to San Antonio, a small village about a half-hour around the lake where he was going to a meeting with several government officials. It seems that a local person had unearthed an ancient Mayan site while digging in his garden. Tata Pedro, one of the most respected traditional elders in the Lake Atitlan region, was meeting with the officials to ask them to leave it undisturbed and that the artifacts found would stay in the town. On the way over, they told us they had heard on the ferry that the heavy winds had thrown many people off a narrow foot bridge in Pana earlier in the morning. Several had died.

We dropped Tata Pedro and his friend off at the town hall where the meeting was being held and Chus and Julia and I wandered the village and settled on a rock outcropping overlooking the lake.

"Several months ago, Tata Pedro walked to Mexico and El Salvador with a group of people," Chus said as we settled in. "It was not just elders, but the youths, too. He carried a sacred medicine bag and handed it to the elders in El Salvador who will pass it on to the elders further south. The journey had taken them eight months. There were fifteen people and eight horses at the start, but only eight people finished the trip. Everyday, they would stop at a school and ask to teach the children about the Mayan traditions. Some were willing, but others resisted, some quite rudely, feeling that this traditional knowledge would undermine the children's Christian beliefs."

"Did it get much press?" I asked.

"No. No. But he is well-known and well-respected in the Lake Atitlan area because people know with everything that is happening, he's fighting for their rights. Many people respect him even if they go to the evangelical or Catholic Church. Tata Pedro is fighting for the rights of the Mayans and that's something really beautiful. He is never selfish. He believes in his responsibility for changes. He always says, 'Changes will come and we have to be ready.' He does these things because he loves the planet and he's really conscious about his love and he's proud of his roots. Five years ago, many, many people from the States came and invited him to go there and one of the women fell in love with him and invited him to stay. He told her, 'My heart would be really happy here with you, but my soul would not be happy. I must be with my people.' So he came back. His wife died nineteen years ago, so he was a little sad, but he has so little time. He has so much work to do.

"People now know about him from the 2005 and 2006 Activation Maya. This year, he left the Activation Maya the day before you came there because the organizers wanted shorter ceremonies, but you can't do these ceremonies shorter. They have to be long because we invoke the four directions and then count the *naguales*. These are the spirits of the day. We have to count each of the twenty *naguales* thirteen times and to say all the names—north, south, east, west—with each name, each color. It takes time, especially with translating."

"These ceremonies are beautiful," Chus continued. "He is a *zahorin*, somebody that can talk to the spirits. I don't mean the dead people's spirits. I mean the spirits of the mountains, the lake, the trees, the earth, the animals. The presence of the spiritual energies is really important in a Mayan ceremony. These spirits of Mother Nature exist and the *zahorin* talks to these spirits and Tata Pedro understands their language. Tata Pedro is in direct contact with these spirits. They are talking to us all the time, but most of us don't understand. We don't listen to their whispers or give this enough time in our busy lives.

"Fortunately, in this world there are people who do listen and understand. Their mission is to communicate their message to the ordinary people. We all have this power and the power to heal but we have forgotten about it, but it is in our DNA. When we talk about the awakening of the consciousness, it's just to remember who we are and where we are coming from. People know that these times are different and many are afraid and in some ways this is good because they are seeking spirituality. The Mayans have a lot of knowledge, but Maya is also a state of mind. If we awaken our consciousness and vibrate with the spirits of the natural world, then something beautiful will happen through all these prophecies. Between now and 2012, you will see the changes, the great awakening of human consciousness."

After about an hour, we met up again with Tata Pedro at the town hall. He was in good spirits. The government agreed to stop digging in this area. Tata's friend, Tata Jose, peeled off and Chus, Julia, Tata and I sat on the grass in a pleasant lakefront park at the foot of the village. We sat under the shade of a tall tree. It was warm and sunny with a breeze coming off the lake—a perfect place for a quiet reasoning. Wild doves were cooing in the background.

"Tata Pedro, for many years now, we have been bringing forward a message of One Love, of unconditional love for all humanity," I said, wanting to find out if he, after witnessing so much more suffering and cruelty as a poor Guatemalan farmer, had reached similar spiritual conclusions. "In our books and talks and concerts, we try to remind people no matter who they are or what has happened to them or what they have done, they can always claim their assignment given to them by the Creator to teach and learn love. Is your message similar to this?"

"Si!" he said loudly and distinctly after a long pause. "Congratulations!" We all busted out laughing.

"Well, I guess 'si' says it all," I said, knowing our search over two months and thousands of miles had not been in vain.

"I had a revelation in May and June in California," he said. "I was crying, not on the outside but on the inside, to see the world too complicated. There have been many things you see around this planet and it is really easy to find a solution. In life, there are not so many problems. If I want respect, I have to respect first—humanity, the grandfathers, the animals, the trees, the sky, the clouds, the lake, the fire—all the Universe. There are few words that offend me now. When the people treat me badly and give me bad treatment with words, I don't get angry. People compare me with an animal, like a donkey. White people use different words to offend me. The white people always find a way to offend indigenous people. That doesn't offend me. I don't get offended because it could be *true*! [He says this with an impish grin and a shrug of his shoulders and we all crack up laughing again.] They will try to offend me with the animal, but the animal is a part of me. It is my brother. To be honest, to be like a donkey is no problem. It is easier. The donkey has four qualities, not like a human. This is where the peace is—when you don't get offended. I want to be honest with myself. My fight is not to give attention to everything that comes from little things.

"I am going to be talking about love, but what is love? In the field of life, where is love? If you listen to the word 'love,' the first

129

thing that comes to many minds is a woman's body, sexual love. They go together for most of the people, but love is big and takes in everything. When couples start loving each other, they want more and more. There are couples that cannot convert the words 'I want you' and 'I love you' into action. The words 'to love' comes from inside and is born inside, as a special feeling. We must convert words into real love.

"Love is love. It comes from spirit. Love is respect. That is why every morning, like a spiritual guide, I take the energy from heaven and from the earth, from the water, from the fire, from the heart, of those four elements and four winds. That breathes strength into my life. Before the sun rises in the morning, I pray for my family, for my community and all the cultures around the earth. That is love. I ask for peace for my friends and for all my enemies; for the ones that make wars, that they will say they are just an instrument of peace. One day that will happen—the peace, the equilibrium. It is not possible to be rid of the negative, but look for positive energy to have a balance.

"People say to me I speak too much about spirituality and that I do not know anything. However, the reason I like teaching is because I learn every time I teach. Where is the peace in my town? People tell me that my message, my energy for peace, doesn't work. I want to be honest. In my family, there are different kinds of people. Some that really work hard, some very intelligent, some full of love, some that have amnesia in their brains. I have everything in my family—lazy workers, alcoholics, drug addicts, all kinds. But my family is the world, humanity and the animals. The animals understand me. The stones listen to me. They cannot convince me not to talk. One day, some will listen. Somewhere my message will be heard. I do not talk about religion. My words take the whole concepts of the ancestral knowledge and spirituality, in general, with love.

"I felt so good when you were talking about forgiveness and peace and love and kindness. I do not share the idea of forgiveness with my brothers from the other religions. I respect my brothers and sisters if they want to go to confession, but just to say 'sorry' is not asking for forgiveness That does not mean 'forgive me.' You need to ask for forgiveness to AHAU, the Creator. Sometimes I ask for forgiveness from AHAU and promise I will not do the same thing

130

again and sometimes I do the same thing again and I feel guilty. To forgive someone by words but not by heart with action is hypocrisy. I can be happy with someone and hug him and say I forgive him, but around the corner I will say something bad about him. That is not forgiveness. The mouth and the conscience go against each other. I can be happy with him with peace in my heart. I am speaking in general. We are part of the play. Now we are the actors of the play. If I ask for forgiveness and I do the same thing again, I am not keeping my word.

"We are preparing ourselves to create paradise here. It is here, now—to enjoy my life, my happiness, my love inside, to be okay with myself. It doesn't matter how others are speaking of me. When AHAU says my mission is done, my spirit doesn't need any preparation because it is pure before it comes into my body. My body will go into the ground as an offering. I believe in reincarnation. The spirit takes a different body. Sometimes people ask me, 'When are the ancient Grandparents, the original Mayas, going to return?' Many of them are still waiting, but the Mayas are here now—through us. You and your wife, looking for the love or for the peace, Mayan ancestors are living inside of you. Chus is studying the Mayan culture because the Mayan ancestors are back and are prompting him.

"People tell me that they have seen me in other places all around the world. I interpret this as my spirit traveling during my meditation or dream time. I feel free to talk. When I am receiving the divine messages, I do not feel limits because I didn't have a teacher to ask for orientations—what I have to do, what I will be, how to do the spirituality. My teacher was my grandfather. When I was seven years old, my grandfather took me to the sacred place and he taught me my mission for when I grew up. A half an hour I talked to him. Then he moved away. At eight, nine and ten and eleven and twelve years old, I was alone and I was crying because things did not function in the way I expected.

"I like the thoughts of the other brothers, but everything I receive comes in the form of a divine message in my dreams, not from books. Since I was a little boy, I have been able to interpret dreams. I hid this for more than forty years. I am 64 but this is the beginning of my life. I want to talk about my life on this planet. When I came into this world my parents got separated. I was born in my grandparents' house. My mother nursed me for just seven months and left me there and she left with another man. My mother left me. I could not feel the warmth of the love of my parents. I would cry and cry and cry. In the night, my grandmother told me they could not sleep because I was hungry so they gave me a little alcohol when I was eight months old. I have had many troubles in my life. I have suffered a lot. My grandparents would not take me to school but I would go different places for planting and farming corn.

"When I was fifteen years old, I went into the army. My spirituality started to develop more in the army. I began to walk in the mountains where I connected more with the natural things, nature. When I was seventeen, I left the army. I began to know the organizations. In 1962, I started sharing with the organizations of the Maya, with the other elders. I was nineteen. Then the religions came here really strongly, Catholics and the Evangelicals, and they were fighting over who was the best. None of them came inside my brain. I didn't allow them to confuse me.

"I always believed in the Mayan culture. There was not a minute I doubted. The religions came and complicated things for us Mayan spiritual guides, but then the moment came to say, 'I am going to preserve the Mayan culture.' It does not matter what the others think. This is meant to be public. I began to act in plays of the Mayan culture and after that, I became a director of a theater group. My intentions were to preserve culture in the theater. I was always a dramatic actor, never a clown. For sixteen years, since 1990, I have been recognized internationally and in Guatemala as a spiritual guide. There have been many confrontations with the ancient Mayan ways. I do not call myself a Mayan priest. I am a spiritual guide. Another word I am hearing now is 'shaman.' There are people that call me a Mayan priest, but inside I do not accept it because a priest is a term used by the Catholic Church and 'shaman' is the word used in other traditions. I am not a shaman because I do not do anything bad. I like peace and love.

"I am one kilometer from where you started your question. Thank you, Julia, for giving your support to me and thank you, Robert, for giving your support to Julia. I love you both. Thank you for sharing with me. I am single, always alone, but when I am here with you, my friends, Chus and both of you, now I do not feel alone. My wife died nineteen years ago. She was my right hand. We had thirteen children, four died, nine are alive. Now my staff and my sacred bag are my wife. I walk alone."

"We too feel grateful for you and feel less alone on our journey with all of us together here," I said, understanding how sparsely populated, and at times lonely, is the path of the peacemakers, at least for now.

"Thank you," Tata Pedro said, smiling.

"Tata Pedro," I said, "how did you learn about the calendars?"

"In 1950, when I was seven years old, I began to investigate, to listen to my grandparents talk about my *naguales*. I heard them speak about *Toj* [offering *nagual*]. I began to realize that *Tak* was my future. I didn't understand the *nagual* of the corn. Then my grandparents began to talk about the *naguales* of the corn and *T'jax*, so I was wondering about just three *naguales* at first. What do they represent? What do they mean? I used to dream and receive revelations about each *nagual* being in a circle. First I dreamed of thirteen, then later with twenty. I couldn't understand when I was less than ten but I was trying.

"When I went into the army is when I began to discover which *naguales* are the other ones. At the beginning, I had only three *naguales* and then I had five symbols. In the sixties, I had thirteen *naguales*. I knew what these thirteen meant and their representation. In the circle, there are twenty and I began to feel as if I knew how AHAU existed, the Creator existed. Then I knew the difference between the night and the day. In the same instance, I knew about one day, one week, one year, twenty years. I was asking at thirty-five, 'Why He didn't give me the answer about all twenty. You are right. We as your sons have many necessities, but You will give me the answer.' That answer came when I was thirty-five years old. I could complete the twenty *naguales*. I knew all the names of each one and the specific meaning of each. The conclusion of my grandparents' teaching I got in a revelation. I got the symbolism of creation."

"What do you think will happen in 2012?" I asked.

"People are saying the world is going to end," he answered, his smiling eyes turned toward the sky. "People are getting sick just thinking about it because they do not want to see the world end. What is going to happen is a change of time, a cycle of time. That is why people around the world are afraid. We will end a baktun in 2012. It is a big change of the time."

"A positive change?" Julia asked.

"Yes. We are doing things really good. We began to search in 1999, with 13 years for seeking up until 2012 or 2013. It is important to have people around that know peace and have more light, more illumination. There are people inside the circle and this mission is to spread the word in those moments. If we don't stop now to protect the planet and stop the pollution, there will be some destruction."

"People will wonder," I said, "with so many problems in the world, how will there be love and peace in five years, in 2012."

"There will be more understanding, more peace, more love," Tata Pedro said with certainty and calm in his voice. "It doesn't mean that the earth will change, the trees, the mountains. The world will receive a revelation. It is just a small percentage of the people on this planet that now have an interest in the ancient knowledge. We know this planet is so big, but we can make it smaller, to have it inside of us. And we must share this world within us with others, but if we have a war inside of us, we cannot share that with others."

"What will happen to those who don't have an interest?" I asked.

"For them, it will be the same—more war, more terrorism, more problems. The world will look the same, but we will have more people with consciousness—for those that can see it. The changes of this planet are gradual, not just from one day to another. If we continue doing the ceremonies and opening the portals and the gates, more people will know about what is happening and maybe they will change just because they want to change, not because they are afraid of the destruction of the planet. They will change because they will see more people that are more loving, not just people that dance with death. The energy will be more positive and those that want to come into this envelope of peace and love are welcome. Those that don't want to come in, they will be out. Now we are receiving the messages for 2012 that we have to change, that we have to open our hearts; that we have to be more conscious. The changes are now, in this moment."

"Will there be major earth changes, too?" I asked, thinking about the predictions of rising sea levels, global warming and the earth shifting on its axis and creating worldwide cataclysms.

Research has recently shown that the earth's magnetic field has flipped 171 times in the last 76 million years. There is no predictable order to the reversals but they are always preceded by a dramatic change in weather patterns and a weakening of the planet's magnetic field—both of which are now occurring.

"Our mission is to spread the word to have more people around this love by 2012," said Tata Pedro, staying on this message. "It will not be the end of the world. The energy now is very strong. There is much strange weather. The rays of the sun are changing the weather. This is the energy that we are feeling now, these changes in our planet, radical changes in the weather. We must find equilibrium with the sun and the planet and stop polluting because the rays can give us life or death."

"Will we change soon enough to prevent this when so few of the leaders are awakened?" I asked.

"We must reach them. I tried to reach Bush when I was in America, but I was not lucky because you need some money to reach him. We are receiving a message from heaven now that Bush will fail in his bad intentions. He is not doing the work for the peace of the planet. He has a personal plan. They are fighting spiritually against us, against this spiritual energy. They will not win. The good ones are more now. Shake away our doubts. It is very important to begin putting good things inside your head, not hate, greed, bad images. Many people think life doesn't mean anything. It is not me that is talking. It is the spirits."

"Are there enough of us to change the present course?" I asked.

"There is a small percentage of the people now that are truly interested in having spirituality and on April third, the beginning of the sacred calendar in 2007, we will receive a new percentage. It may be more or less, up or down. In the temples, they have just the Mayan Calendar. They have many calendars for everything and we are just learning about them. We cannot understand them all. We studied the glyphs, those codices, but we cannot understand it all."

It was getting late in the afternoon and we had to get Tata and Chus back to Pana so they could catch the last ferry back to San Marcos and to nearby San Pedro, where Tata Pedro lived. Tata Pedro wanted to take us to a cave near San Marcos the next day to do a special ceremony. The cave was sacred to the Maya and Tata Pedro and a group had put together money to purchase it. We all agreed to meet at the Unicornio the next morning.

"Why do you think so many people are interested in the Mayans now?" I asked as we drove toward Pana.

"Because this is the center of all the spirituality," Tata Pedro answered. "We were here before other people in other civilizations."

"Tata Pedro, the Hopi elders believe the Mayans are their ancestors," I said. "Do your ancestors say that?"

"Well, it was a long trip," he said, as if completing a partially-told story, "thousands and thousands of years. Much information was lost. People now believe what the Bible says, about Genesis and all those things, but those are confusing words. The book of the Maya, the *Popol Voh*, is almost the same as the Old Testament. A lot of the wisdom is inside of the Mayan calendar, the 260-day calendar, with the *naguales*. Each day has a meaning and now many people want this knowledge. I am opening that way inside of me for other people to share it and receive messages through their dreams.

"In 2005, I walked for seven months with a group of eight people across Guatemala to the Mexican border. In the beginning, there were fifteen. In the end, there were just eight. I was looking for the information of the sacred pyramids, the temple. Sometimes I was dream-walking. Now I am opening up a different consciousness of my own tribe. I was in Santa Fe, San Francisco, Santa Cruz, Mesa Verde and there are similarity between our people and the people in the States. We are you and you are us. Many Mayan people immigrated to many countries. *Paxel* was the original name of this land and in the dream I had when I was walking was that it is better to call it 'Guatemaya' because 'Guatemala' sounds like it is sick ['mala' means sick in Spanish]. I was in India for three months and I was interested to see how the Indian people respect each other. We are all one blood, one love, one nation. In our ceremonies, the colors are the different colors of the human kingdom—white, black, yellow and red."

On the return to Pana to take Chus and Tata Pedro to the ferry landing, we stopped in a store in the middle of the village so Tata Pedro could get his candles and incense for our ceremony the next day. The store was small but well-lit, crammed to its tall ceilings with bags of incense and multi-colored candles of all sizes. The aroma of thousands of fragrances hung gently in the air. It was a pleasant oasis in the otherwise franticness of Pana's central business area. We spent almost a half-hour there as Tata Pedro slowly, methodically, reverently selected his candles and incense.

∞∞∞∞∞∞∞∞∞∞∞∞∞∞∞∞∞∞∞∞∞∞∞∞∞∞∞∞∞∞∞∞∞∞∞∞

Early the next morning, Julia, Alicia and I took the ferry over to San Marcos to join Chus and Tata Pedro for his ceremony at the sacred cave. These small ferries hold 15 to 20 people and they stop at every village and a few private docks along the route, basically wherever passengers want to get on or off. It costs locals about fifty cents and tourists about two dollars, no matter how far you go. Along the way, you pass quaint mountainside and lakefront villages and architecturally-designed weekend homes of the wealthy. Many of the small hotels have their own docks, set inside lush, landscaped gardens. Everywhere your eyes rest, there is the crystal-clear lake surrounded by the three huge volcanoes. Our boat was full. The last passenger, a petite Mayan woman in traditional dress, walked out on the dock with two large cases of Dr. Pepper balanced perfectly on her head.

We met Chus and Tata Pedro at the small outdoor cafe across from Chus's hotel. We all settled in comfortably together. As always, I am impressed to see how Alicia feels at ease with people and situations outside her usual lifestyle. I really shouldn't be surprised. She has Rastafarian grandfathers, hugging relationships with many of Jamaica's conscious recording artists and speaks comfortably in front of groups, both large and small, here and abroad. We love traveling with her and her sister.

After breakfast, the five of us hiked up the hill behind the village a mile or so until we came to the cave. It was more like a large rock outcropping that created a sheltered area around 10 feet high and 30 feet in length and 12 feet in width. The ceiling was blackened from centuries of sacred Mayan ceremonies. It was cool under the outcropping, a respite from the morning heat.

"Here we will talk with God," Tata Pedro said, "and pray and ask for blessings. Please let us not forget our parents and grandparents and we will not forget about AHAU. We pray. We offer something to the Mother Earth and we will say a prayer for your brother-in-law and your sister and their family."

The night before, we had received an email from my nephew saying he thought his father, my brother-in-law Alan, was close to making his transition. For Julia, Alicia and me, so far from home, this ceremony was a comfort, allowing us to say goodbye to a man we all loved so dearly.

"One thing I want to say, to be really clear, *Toj* is my future, my hope because I am *Imox* and *Imox* receives the messages from heaven and are really close with God," Tata Pedro said as he spread twenty sheets of paper out on a low rock shelf in the back of the cave.

Each page had the picture of a *nagual* on it with its brightly-colored symbol. He then asked Julia, Alicia and me for our birth dates and that of our older daughter, Julie. He told us our day signs and which *nagual* and number we were born under and how that affects our individual life and mission. He explained that today was a 6-Aq'ab'al—a day for sunshine, a day with a lot of meaning, a lot of energy.

Using sugar, he created a two-foot wide circle with a cross in the middle facing the four directions. Within each quadrant, he poured a circle of cornmeal, creating a cross-inside-a-circle symbol that we had seen often in Hopiland. Years ago, Julia had created a mandala of the same symbol using white crystals in our backyard. An ancient white pine is on one side and our small pond, the highest point— the headwater—of the New River, the second oldest river in the world, is on the other.

He then laid out the candles and the incense for the ceremony—four large candles (red, black, white, and yellow) in the four cardinal directions and one green candle in the middle with a hundred or so small multi-colored, pencil-width candles laying flat on the ground between the larger ones. Between the candles were many two-inch wide small resin saucers made of their sacred copal incense. As he laid everything out, his movements were slow and methodical, done solemnly and with great deliberation, his vibration setting a peaceful and reverent tone in the cave.

"This large red candle is for the red cultures, for the Hopis. The black one is for Africa. The white is for Europe, the invaders, and the yellow is for China, Indonesia, Asia. I consider myself yellow for Maya. This is not a prayer for the Mayan world. We are a part of the whole world. This invocation is for the whole Universe. We will pray to the cardinal directions—the Heart of the Wind, Heart of Fire, Heart of Water, Heart of Mother Earth. We ask for equilibrium for everything. You are our ancestors and we thank you for your words of wisdom. We will follow your footprints. We ask for forgiveness for all the bad things, all the limitations, the exploitations against the physical bodies of women. This is a special moment to ask for all the debts of our ancestors that are underground now. There are just five of us here; there are many spirits here too. We need to be strong to send our message of love and peace to reach the ears of all the five continents. We are always searching for love and unity, love for everything, the trees, the animals, the rocks. If I die, someone else will come behind me to do the ceremonies. It will not die. Paradise is here, not in another world."

We gathered around the candles and Tata Pedro began to pray, sometimes holding his hands bent at the elbows with palms up, other times above his head, stretched toward the sky. His eyes were closed, his face in earnest communication with the Creator. He prayed for AHAU—the Creator of the Universe—to not leave us alone, to give us a useful life, to bring peace in our hearts and in the hearts of all people, all countries, all continents. He asked for forgiveness for our negative feelings, for envy, for anger. He prayed for wars to stop and all to live in peace. He thanked God for the corn, the fruits, the herbs, the sun, the rain. He blessed each of us individually, using our Spanish names, asking that we receive guidance in our lives. We did this in all four directions, bending down, reverently kissing the earth after each directional prayer.

Then, he said a blessing for the International Day of the Woman, scheduled for the following day. He asked for forgiveness from all the women around the planet for the bad things men have done to them and prayed that men would remember that women are a gift from God. After these prayers, Tata Pedro began a quiet rhythmic chant in his native Tzutujil language, while playing a small drum. Chus began lighting the candles and Tata Pedro invited the ancestors, the "grandfathers from the stars,"—the *abuelos*—to join us. The candles burst into flames, with the hundred or so small candles flaring up, melting the sweet smelling incense. At times, he would give us some incense or a small candle and ask us to make a special prayer and throw it in the fire.

He closed with a special prayer for my brother-in-law, Alan, who he said was "between life and death" at that moment, reminding us that life is eternal and our bodies only temporary vehicles for our souls. He asked that God not take him unless his mission on earth was complete. If his mission was complete, it was okay. He quietly said prayers for Alan in Tzutujil as he spread the embers of the dying fire.

The ceremony went on for almost two hours. With the intense flames from the candles and the rising morning heat, I found my mind wandering and then I would refocus on what was happening, the sacredness and reality of communicating with our Creator, something that I often forget to do. At times I would focus on my brother-in-law, my sister, my nephews, and send love and comfort their way. Often I was in tears, as were Julia and Alicia.

When we returned to our hotel several hours later, there was an email from my nephew, Adam, saying his father had passed. Though it was expected, it hit us all hard. The funeral was scheduled in two days, on the day we traveled home. We would not make it. Our tearful goodbyes were said in private, in that sacred cave.

Chapter 7

Return to the Umbilicus of the Universe

Once you grasp the nature of unconditional love you realize that there is a galactic agenda. There is a higher order of complexity that is unfolding within human consciousness as a whole. Then you receive the next gift of the angel light—humility, perhaps the hardest gift to accept. After all, we learn to function within the planetary dream because we have an ego, and the better we function, the higher our self-importance. But in the angel light, there is no room for self-importance—it is, in fact, a major obstacle. Instead, it is necessary to surrender all our false pride.

- Judith Bluestone Polich, *Return of the Children of the Light:Incan and Mayan Prophecies for the New World*

February and March rolled by slowly. I spent my days writing this book and nights by the fire with Julia, punctuated by visits from our daughters or friends. About six weeks after our return from Santiago Atitlan, I had finished transcribing the talks with Tata Pedro and Chus and telling this story to this point.

"I feel we need to go back to get more from Tata Pedro," I told Julia one night by the fire. "Two times with him just isn't enough. There is so much more I want to ask him."

"I've been feeling the same," she answered. "Let's go soon. You're kind of hard to live with if you're not writing anyway."

"Well, we still have frequent flyer miles," I said, "and Chus said the rooms in San Pedro are only a few dollars a night, so let's stay there, where Tata Pedro lives."

Through Chus, we contacted Tata Pedro and he said he would be around, as would Chus and Louise, who would be our interpreters. Two weeks later, we were on a flight to Guatemala City, having made arrangements to spend seven days in San Pedro.

Leaving the traffic and urban sprawl of the capital, we were soon on the road through the beautiful Guatemalan countryside. We spent the first night in Pana and the next day, we took the early ferry to San Pedro.

After a forty-five minute ferry ride from Pana, stopping at several villages and private docks, we disembarked at San Pedro. The highland air felt fresh and clean. Lake Atitlan is known for its favorable weather—seldom too hot, seldom to cool. It's called "the land of eternal spring."

A very friendly guide walked us around to all the local hotels and we chose the Maria Elena, a brand new lakefront hotel with basic but clean, well-lit rooms opening on to large covered verandas overlooking the lake. Our guide seemed surprised when we gave him a tip. He was just being friendly—a welcomed change from the hustlers of Jamaica. We had arranged to meet Louise in front of the Catholic church later in the day, so we dropped our bags and set out to explore the town.

All the villages around Lake Atitlan have their own character and San Pedro is no exception. The upper part of the hillside village is Tzutujil Mayan, with cinder-block homes rebuilt after a fire destroyed most of the village and its traditional thatch and wood structures. The lakefront area is quite different. It is the hippie/backpacker/eco-tourist Mecca of Lake Atitlan. This section of the village, from the lakeshore inland about one hundred yards and stretching over a mile or so down the lake is complete with twenty or thirty small hotels (from five to twelve dollars a night), quaint open-air restaurants, a few craft stores, mostly selling easy-to-carry items. Everything is spread out along several narrow, winding pedestrian paths in such a way that you feel as if you've been transported back in time and entered some fantasyland mixture of the 1960s counterculture and traditional Mayan life—and in many ways you have.

Since there are also 15 or 20 Spanish language schools in San Pedro, the tiny village has established itself as an inexpensive place to live while you learn Spanish as you prepare for your backpacking trek through Central and South America and/or Mexico. Its two main cobblestone streets cross immediately above the ferry landing and are lined with shops, internet cafes, tiendas, a reggae club and several open-air restaurants (two to five dollars a meal!). Since there are few TVs in the hotel rooms, several of the restaurants show movies each night. Local street vendors sell small cakes and pastries, fried chicken, french fries, fruits and nuts. The sweet smell of marijuana completes the vision. We liked the village instantly. (What would you expect from the guy who wrote *Memoirs of an Ex-Hippie?*)

We wandered uphill toward the church, cutting through the marketplace, crammed with every fresh fruit and vegetable imaginable. There were also baskets of dried fish, some a foot or more in length and others just an inch or less. Several stalls were selling cuts of meat, including full pig heads and cow tongues—all profusely covered with flies.

The locals were friendly. A warm smile and friendly "Hola!" was quickly returned. The village youth drum corps was marching through the town, much to the delight of the villagers, who greeted them by setting off long strings of firecrackers. There was one policeman in town who seemed rather bored as he lounged outside the small police station. Though hard drugs had started to creep in and there were reports of a few robberies of tourists on back roads, the town seemed peaceful and safe.

As planned, we met Louise at the Catholic church. Louise, an attractive, energetic, and articulate woman from Liverpool, England, operates the holistic health center next door to Chus's Unicornio. She is a kinesiologist and teaches seminars which blend the ancestral wisdom of the Maya with practical techniques for attuning personal energy and maintaining health in the countdown to 2012.

After getting to know Louise a little, we headed down to their hotel, directly across the street from ours to meet Tata Pedro and Chus. This week was the big festival in their village of San Marcos and Chus and Louise had decided to stay in San Pedro to get away from the all-night music and fireworks that continue all night during the festival. With all of us staying in San Pedro, where Tata Pedro lived, it worked out perfectly.

Tata Pedro and Chus were at the hotel when we arrived. It was good to be with him again. It seemed familiar, like a long-time friend rather than a new acquaintance. We soon learned that in the week before our arrival, Tata Pedro was so sick from gastritis, he had almost died. Louise said he was very weak and had to be taken to the hospital in an ambulance, something that is rarely done in this

143

impoverished village. As Louise later told us, "There is no health insurance for the Mayans. They just die." Though he seemed a little weak, he was definitely on the mend and by the time we left a week later, he was back to full-strength.

Not wanting to push him, we all settled on plastic chairs on the lakeshore in front of our hotel for our first of many reasonings. We gave Tata Pedro some organic cherry juice we had brought for his occasional gout and a clothe bag full of Hopi blue corn that was given to me in Hopiland. We also gave him and Chus and Louise a leather Native American totem bag like the one we had given Luis in Tikal. I had also brought them each a small handmade ceramic bear I had bought at the Cherokee Indian reservation near our home in North Carolina. Much to my surprise, Tata Pedro starting blowing in one of its legs and played it like a melodious flute.

"These three symbols represent the past, present and future," he said, pointing to three spiral symbols carved on the side of both bears. "It is significant that you gave us this. It shows where you are coming from and where you are going. It talks of our path. There are not many differences between the religions of the world. There are many pathways. We have many days when we communicate with our ancestors. We talk about light and dark, the world of the Creator and the world of materialism [the Hopi use the exact same terms for the two paths they say everyone must choose between]. We ask for forgiveness, to get rid of our fears, our fears that we are going to die. I am not afraid of death. It is not the end, only a transformation. Until God says I have completed my mission, I will continue to take my medicine [holds up the cherry juice and we all laugh].

"This week we will do a ceremony at the Grandfather Trees on the other side of the volcano. They talk when you cut the branches, but you must ask permission. I have received messages, but I didn't know what I was waiting for. The Grandfather Trees talk to me even though I wasn't expecting it. It was from the Grandfather Trees that I received the messages."

"Tata Pedro, what do your people say of Quetzalcoatl?" I asked. "Like Christ, he seemed to be a great teacher of love."

"In our language, he is called Q'uq'kumatz [pronounced 'Ku-ku-mats']," he answered. "It is the same as Quetzalcoatl. Jesus was talking about an ancient knowledge—something that came before. The religious leaders are afraid of this ancient knowledge coming

144

back from the ancient Mayans, all that wisdom."

"Radford, the Hopi elder, says that most Hopis still hold to their ancient beliefs," I said. "Is it the same here?"

"I dreamed about Radford, about the reunion. In San Pedro, a town of eleven thousand, I am the only one who keeps the ancient ways. There is a big discussion now because twenty days ago, I did a special celebration at one of our sacred sites where the Grandfather Trees live. Several hundred people came. Many were students. It was about peace and love. They will broadcast this ceremony on local TV this week in San Pedro and Santiago Atitlan. There's been a big commotion. The Christian leaders forbid people to participate in these ancient ceremonies. They put pressure on the people not to go to their own ceremonies, their own celebrations. In the past, five or six people were preparing to be spiritual guides, but now we walk with the door closed.

"I am the only one to talk openly about the *naguales* [the spirits of the days], the changes in the weather and the changing times. There are a few others that practice the old ways in secret. They are afraid of the Christians, of what they will say about them. They communicate with their spiritual guides but not here in this town, but outside. There are about seventy thousand people in the whole of Guatemala that still follow the old ways, out of eleven million Mayans [less than one percent]. It is good that the Hopis do better [Radford had told us about eighty percent of the Hopis still follow their old ways]."

"Years ago, how many people in this village followed your traditions?" I asked.

"Forty years ago, when this town was traditional thatch-roofed houses, people believed in the ancient traditions," he said with a nostalgic sigh. "During one of the Christmas celebrations, a firecracker caught a house on fire and the whole town burned. The Christian leaders took advantage of that to convert the people. There was a big struggle for the people between the Catholics and Evangelicals. The Catholics would sing 'We don't want Protestants. We don't want Protestants.' "

"Why do you still keep to the old ways?" I asked. "It must be disheartening, lonely."

"I am the *only* survivor from the eighties. I was in jail during the war and there I heard a voice say to me, 'You are not going to die because you have a mission.' I was kidnapped two times by the army, but it was not my time to die yet."

"Your story is similar to the Hopis' but they are much more remote," I said. "Maybe this was the Creator's plan knowing that this wave of conquest was coming and the Hopis were sent from here to such a remote place to keep the wisdom alive. They still have their year-long Ceremonial Cycle intact in Shungopovi, their Mother Village. Radford told us the ceremonies are a repository for all human wisdom. There is a ceremony for love, gratitude, abundance, respect for women, co-operation, generosity, courage, trust, honesty—all wisdom. They were told that one day the entire world would go into chaos, they call this *kyonisquatsi*, and then they were told to share this wisdom with the whole world, which they started doing fifty years ago. They believe that a time of purification is coming to balance the world, but they do not know when. They said it may be tomorrow or in a thousand years. Maybe the Creator's plan was to entrust your people here with the calendar, with the timeline. You are the daykeepers, the timekeepers of the path to enlightenment. The Hopis are the wisdom-keepers."

"Maybe one day, I will meet with Radford," Tata Pedro said. As soon as he said it, I started to wonder how to put these two elders together. "It is lonely here. One day, the church leaders told me that I was an enemy of Jesus Christ. But why? Why do they think like that? They confuse our people. They retell our history about Maximon [the wooden Mayan icon we had visited in Santiago Atitlan]. His real name was Francisco Socuel, one of our ancestors. He lived in Santiago Atitlan and he was the headman. The Christians came and said he was a white man, Juan Simon, that wore a hat, dressed in black and smoked a cigar. This was the Spanish version of the real Maximon. That was not Maximon. Maximon came and taught us peace and love.

"With my Hopi brothers and sisters, there is not so much confusion within them, not so many things coming in from the outer world. That's why we are beginning with the youths today. The people my age push me away. They do not want to share the information. This is not about fighting among ourselves. By the middle of this century, this will all finish anyway. This conflict, this mixing, is going to finish. Now the Mayan priests have a lot of influence coming in from the West and Christianity. Really the

146

Mayan priests' spirituality is part of the ancestors. They've got to find the way of culture in our life. That's why we need to teach the children, the new generation. So these children will begin to flower, to bloom in the middle of the century. This is the way the *tatas* and the *nanas* are still here. They have not left. They are still here within us. Only when they take me to my grave and I am cold, will I stop talking about the ways of our ancestors, the elders.

"The Mayans, the Hopis, the Aztecs, and the Incas are all over the whole world. They go and they come back. It is really important to see this message [he holds up the bear] of where we go and where we come from. So when these things are presented to us, we need to do something practical about it. It is not a coincidence that I am completely convinced that the pathways of the Mayans and the Hopis are in complete agreement. When this message from me gets to Radford, I am sure it will give him more tools to take his words and apply it to his own philosophy.

"The Hopis left here when there was a lot of conflict like there is here now. The flood that Radford is talking about and why they left, there was a lot of pressure when they were massacred and it was prohibited to practice the spirituality of the ancestors. [Radford had asked us to ask the Mayan elders about a flood that he was told caused his people to leave Central America.] So the *naguales*, the spirits, they had to change their names and their images. [The Hopis call their spirit guides *kachinas*] People began to say one thing is devil, another is saint. That's what is called materialism. That's when they started to war."

"The Hopis have held strong in spite of much suffering," I said. "There has been much suffering here also—with the invasion, the civil war, the earthquakes, and hurricanes. How bad was your village hit during Hurricane Stan?"

Hurricane Stan hit this Guatemala on October 5, 2005, dumping so much rain that it caused deadly mudslides in many areas. The worst hit was the small village of Panabaj, a community on the outskirts of Santiago Atitlan, instantly buried by a mudflow a half-mile wide and up to 20 feet deep. Estimates of the dead were between several hundred and two thousand. After some initial digging, the town stopped and decided just to declare the entire covered area a mass graveyard. Julia and I had walked to the area which was a few hundred yards from our hotel in Santiago Atitlan.

Ruined homes and buildings, including the army base where the citizens from Santiago Atitlan were gunned down as they protested the army's brutality during the civil war, were everywhere—still half-buried in mud. The tragedy was mostly ignored by the international press.

"Hurricane Stan came here and a journalist called it The Assassin," Tata Pedro said. "I got really angry about this. For me, nature is never an assassin. Just like people need to have a bath, to feed ourselves, our bodies need attention because it's a sacred body. Nature does not look for good things or bad things. It looks for balance, for cleansing, for purification. In our cosmovision, nature was made for love, for sharing, to cleanse us, to feed ourselves, to give us all we need because we live within nature. It is the same with death. We need to be reformed. We need to feel a new breath, like a new beginning. Nature is just the same. The rain, the wind, the hurricanes, it's like nature's party. Nature is part of us. We come from the lake. Our First Mothers, they all came out of the water. The lake is part of our life. I wrote to thank all the waters of the world. Three nights ago I had a revelation. The word 'gracias' [thank-you] is used because that's what gives us love. We offer our sincere thanks, to the lake, to the rivers, to the waterfalls, to the rain, to little streams, to the sea, because they have got to be there. So we give thanks.

"One of the prophecies I want to leave the knowledge of so that it can blossom in the middle of this century is that all the pollution and conflict has to finish first, which is part of the Western doctrine. In my personal case, you can look at me with good eyes or bad eyes. I don't want to mix it up. I want to say things exactly as they are as a Mayan descendant. I am working based on the philosophy of my Mayan ancestors. I am walking with the sun, following the footprints of my Mayan ancestors. I am not trying to create conflict with my Christian brothers, the church leaders, but one day these ideas are going to be finished, the ideas that have come to them."

By now it was late afternoon and our reasoning felt complete. A cool breeze had picked up, a peaceful time around the lake. We all wandered toward the ferry landing and entered one of the open-air restaurants for dinner. Bob Marley was singing "One Love" over their sound system. A small ferry was pulling into the landing,

"Marley" painted in large block letters on its side.

∞∞∞∞∞∞∞∞∞∞∞∞∞∞∞∞∞∞∞∞∞∞∞∞∞∞∞∞∞∞∞∞∞∞∞

"We in the Western world live in here," Louise said pointing to her head. It was the next morning and we were all sitting on our veranda at our hotel. "The Mayans, wherever you go, live from here [she points to her heart]. You'll see it in the little old lady. You'll see it in the child carrying boxes on his head. When you ask directions from someone on the street, they don't just answer you, 'left' or 'right.' They beam it from here, from their heart. Even in Guatemala City, in the middle of Zone One, which is a really rough area, and when you ask somebody and a smile comes over their face and they just open up. To me, that is the message of the Maya. One Love is absolutely here and people ask if the Mayans are gone. To me, they haven't left. Even if they've changed the way to do their worship, it doesn't change the way they are. I've traveled in many countries of the world and there is something special about Guatemala. They live from the heart. This land is the heart, where the condor and eagle will meet—in the heart of America. We live in harmony day-by-day with them. They are a *living* calendar."

"We talk about the Mayan calendars and the Mayan culture," Tata Pedro said. "The calendar is at the center of the culture. It is the creation of the planet and the necessity of the human beings. All that AHAU created—the plants, the animals, the sacred elements—He named each one and gave them a use. There is a need to survive, to understand this Creation. That is the calendar. The sacred calendar is 260 days—the short count—thirteen months, the period of gestation for a baby."

"Why are there thirteen months?" I asked.

"There are twenty days in each of the thirteen months, 260 days," Tata Pedro continued. "Today is *I'x*. It is a day to receive spiritual revelations. This is when we began to say 'gracias' for everything. Even when my own people say, 'You are Mayan,' I don't accept it. There are no limits, no frontiers for the Mayan blood, for the Mayan race. In the red Indians is the same Mayan blood. In the ceremonies, we use the four colors of the skins of the world but we do not believe that Maya is only one color. All of this is related to the calendar. We have many, many calendars. We have been talking about our lunar calendar of 260 days. Our solar calendar has 360 days plus five, eighteen months with twenty days and one month with five days to make offerings, to give thanks for the other eighteen months, even for the mistakes. This is the time the Mayan elders go up into the mountains, to the highest point, and fast, just water and fruit. So there are nineteen months in all. This calendar tells us when to plant the corn, the beans, the plants and when to harvest them. The corn that you brought me from the Hopis, we cannot just plant that anywhere. We have to plant it in a special place, where we are going to go tomorrow. There the corn will be harvested in December or January. Some beans take three or four months to grow; the vine beans take a year.

"So we use the solar calendar to control our planting. We call this the agricultural calendar. It is about our life, our health and the food we eat. It took me many years to understand these calendars, these sacred calendars, the most complete in the world. When I was seven years old, my grandfather took me to a sacred site and told me my mission, but after that I had nowhere to get the information because he left town. So in my dreams, feelings in my body, when a woodpecker sings, when a lazy bird flies in front of me, all these things bring messages. A tremble in my left eye—is it positive or negative? What my grandfather didn't give me, I received in my dreams. When I used to wake up at five o'clock in the morning, my grandparents were on their knees looking up at the sky. The agriculture was in the sky, in the rain, in the clouds. We didn't have clocks. We just watched the ducks on the lake.

"In the fifties, there were no machine noises. In the sixties, you started to hear the electric corn grinders. In 1965, you started to hear the sound of the cars and then the beginning of the boats. Before all that, you could only hear the people rowing and talking. You could hear the mountains, the hills [he looks rapturous, eyes closed], the sound of the wind, the sacred singing of the wind. The volcano would shake and you could hear it. They would tell you when the hurricanes would come. You could feel the weather coming.

"This town was not called San Pedro then. It was *Tzun'un Ya*—the hummingbird. This is the knowledge from the Creator. But where is all that knowledge now? Now you cannot hear the little

150

ducks that tell you summer is coming [almost on cue, a large loud truck rumbled by]. My grandparents would light their incense to thank the ducks when they came and when they went back. My ancestors could invoke the lightning, the rain, but now they cannot do that anymore. Now they are all Evangelicals. They are all Catholics. This is the real Mayan knowledge and it is all related with our sacred calendar and the solar calendar.

"The moon calendar knew when a woman could get pregnant and the people would not let her walk in the streets during that time. Any project that you wanted to begin, you started on the new moon. If you wanted to build something or you wanted to maintain your crops, it had to be on the full moon. You choose the seeds for your crops on propitious days. You do not plant your crops on certain days because they will germinate, but not give any harvest. You harvest the corn on a full moon. You have to consult the spiritual guides to know when to make love and whether you will have a son or a daughter. You have a ceremony. If you make love on *Tijax*, the child will be born on *Q'anil* and the mother will be between life and death. There is a lot of bad on that day. You must be careful. Now there are clinics and pills, but before, the elders taught the birth control with the calendar.

"Before the couple unites, when they fall in love, the elders did not let them be alone together, maybe for only ten minutes during the day. It was very controlled. They saw what the couple's day signs were, to see how they would get on—to see if they were compatible. This way, there will be no divorce. If a beautiful woman comes along, his heart will start beating but his wife's name is in his heart so he'll behave himself. However, when they look at the couple and they are not compatible, it is really bad news. They like each other a lot, but they're not compatible with the calendar. It's like toothaches for everyone. The parents try to talk them out of marriage. You might marry, but you've been warned. The parents won't stop it. It is a spiritual assessment and the parents will help the couple keep equilibrium.

"I was born in the forties. By the fifties, I began to realize that these traditions were being lost. In the forties, there were no killings, no conflicts; no jealousy here in the village like there is now. Now, this world is all about separation, divorce. It is the women that suffer most in all the continents of the world, but now the young women

151

are awakening and when they find their love, they find out what his day sign is to see if they are compatible. This was the life of the Maya. Lot's of things are happening now. They are all related to the calendar."

We were getting hungry, so we all wandered down a winding back lane, past little juice bars, internet cafes and tiendas, to an open cafe serving organic vegetarian meals for a couple of dollars each. Over lunch, Tata Pedro told us about his daughter's problem with her marriage. He had warned her not to marry her husband, not only because of incompatible day signs, but because his family had kidnapped Tata Pedro twice during the civil war and had him thrown in prison. He was released after an investigation and sought no retribution toward the family. Now, his daughter and her husband were separated and involved in a custody fight over their two year old son, Tata Pedro's grandson.

∞∞∞∞∞∞∞∞∞∞∞∞∞∞∞∞∞∞∞∞∞∞∞∞∞∞∞∞∞∞∞∞∞∞∞∞∞∞

After lunch, we all went our separate ways and agreed to meet again at our hotel late in the afternoon to accompany Tata Pedro on his next ceremony. Blake, a young American from San Francisco, was opening a new restaurant, La Puerta, down the lakeshore from the hotel and had asked Tata Pedro if he would do a blessing for his new venture. He had attended a ceremony with Tata Pedro at the beginning of the solar year a few months earlier and was moved by it.

We met at the hotel and walked through the winding paths of the village. The restaurant was a small concrete open kitchen covered by a thatch roof and several tables set on small grass terraces cut into a sloping bank that looked across an open meadow that blended into the lake about fifty yards away. It was very roots, very natural.

Louise, Tata Pedro, Julia and I gathered at the lakefront in front of the restaurant where there was a fire pit surrounded by several chunky logs that served as seats. In the grove of trees next to the field, a young American was taking lessons in Spanish from a Mayan woman. He sat in a plastic chair under a tree while she stood by a small blackboard set on an easel. A traditional hut, made of bamboo with a thatch roof with a large clay pot covering the peak, stood nearby. Except for the occasional fireworks coming from the festival in San Marcos, the scene reflected Lake Atitlan's usual unhurried calm. Doves cooed in the background. The rhythmic bass drum beating of a student drum corps from a nearby village wafted gently and quietly by.

In the same tranquil, deliberate manner as he did in our cave ceremony, Tata Pedro, with Julia and Louise's help, began laying out the numerous candles, large and small, and a copious amount of incense. When that was complete, Tata Pedro put on his brilliant red ceremonial headdress and his massive necklace and took up his carved wooden staff. He looked ancient, wise, powerful.

"Good afternoon, everyone. Welcome to this sacred site," Tata Pedro said to the twenty people who soon gathered for the ceremony—Blake, his friends, several Mayan locals including four children and two women in traditional dress and several interested tourists who just happened to be wandering by. "People ask me which is the most sacred site. Every step that I take is a sacred site for me. Mayan ancestors looked for observation points in the mountains for our astronomy. All the hills have a function for this.

"As Mayan descendants, we follow the footprints of them. That's why we are giving the welcome to this sacred site. The fire that we are going to have is not just any old fire. It is something you are going to feel. We are talking about love, peace, harmony, unity and brotherhood. Our Mayan ancestors, they leave an inheritance, these ancestral spirits. There is nothing new. It has been around since the creation of man. When the world was created, there were three generations which didn't work. The fourth, of corn, worked. We are made of corn.

"These candles are the four colors—red, black, yellow, white—important colors in the Mayan world and on this planet earth. These are the colors of humanity and they symbolize the colors of our corn. There is blue and green for the sky and earth. We didn't get all the colors. Also, there is light blue, red, pink, and purple. These are all the colors of the Mayan world and of the planet earth. This gives us the strength to refresh our minds and our bodies.

"We thank Blake for inviting us. This is a spiritual banquet. I would like to remember our elder, Philipe Chavajay. I talked with him and I lived with him. We always did ceremonies up there [he

153

motions toward his right] and down there [he motions toward his left]. We are here to bless this new business. It is an honor to be here. We are going to receive many blessings. We are here to thank God. It is not a different God. For Mayans it is AHAU. For others, it is Jehovah. It is all the same. We all have the same God that we invoke. We all have needs. We all have different things to ask and we can ask the ancestors here. This is not witchcraft, negativism. It is ceremony, fire. The fire symbolizes the spirit, the spirit of the sacred lake.

"We are going to ask AHAU to bless each of your families, your communities. We are looking for the pathway of love and peace. We are going to concentrate as much as we can and feel God, AHAU, in our own way. We are going to ask to the heavens and the earth and the fire and the water and the wind that we breathe in. All these symbolize the spirit of our being. We are asking for well-being and health, positive energy in each of the thirteen joints of the energy that moves around in our sacred body so that it all works. Let's ask for harmony, patience, friendliness. In a project like this, you need love and appreciation. People will come here from all over the world. That's what I think and that's what I want to ask for and for each one of you here, that you have good health in your families. We are asking for peace in the world. As Mayan descendants, we are not on the side of any conflict.

"Concentrate a minute. The ceremony will be in three parts. In the first part, we are going to invoke in the four directions. In the second part, we are going to make our offerings, with *Toj*. That's when we ask for the cosmic strength, mental and spiritual and material, for each one of the *naguales*. In the third part, before leaving the sacred fire, we are going to give thanks for the moment that God has given us."

As the group watches quietly, respectfully, Tata Pedro begins the lighting of the candles. Soon the fire flares up, set off by the many small candles laid flat in the fire pit over the combustible saucers of resin holding the incense. He invites us all to turn toward the lake, toward the sunset, toward the *abuelos*, the ancestors. He says a quiet blessing to the lake, the fire, the four winds, Mother Earth, AHAU, in all four directions, bending to kiss the ground after each one. I notice he has calluses on his elbows from a lifetime of doing this. He then starts to speak of the *naguales*.

154

"Come toward the fire. Feel the energy. It will get rid of all the negative stuff. We all have the ability to make this offering, not just me, so we will all make the payment. Blake will make the first payment [he hands Blake some incense]. Today is *E*, which is a great day for opening the pathway in his new business. It means destiny or sacred road. Next is *Aj*, which is the corn husk and represents the family and the children. He's going to pay the ancestors. This is about family. It is a symbol of the home, a symbol of the children. You have to have lots of patience when there are children at the ceremonies, not hit them. Even if they're naughty during this ceremony, don't hit them.

"*I'x* is next. It means the sacred places, the sacred Mayan temples which are the Mayan altars in the hills. Next is *Tz'ikin*, which is when we offer these sesame seeds to the fire. We will pass the bag around and take some seeds, the sacred seeds. This is for all of the things we have to say thanks for in our lives. It is a symbol of our richness. We say thanks for the food, the seeds, and say thanks for everything we have—our clothes, our food, everything we use in our lives. Do it with lots of faith and get close to the fire and make a noise like I do."

He takes some seeds and gives a little to each person and throws some in the fire. As he throws them, he makes a fluttering sound with his lips. The seeds crackle and pop as they hit the flames.

"*Tk'ikin*. This is a symbol of projects, the bird that flies half way between heaven and earth, the messenger from the heavens. This is a good project, a communication with humanity, nature and the spirit of God. Come toward the fire and offer your seeds."

One by one we throw our seeds in the fire and make a fluttering noise like a bird.

"Now we will talk of the rest of the *naguales*. *Ajmaq* is next and it means sin and forgiveness. As Mayan descendants, we recognize that we also dedicated this day to our ancestors, those who have gone on to another world, the dead ones. We dedicate and ask help from all of those who have left this earth and that those who are still with us here in this world. That's why they say it's a big spiritual banquet. The *no'j* follows next. Its meaning is wisdom. This is where our spirit from God is housed. *No'j* is the brain. We are going to take some pure amber and hold it over your brain."

Tata Pedro takes some incense from a small plastic bag and

gives some to each person and then holds a handful on top of his head.

"Make a request. *No'j* is the symbol of goodness, of wellness. Do this with faith, but you don't have to do this if you don't want to. If you do, do it with all your will. We don't ask for money from the fire. We ask the fire for health for our thirteen joints of our sacred body. Why do I say this is a sacred body? I say this because there is the spirit of God or Jehovah or whatever you want to call it, inside our bodies."

A loud fireworks explosion echoes from the San Marcos festival directly across the lake.

"Please come up to the fire and make your request. This is a symbol of wellness. We all know that good overcomes evil. This is a symbol of goodness."

Another explosion echoes in the distance.

"The next symbol is *Tz'I*, which I will talk about later as the symbol of badness. That is why our ancestors needed to create the nagual *No'j*, to compensate for the other one, to dominate the badness that hasn't finished yet because within all areas there's positive and negative. If we only think in the positive, it doesn't work. If we only think in the badness, it doesn't work. That's why every *nagual* has a positive energy and a negative energy.

"Next Julia is going to pay the *nagual Tijax*. *Tijax* is the obsidian rock," he says as yet another explosion emphasizes his reasoning and the dogs around our fire circle start to bark. "It's the skeleton of the sacred temples. When we invoke *Tijax*, it takes all the negative influence away—all the bad shadows. *Kawoq* is next. She is Mother Earth, a symbol of woman. That's why we give a bit of honey and a little sugar to our fire and Mother Earth, as we always have. We all come from the earth. She gives us everything, our Mother, everything we consume. That's why we thank her. We ask for forgiveness for all the exploitation caused by humans to Mother Earth."

He is silent for a moment and then he bends down and takes some honey and sugar from his backpack and pours it on the fire. I look at the group. Everyone seems to be captivated. No one is shifting around or looking off. For this moment, in this place, he is our spiritual guide—our elder.

"*Ajpu'* is the sun, the fire," he continues as he stokes the fire

156

with a long branch. It is now getting dark. The surroundings fade into the twilight and only our circle is illuminated by the fire, with Tata Pedro in his white shirt in the center. "We are going to ask the fire, 'Please, don't go out.' Give us the divine light that there is always positive energy in our lives and for this new project of Blake's. For *Imox*, you always offer thanks to the lake. *Imox* is the *nagual* of the lake. If there is no water, there is no life. This is what sustains us. We are going to ask Robert to pay his *nagual, Iq'. Iq' is* the wind, our breath. If we don't breathe, we don't exist. It is the cleansing of body and mind, for death in another world."

Tata Pedro gives everyone more incense to throw in the fire, which we all do. Its crackling noise breaks the deep silence.

"Bill will pay for *Aq'ab'al. Aq'ab'al* is the dawn, the name of the place where we are now. It's the dawn and the sunset. It's the light of the day and the dark of the night. When *Aq'ab'al* arrives you discover many things, hidden things. It is followed by *K'at* which is the sacred fire. It's the spirit of AHAU, the spirit of life. It's a moment to ask for cleansing of the body and mind."

"Lobo will pay an offering to *Kan*, the feathered serpent. For our Hopi brothers, waiting for the white man, it's the symbol of the wisdom of our Mayan elders," he says. Quietly praying in Tzutujil, he throws handfuls of incense on the fire, which flares up and pops in agreement. "Now we are paying the offering of *Kame*, the symbol of death. All of us are afraid of dying because to die is to die. It is really stopping to exist. We think that death is the end. To the descendants of the Mayans, death is a symbol of the spirit, a symbol of rest, a symbol of hope and love. For us, to die is a transformation. The body grows here, does all it's stuff and it also dies here and goes back to the earth.

"Yesterday and today, people from our community have died. The families are grieving, but they offered their relations back to Mother Earth. It's confusing. It seems contradictory to listen to it, but that's the way it is. This is the wisdom that has been left to us by our ancestors. This is the life, the philosophy and the science of the Mayan civilization."

He throws more incense in the fire and it enthusiastically responds.

"This is the moment to ask for our parents, our grandparents, for all our loved ones that have passed to another world. Their

157

bodies, their bones are dust now but their spirits are still here with us."

"Now we are paying *Kej*, the deer, the symbol of the four directions, the sunrise, the sunset, where the wind rises and where the wind is hidden. It is where you receive the strength of the cosmos, of the spirit of the Mayans. Now we will pay an offering to *Q'anil*. *Q'anil* is the symbol of the seed, of all the production of Mother Earth. [He gives a few more seeds to everyone.]

"It is the offering, the symbol of the fertility of Mother Earth. *Toj* is also the symbol of the sacred fire. Our ancestors, every twenty days, they say 'Thank you' for everything that's been received, all the benefits, all the harvests, all the children, for everything that is harvested in this life. We also say 'Thank you' for all the pain, all the suffering. We don't wait until we receive the harvest every year. We say 'Thank you' every day, every dawn, every sunrise. Symbolically, this is the *Toj*, to really say 'Thank you.' So come forward with all your faith and throw your seeds in the fire and say 'Thank you.' "

"Now we are going to offer to *Tz'i*. It is the symbol of evil or badness. For the ones that are born on this day, these are the ones that will fall in different vices, the negative. They're angry but they're also loving. They fall into this. It is their destiny. *Tz'i* is a symbol of the law, of justice—spiritual and material. The people that have this sign, they overcome, they develop really quickly in everything they propose. They're intelligent, very studious, talented in making the destiny of their community and maybe their country. They come with a destiny to have a public position. If they don't know from the beginning that they are born under *Tz'i* and that it is a symbol of badness, of negativity, it is harder to control it and if they don't balance their energy, they go astray. [The fire is fading; the night is enveloping us—slowly, gently.]

"We will finish making our payment now to the last of the *naguales*. *B'atz'* is the thread. It's the beginning. It's the creation of humanity. It's a very symbolic day to arrange a marriage, to look for a partner, to begin something, anything—like this one [he begins to quietly pray in Tzutujil]. United we can form a circle before we leave to show unity and peace, to be in harmony "

We all gather around in a circle—old and young, Mayan and foreign, poor and not so poor.

"It doesn't matter if it's not a round circle. It's a circle of love, a symbol of unity and understanding. Now we have finished our ceremony. Thank you very much for being here with our elders. We say our thanks again. The sacred fire is going to say 'Goodbye' to us."

After the ceremony, Blake invited everyone to join him at the restaurant where he had prepared a meal for us all—the first of many to be prepared and served there. After everyone had gone up to eat, I stayed around the fire awhile packing up my camcorder and watching Tata Pedro pack all his sacred items in his backpack. He seemed a little tired, but at peace with himself. He had completed that day's assignment of sharing the wisdom of his *abuelos*—his ancestors—with the few people AHAU had sent to him.

I wondered what it must be like for him to do these ceremonies for a few tourists. Forty or fifty years ago, the entire village would have joined in. The *tatas* and the *nanas*—the leaders of the ceremonies—would have been the most respected elders in their community. Their leadership in their ceremonies would have earned the same respect that devout Muslims, Christians or Jews offer their spiritual leaders. Now, he was often held in scorn and contempt, sometimes by the very people who in their youth had joined in these ancient traditions. Over the years, he had personally watched the numbers decline from several thousand to a few hundred to a handful until now there was only he and a few curious tourists and seekers. He was the *only* one left in the village willing to stand up and say, 'I practice the ancient ways of our ancestors. I still embrace their wisdom.'

I thought how he had almost died a few weeks earlier and I realized how close we had come to losing a lifetime friend and co-worker but more importantly how close the world had come to losing the strongest link to his people's ancient wisdom and ceremonies. He was the last unbroken thread in his village and it had come very close to breaking. However, now we both knew that through our book and posting our reasonings with him on the Internet, it would be safe forever.

He finished packing his backpack, slowly, methodically. He looked over at me across the fires and our eyes met and we smiled at each other and walked over to the restaurant, our arms around each other's shoulders.

Chapter 8

The Grandfather Trees

To surmount maya was the task assigned to the human race by the millennial prophets. To rise above the duality of creation and perceive the unity of the Creator was conceived of as man's highest goal . . . To remove the veil of maya is to uncover the secret of creation . . . let man learn that there is no material Universe: its warp and woof is maya, illusion.
      - Paramahandasa Yogananda, *The Autobiography of a Yogi*

     The next day, Julia, Louise, Chus and I walked up the hill to Tata Pedro's house at the top of the village. We had arranged for two of the small three-wheeled taxis to meet us there and take the five of us around the backside of the volcano to do our next ceremony at the Grandfather Trees. To get to Tata Pedro's from our hotels is about a fifteen minute walk straight up the steep slope of San Pedro— past the commercial area with it's small shops selling everything from candles and incense to cellphones and CDs, past the open marketplace, the large ancient Catholic church, the large new Baptist church and it's adjoining infirmary, the large new orange-colored Evangelical church, through the ancient narrow lanes of the residential section. You finally arrive at a cluster of thirty or forty small homes built on the hillside directly below the road that leads to Santiago Atitlan in one direction and Pana further around the lake.
     Like almost all the homes in San Pedro and Santiago Atitlan, Tata Pedro's home is a low cinder-block, corrugated tin roof house. It is built in an "L" shape, with a kitchen at one end and three bedrooms in the middle. All the rooms open on to a covered veranda that surrounds an open courtyard. In the center of the courtyard was a fire pit and off to one side were a clothesline and a ten-speed bike.

At one end of the covered veranda, small pieces of firewood and dried corn cobs were stacked for fuel for the family meals, often cooked over the open fire. At the other end of the "L" was Tata Pedro's altar room, a small open room with three walls and no wall separating it from the veranda and courtyard.

When we arrived, a man wearing a white dress shirt, slacks and a tie, seldom seen in the village, was talking to Tata Pedro in Spanish. Tata Pedro looked concerned. Nearby, one of Tata Pedro's adult daughters was listening, her face anguished. Two of his small grandsons played in the courtyard and one of his adult sons stood nearby staring off into space, looking as if he was wrestling with intense inner demons. Tata Pedro's other daughter, Marina, greeted us warmly and ushered us into his small altar room, where we made ourselves comfortable on plastic chairs and five-gallon buckets. Marina, a recent university graduate, is a bright spirit who is also well respected for her Mayan massage. Her massage table stood nearby, next to a door that led to a small bathroom with a toilet, sink and cold-water shower.

As Tata Pedro and the other man talked, I looked around the altar room. It was very full, very roots—intense and yet welcoming. Off to the right was a low arch-shaped entrance to an igloo-shaped, wood-fired sweat lodge. Many wooden ceremonial and walking staffs leaned against the opposing wall, where several color portraits and photos of Tata Pedro hung on the wall. Some were recent but one showed him as a young man looking determined, idealistic and defiant.

Above the photos and portraits, and running on to the intersecting wall, were individual color paintings of the twenty *naguales*. Brightly-colored ceremonial candles hung nearby from a nail on the wall. The altar itself was so full of various objects that it was hard to focus on any of them individually. There were crystals, stones, corn, fresh flowers, carvings, and pottery. Two low bookcases holding various ceremonial items stood next to a large native drum. In one corner were several stone carvings with a candle burning in front of them. In the center were several ears of corn with another candle burning in front of them. Nearby was a wooden replica of the *Tzolkin*, with its two inter-meshing cogged wheels that rotated to align each day's day sign and number. It was set to that day's sign and number.

We chatted awhile with Marina and she told us of her master's thesis that she was working on to record the remembrances, beliefs and traditions of the elders of the Atitlan area. She had enrolled several of the local youths to work with her visiting the elders. Knowing how much easier it is to do interviews when you record them, I gave her an audio microcassette I had in my video bag but seldom used and promised to send her the spare camcorder that we had at home, along with cassettes and spare batteries.

After a few minutes, the man left and Tata Pedro and his other daughter joined us in the altar area. Tata Pedro explained that the man was an investigator from the court working on his daughter's child-custody case. There was a possibility of her losing custody of her three-year old son. She was distraught and at one point, she broke down crying on Julia's shoulder.

We offered what comfort we could, but soon we had to go as the two taxis had arrived. As we chatted with the drivers up on the road, Chus introduced us to Vincente, one of Tata Pedro's neighbors, a painter who offered to paint a portrait of Tata Pedro to use on the back cover of this book. We agreed on a price and he promised to get it to us before we left in a few days, which he did.

With Julia and me in one taxi and Chus, Louise and Tata Pedro in the other, we headed out for the thirty minute ride to the Grandfather Trees. With an occasional dramatic view of the lake, the road wound uphill for a distance, then looped around the volcano and leveled out. The weather changed to cool and drizzly and we started to pass through acres and acres of corn fields that covered almost every inch of the flat areas at the base of the volcanic hills. The soil looked dark and fertile; the plants, one to two feet tall, were lush and green.

Everywhere farmers, most in bright orange rain parkas, were tending their fields with hoes and rakes. There was no sign of any mechanized farm equipment. It was quiet, restful, ancient. For fifteen or twenty minutes, we drove through miles and miles of corn fields. For the first time, I truly understood how vital this plant was to these people. We took several pictures to show to Radford and his family—corn farmers themselves who had to water each plant by hand in their dry, arid small gardens in Hopiland.

At the end of a large corn field, the drivers pulled over by a forested area that had a small footpath leading into it. The clouds were very low and the drizzle was picking up. The two drivers agreed to wait a couple of hours until we finished. We headed across a section of the field and up the path into the forest. I offered to carry Tata Pedro's backpack. I was amazed at how heavy it was. About a hundred yards in, we came to a small sloping opening in the forest. Several large mounds surrounded the opening and at the highest point was a domed concrete canopy, about twelve feet high and ten feet across, held up by several round concrete columns. It was covering an outdoor altar with a large cross on it.

"These are the Grandfather Trees. This one is one thousand and five hundred years old," Tata Pedro said as we entered the opening and he hugged one of the enormous, gnarled oaks that encircled the mounds. "This was one of the ceremonial centers of our ancestors. These mounds are ancient pyramids."

Tata Pedro points to a large pyramid-shaped mound on our right still entirely covered with vegetation.

"There are five pyramids here. The Catholic church came and built that concrete altar here—not because it was their sacred site but because it was ours."

We walked around the backside of the canopy where he showed us a small Mayan altar built into the sloping bank. There were some fresh flowers in a tin can on one of the ledges.

"We used to have our altar up there on the top but in 1996 the Catholics built their altar there. They threw away the sacred *naguales* stones. One of my friends used to take care of this site but he stopped. He said that because I do not talk of Christ, he cannot come to my ceremonies or take care of the site any more. Everyone is welcome at my ceremonies—Jesus, Jehovah, Allah, everyone. That is no problem for me. Last night at the lakeshore, the Mayan people congratulated me saying that they had lost their culture, our ancestors. I do not believe that. When we had our traditional Mayan ceremony here three weeks ago, three hundred and fifty people came, many children, many students. I have never done a ceremony under their canopy, but today we will. It will shelter us from the rain. We can make the fire under there and it will not go out. We will be on our sacred site because underneath every Catholic church, there is a Mayan temple. They continue to invade us, but we can use it. "

We went under the canopy and I looked up at the ceiling. The underside of the dome was painted with various Biblical scenes including ones of Jesus, Mary, angels, and one of a God-like white man with a white beard, with a shirtless younger man at his feet self-flagellating himself with a leather whip. The altar was a large cross and some live flowers in vases.

As Tata Pedro prepared the candles and the incense on the flagstone floor, Chus played a small drum and sang in Spanish. Tata Pedro would stop and play the ceramic bear we gave him as an accompanying flute. This was my third ceremony with Tata and I found myself looking forward to the next two hours of peace and reverence. At one point, Chus took a fan made of large bird feathers held together by leather strapping and "feathered" each of us by vigorously fanning us from head to toe, back to front.

The ceremony for the first half-hour began much like the other two, with Tata Pedro offering prayers in the four directions and ending each prayer with all of us kissing the flagstone ground.

"Thanks to God for flowers, rain," Tata Pedro said in closing this part of our ceremony. "I am always bringing light to the pathway, trying to leave everything that God has given me. I am trying to be sure that the wisdom that was given to me stays here. This was my university. It was this place here. That's why I feel that I have a right to be here. So I want to thank my Christian brothers for this roof that they built. This is the first time I have ever done this under this roof. These are the trees that have taught me. I call them my Grandfather Trees. These trees talk to me. Here, I have traveled to another dimension, another world. This place is full of natural forces, ones we do not see. This is why I feel good here. Each place gives me a very good message."

At this point, we all sat on the flagstone floor underneath the canopy, facing Tata Pedro as he displayed the brightly-colored *naguales* he had brought in a three-ring binder.

"Today, during the ceremony, I want to talk of the *naguales*, the day signs," Tata Pedro said. "The Grandfather Trees talk to me. There are lots of natural resources and each place has a message. The ceremony, the petition, the invocation, the meditation, is according to the necessity, according to each day."

Tata Pedro let out a long breath of gratitude and a sweet smile. He seemed childlike and vulnerable and wise and powerful all at once. I had quickly come to love this man.

"I will give a short explanation of each *nagual*. They will be

164

short. I could write a book about each *nagual*. Now, I will refer to each of the *naguales* by its Tzutujil name rather than the more common Quiché Mayan name. [The spellings of the *naguales* are also different as noted.] The *nagual* of this day is *Aaj*, calm, cave. It is a symbol of family, of home, a symbol of children. This is the one that rules over the life of our children. This is why it is a really special day and why we are here. So the people born on this day are spiritual people that heal. If they don't take up their mission, they will have the consequence of having not done so and can suffer illnesses.

"The next one is *Ii'x*. *Ii'x* is for the sacred temple, sacred sites like this one. This is the day to ask for forgiveness for everything, for all the erosion, the exploitation, that man does. It is a day to request, to ask for forgiveness of all the Grandfather Trees, for all these grandchildren that cut down all these trees without asking permission. To cut a branch, you need to ask permission. So you or me, to cut a branch here and there, I ask permission first. You have to ask permission and if you take it without permission, it has consequences. This is the symbol of all the plants.

"Next is *Tz'ikin*. It is the bird, symbol of spirituality, the intermediary, the community, the interrelationship between God and man, a symbol of richness, a symbol of humility of our brothers to discover and show us the way home. When humility was discovered, this symbol was here already. This is the colors of red, black, yellow, and white, the symbols of directions of richness, of spiritual and material richness.

"Then we go to *AJmaak*, the symbol of sin and forgiveness, but for us, it is the symbol of the grandfathers, the elders, Francisco Socuel. We are talking about the elders who have gone on to the next world. We ask them for all the things they could not achieve in their lives.

"The next is *Na'ooj*. This is the brain, the mind. This is the wisdom. This is the symbol of wellness. It is a symbol of peace, a symbol of love. It is the first petition from our ancestors. The Creator informed us that there is a brain, a symbol of the mind, to think good things. So this is a symbol of goodness and wellness. Those that create horror and terror, those that cause problems in life, on Mother Earth, in humanity, have not used this name of this *nagual*. We have lost them."

"Now we will talk about *Tijaax*, the rock, the stone," he said, blowing air on his right hand that is wrapped in his sash. "It is the bones, the skeletons of the temple, which are the hells. It is the point of the knife, a very strong instrument. We are here looking at this suffering. This is why I say once our ancestors were spending the night meditating for their friends. This is the day. There is no suffering. This is a day for healing, a day to get rid of all the negative influences. This is a day of sacrifice, human sacrifice, not Maya human sacrifice because we did not sacrifice people. They sacrificed themselves.

"This is *KaWoq*. This is Mother Earth. This is the one that gives to us. So let's say hello to Mother Earth. That is better, isn't it? This is the one that helps dress ourselves. It gives us shoes, gives us hats so that we can cover our bodies and gives us a way of walking. This is Mother Earth. This is why it looks like grapes so we say 'thank you.' It continues to sustain our feet and give us a cover to walk upon.

"Let's talk about *AJPU'b*. It is the ending nagual of all the days which is the symbol of love, the mouth. This is the father sun, the one that sends us energy. It makes the night go away. It is positive, the one that sends the warmth of our blood and we begin to move, to work, to sing, to dance, to make love. This is our movement and also of Mother Nature to all the plants. This is where all energy comes from—nature, the plants. We need not just to water it. It needs water and fire which is our life.

"Let's talk about *Imox,* a symbol of water. It takes this energy of water. This is my symbol. That is why I am called 'the Heart of the Lake.' That's why when I don't feel good in my stomach; it means the lake is suffering. Today, I feel OK so the lake is OK. It's crazy, but the craziness is in *Imox*. When the lake is stormy, it listens to me because I have this *nagual*. When I was traveling, I was at a sacred lake. I came singing across the lake, singing about the lake, about my life because it cleanses me, it gives me food [he says this with a hushed sacredness and a smile].

"The lake was strong with wind and big waves. A girl came up to me and interrupted in the middle of my song and said, 'Say something to the lake.' We were all scared. It was too strong. So I said to everyone, 'Stay with me. Let's ask together. If you help with a lot of faith together, that will calm it down. So let's ask it to calm

166

down.' Little by little, and in five minutes, it was calm, the blessing of God. I am not just talking in vain. The spirit listens. The spirit lit the fire and in me. This is the meaning of *Imox*.

"Now we are going to talk about *Iiq'*. This is the symbol of wind. So the four winds from the same lake have taught me. I have not read this. It is the same lake that has taught me this. From nine in the morning, the wind begins. At ten in the morning *XOCOMIL* begins in San Juan. At ten in the morning, the *XOCOMIL* starts in Santiago Atitlan. At one or two in the afternoon at San Lucas the wind forms. At four, it forms in Panajachel. In the middle of the lake, it forms the four winds. It taught me. My 15-year old brother sank to the bottom of the lake between San Pedro and San Juan. I looked for him a long time. I went down to the bottom of the lake to prove that he was down there. The palaces and the great houses where you keep the most precious relics, which were hidden from our Maya Tzutujil ancestors, are now in the lake, under the lake. That's where the richness is. It has not been found because of the invaders.

"Let's talk about *AQ'ab'iil*. It is also the sunset, looking at the candles. This is the light. Light begot light. From where did it come? Look at the flames of the candles. They are not all blowing in the same direction. One goes here, one goes over there. So they go to the four directions. Each one goes to the four directions so this one represents divine light. It is the *nagual* that protects us from all negative influences.

"This one is *Q'aaq.*' It is also fire. When we do our ceremonies, like last night at the lakefront, and make our offerings, it is an energy—very positive and very negative, very strong. Those that have the *nagual Q'aaq'*, if you offend them and you say 'I have done nothing wrong,' it will have consequences. We should be very, very careful in what we say in meetings with them, very careful. Try not to offend any because there will be consequences of this. It causes incurable diseases. In forgiveness, take a hand and kiss it and ask forgiveness.

"The *nagual Kaan* is next. Not that long ago, an evangelical pastor, a preacher, came here and asked, 'What do the Catholics have here in this altar?' So I said to him, 'Don't go there.' But he said he has to go see what they are up to. He saw the feathered serpent when he was here resting and was completely frightened so

167

we had to give him water to help calm him down and he returned to his brother. It is the symbol of the elder of wisdom.

"*Kamik* is a symbol of death, the end, but for us it is not the end but a symbol of transformation. Death is to begin to live again, the spirit of peace, of love and going in quietness, with no jealousy, not thinking negatively, with spirit. The body goes back to the earth and the body is an offering to give back to Mother Earth. One day, our ancestors said, 'Let's be one. Let's all love each other, never to be behind or in front. Let's all be together, to our father, to our family, our children. First walk and then know where we come from.' Here are our ancestors. This is a symbol of the resting place.

"Let's talk about *Keej*. It is the deer. It is the symbol of the four cardinal points, to take force. Take a fist like this and see the four points, four strengths and four directions. After doing the movements in the four directions, concentrate, then feel like a transformed person of energy.

"Now we talk about *Q'aniil*, the symbol of the beginning of the seed, human gestation, the symbol of all the production of Mother Earth. *Tojooj* is the offering, the payment to give something back to Mother Nature. Instead of going to another place, give back to Mother Earth. Give back for everything that has benefited you in your life. For suffering, for failure, you also have to give thanks and ask God so suffering is not repeated. You have got to ask for love, for peace. Everything you are talking about is the thread. It is about the roots. Just like these pages of paintings. It is like branches and leaves and it is about the love between a man and a woman. That is why we are here to love.

"Now we are going to talk about *Tz'i*. It is the dog. The dogs in the street, they are barking and barking all around. They only bark to make noise. This is the symbol of badness of spiritual and material law. It is a symbol of an intelligent person and they develop rapidly in everything. They are predestined to fall into vice, drugs, alcohol. But when they realize this, they are an intelligent one or a studious one. They've got talent for directing their community and their nation. They develop rapidly. *Tz'i* is a very strong *nagual* for people in public positions. So it is a symbol of good and bad. Each one of the *naguales* has positive and negative energy so we all have lots of love and lots of anger.

"*B'atz* is the thread. It is what rolls up life and the destiny of

168

life. It is the thread that passes from the belly button. Those that are born with a cord around their neck, they can't move. This is significant. Those born with a cord around their neck are going to do lots of things, the good things in the world, loving, intelligence. They do everything that they say they are going to do. A spiritual healer, a midwife. They do everything, all the good in the world. It's a missionary of peace, an artist, a musician, painter, dancer, photographer, all those good things. It's a beginnings counselor.

"This is the last one. It is *Eey*. This is the pathway of destiny, symbol of the tooth and of the road, the pathway, a symbol of what rules over the lives of human beings. This is significant, the stones along the road of life, the life of the human being and the animals and all the plants. This is what drives us to our destiny.

"Each one of the *naguales* we have talked about, it is a short summary. Afterwards, we can translate this information into Tzutujil. Now, it is being translated into English through your book. Other people are going to become interested and it's going to be translated into many languages for all to hear. I will authorize to translate this into languages all around the world so the message will get out there. Thank you very much for coming here. This is what we have talked about in this sacred site where we find ourselves. It is not an invasion here on this sacred site. Our brothers continue to invade us, but I am joyful about this. I am not angry. I am the opposite. I am very happy. Thank you for coming here. That's why I am resting here because I am very happy."

We all stood up and stretched and Tata Pedro started to play a happy, whimsical song on the drum. His eyes were closed. "This is the song of the lake, I feel more positive when I sing. That was the original language of our people. "

After Tata Pedro closed the ceremony, we all smiled at each other and hugged. We had all shared something sacred, something moving. This was the third ceremony we had shared with Tata Pedro and we had recorded them all and they would soon be posted on the Internet to be shared by anyone who came across them.

As we walked from the Grandfather Trees back toward the road, I could not help but reflect on the religious ceremonies of my youth in my synagogue in Atlanta where I dreaded the services, mostly done in Hebrew, a language that almost no one in the congregation understood. The only part of the service I enjoyed was the closing Hebrew song that indicated the service was over and we could soon go into the assembly hall and eat pastries.

For me, my spiritual training at this synagogue was empty. It was the years soon after World War II and the brutal death of six million of our "tribe." I sensed many of the adults doubted the existence of a loving God, even our rabbi. As I reflected on the intensity and exquisite guidance of the ancient Mayan initiation of their young men, I thought about my bar mitzvah at thirteen—the epitome of my spiritual training. I spent a year learning to read a Hebrew passage from the Torah—the meaning of which was never explained to me. On the day of my initiation, I nervously sang it in front of the whole congregation, for which I received many gifts including dress shirts, fountain pens, stocks, socks, a watch, luggage, and, my favorite, a set of golf clubs.

In front of my tribe, my elders told me my initiation was complete and I was now a "man," but nobody, including myself, really believed that. After all, how could learning to sing one passage from the Torah have anything at all to do with preparing a young boy for the responsibilities of manhood? Everyone meant well. It was the best we could do, for like the present-day Mayans of San Pedro and Santiago Atitlan, we were too far cut off from our roots.

We headed back to Tata Pedro's house only to find another necktie man there—this one offering to give Tata Pedro a loan, secured by his home, to cover the legal fees needed to protect his grandson.

∞∞∞∞∞∞∞∞∞∞∞∞∞∞∞∞∞∞∞∞∞∞∞∞∞∞∞∞∞∞∞∞∞∞∞∞∞∞∞

Later that day, Chus had to take the ferry to San Marcos to handle an electrical problem at the Unicornio, so Louise, Julia and I went to our favorite restaurant, Zooli, for dinner. We wandered down one of the winding footpaths that meander through the village and then took another footpath a hundred yards toward the lake to the restaurant.

Zooli was started by a young Israeli man who had recently died from cancer and was now run by his widow. It is not your normal restaurant—even by Guatemalan standards—but rather a

170

huge gabled thatched roof, over twenty feet high at its peak, supported by massive poles. It covers an area about 30 feet wide and 100 feet long and is surrounded by a kept lawn and perpetually flowering bushes and trees. There are no walls and, instead of the regular chairs and tables, there are woven grass mats covering the floor and one-foot diameter varnished logs resting on the mats that defined U-shaped dining area, in the middle of which were low thick wooden slab tables sitting around six inches off the ground. As you dine, you sit on the mats and lean against large stuffed pillows resting against the logs.

The kitchen and bar is toward the rear and the eating area toward the lake. There is a small aviary off to one side with birds and rabbits inside, making happy noises. A sign greets you as you enter that says, "Welcome! Sit down and relax and think about what you *really*, *really* want to eat and we'll be by to see you after awhile."

We chose our dining area and I quickly noticed the rich aroma of marijuana coming from the other patrons who were openly rolling and smoking joints. The scene—the mats on the floors, the joints, the long-haired young people quietly laughing and talking— instantly took me back to my counterculture days in the sixties and seventies. Though I was now forty years older than most everyone around me, I felt right at home. After ordering a delicious dinner (for three bucks!) from a beautiful young woman who had come to San Pedro to avoid being recalled into the Israeli army where she had already served three years as a captain, Louise, Julia and I fell into an easy conversation.

It seems that Louise was going through an intense time herself. She and Chus had been recently been separated as she had spent the last few months with her family in England. They had blocked out the next few months to be together and travel around Central America and Mexico, linking up with other members in Chus's band at different places to perform. All the arrangements were made. They were both looking forward to the adventure and being together again.

She had leased her holistic health clinic that adjoins Chus's hostel to a Swiss man so that she would have the freedom and money to travel. She had just heard that the previous day he had been hurt while hang gliding off a cliff near San Marcos. He had

171

seriously hurt his spine as was being flown to Switzerland for immediate surgery. Her heart was heavy, more from the injury of a friend but also from the disruption to her long-awaited journey with Chus. We discussed her options and she decided to see if the remaining few staff people might take over the lease (which they later did) so she could continue on her planned journey.

As I listened to her talk, I realized that all of us had come together with major events happening in our lives. For us, it was the grieving over loss of our brother-in-law, Alan, a source of true love in our lives for over thirty years; for Tata Pedro it was the threat of his daughter losing custody of his grandson and now Louise and Chus were dealing with the life-altering injury of a friend and the disruption of their long-awaited plans.

I was reminded that though all of us were deeply on our own spiritual paths—and had been for years—there was no avoiding the pains that we all encounter in life. However, our spiritual journeys had enabled us not so much to avoid all pain but to philosophically perceive the situations and pain in such a way that it allowed us to avoid the despair, disillusionment and sense of victimization that often accompany major life setbacks. No matter how things seemed, no matter how dark a particular situation may appear, we were able to ask, "What is the gift in this?" And that week together, we all drew strength from one another and silently helped each other answer that question.

Chapter 9

Leaving Home, Going Home

There is hope for humanity, not because we will all suddenly choose to change for the better, but because the consciousness of humanity is subject to a cosmic plan that cannot be manipulated. To be immersed in this plan through the use of the Mayan calendar will further its fulfillment on both an individual and collective level.
   -Carl John Calleman, *The Mayan Calendar:Solving the Greatest Mystery of Our Times*

We spent several more days in San Pedro meeting with Tata Pedro each day, reasoning on a wide variety of issues. All too soon, it was our last day. We knew we would miss Tata Pedro, but also knew that he was now part of our life forever.

"Tata Pedro," Julia said as we settled around Chus and Louise's kitchen table for our final reasoning, "I want to tell you a story that just happened as we were leaving our hotel. A young man came over to see a young woman who was staying in the room next to ours. They were sitting on the veranda so I could hear them talking. He was admitting that he said something inappropriate and that it had put tension in the air and he asked her to forgive him."

"It is not easy to do that," Tata Pedro said smiling. "It is not easy to ask or receive forgiveness. It is important that you include this in our book because this is what One Love is. My daughter told me that if someone comes to you and asks your forgiveness, you have to forgive them. I said 'thank you' to her for reminding me of that."

Knowing that this would be our last hour together, I wanted to once again ask for his thoughts on 2012

"During this transformation that your people have been pointing toward for centuries," I said, "some people are embracing it and seeking love, some are resisting love and unity and the vast majority seem to be too distracted to view much in life philosophically. How will things be for these three different groups during the coming changes?"

"Well, I do not know exactly," he replied. "More people are asking, 'What will happen in 2012?' People in the universities, in the bars, in the cantinas are starting to ask. They are worried because people are saying it will be the end of the world. Many are looking for the answers from the universities. There are answers there, but they are the natural answers like when the eclipses will happen. They are not real answers. They are scientific answers, but in the Mayan cosmovision, we speak of spiritual answers. People are collecting answers from everywhere—from anthropologists, from astronomers, from professors. If you really want to know, you must ask the Mayan spiritual guides. They know the most. Even some of these Mayans do not know the answers. I get my revelations directly from the *abuelos*, my ancestors.

"And this group here, at this table, is being guided by them. We are awakening to the love. We understand that the world will not end in 2012. It will continue with a new cycle. There will be many changes, both positive and negative. It is a short time now and we must be concerned about getting the right information to the people who want it. We need to tell them not to be afraid and that there are people concerned about them even if *they* don't care. When the changes happen we can regret or we can rectify. It will prove or not what we are saying now."

He smiles even brighter and rubs Chus's shoulder affectionately, playfully. He seems to have entered a state of blissful peace. Once again, I am amazed at how he can be so childlike and wise at the same instant.

"When these changes come we can ask ourselves, 'Is this true or not?' The world will not end. It is just a cycle of time and in 2012, there will be new clothes, good food, good music. We will be grateful and we will keep doing ceremonies and keep being happy and praying to AHAU and doing what is right."

"It is going to be sad for the ones that carry the name of being a spiritual guide, religious teachers in the churches," he continued, "and they are not sharing with the people. People like this, with doubts and fears, will get sick, maybe die, because they do not ask the Mayan elders. This is *our* moment, *our* calendar. The people that do not care about anything, they just go to the market and cantinas. When the information comes to them that the world will end in 2012, they will not be worried either. They don't care about anything. They will be like the people in Panabaj that didn't know the mudslide was about to cover them. They never thought to go from there. Others will be away from danger like my daughter who was here because her boss in Panabaj told her to stay here with her family that night."

"So some will be guided and listen," I asked, "and others will not?"

"Si. We are talking about three groups. There is a group that is embracing the love. They want to know, and as we ask, we learn. When I teach one person, two of us learn. I'm learning a lot from you. We are preparing ourselves for 2012 now. If we see the sun rising in the north and setting in the south, we must be prepared. I'm not saying that will happen, but it could be possible because this is the moment for the changes to take place. There will be more love, more friendship, more unity, more comprehension. Maybe that moment will be the moment of transformation and I will give up this body and take another one. If someone kills my body, that is destiny and I will forgive him because he will be more dead inside than me.

"This body is just an instrument. I'm just doing my mission. I am ready to be born again. It is love. It is peace. For the people who are afraid now that it will be the end of the world, this thought is coming from the Western doctrine, not from my people. The churches want the people to be afraid so more people will come to the churches. We must change ourselves and not wait for a messiah. Shame on the man that knows but does not do the right thing and share his information to help others. I share my information freely, but maybe a religious leader cannot. Their leaders tell them not to.

"I've heard lots of things about 2012. When I was in Cleveland in 2000 at the University of Ohio, they invited me to a museum where an astronomy teacher was giving his lecture. There were about five thousand people there. I was one of the invited ones. After he had talked about astronomy, a little girl about eight years old asked him, 'What's going to happen in 2012? My teacher told me the world is going to end.' The lecturer thought and said, 'It's a question I can't give any answer to, but there is a Mayan sitting here in the audience and he will give us the answer.' The people that were with me told me not to answer, that it was not my job to answer. I said, 'Leave me alone. I know what I am doing. I do not want there to be any doubts. The answer is from spirit.' So, I spoke to the audience, the people turned to look at me where I was standing.

"First I apologized to the children and I said, 'Please don't frighten your parents and parents please don't frighten the children. The world is not going to end in 2012. In a few words, we the Maya, we've got money and food, new clothes. It is the happening we have been waiting for. We will be finishing the cycle of twelve *baktuns* and begin the thirteenth *baktun*.' Everybody applauded me. In my imagination that night, in a dream, a small person came and congratulated me. He said, 'Thanks for coming to encourage us because a lot of people are getting scared of dying.'

"I will speak anywhere. My church is the forest, the mountains. My people are the whole planet. When my mission is ended here, I will begin in another life. When this generation passes, another will come. I cannot give money but I am rich because of the peace I have inside. That's why we need to create a world of friendship, of love."

Tata Pedro shakes Chus's hand with one hand and pats him on the back with the other and then kisses Chus's hand.

"Gracias, mi amigo, Chus. Gracias, mi amiga, Julia," he says kissing Julia's hand.

"Gracias, mi amigo, Roberto," he says kissing my hand.

"Gracias, mi amiga, Louise," he says kissing Louise's hand. "This is love. This is peace. This is life. This is the message that the Mayans have been listening to. It roars in the wind, in the rain, in the birds. It is peace and love. That's why we will be at peace after 2012."

Together, we all walked to the dock so Julia and I could catch the ferry back to Pana. From there, the next day, we were leaving for Guatemala City to catch our flight home. It was a beautiful afternoon, the air crisp and clean, the sun shining. Lake Atitlan was laid out in her pristine beauty before us, her three volcanoes rising majestically in the distance. Our work was done—we knew that. The wisdom we had sought in this distant land, we had found and it was more complete, more beatific than I could have ever imagined. As our boat pulled away, we waved to Tata Pedro. With hat in hand, he waved back, a huge grin across his face both ancient and childlike. In some strange and surprising way his contented, almost joyous, demeanor during these last hours together reminded me of the way Alan had been on our last visit with him. There was a sense of sweetness and gratitude about them both that sometimes comes when someone has recently confronted their own mortality—and made peace with it.

∞∞∞∞∞∞∞∞∞∞∞∞∞∞∞∞∞∞∞∞∞∞∞∞∞∞∞∞∞∞∞∞∞∞∞∞∞∞

As we made our final ferry trip across Lake Atitlan, I realized that I, like Tata Pedro, was also becoming more certain as to the almost blessed outcome of this transition culminating in 2012. I was not optimistic because of anything being reported by the mainstream media. Indeed, their worldview only led one to feel more pessimistic about the future. However, there was something powerful stirring below their radar screens—an ever-growing grassroots expansion of consciousness that had the power to transform our world "from the love of power to the power of love."

It was being brought forth by forces the press never considers covering and would probably not understand if they did. Our journey—and it was only one of many—had revealed that this wisdom was carried by Rastas in the hills of Jamaica, by Bob Marley and conscious reggae music, by ancient Indian tribes in the remote Arizona desert and by Mayan elders in the highlands and lowlands of Guatemala.

Looking back over the almost four decades of my own spiritual search, with its roots in the counterculture of the 1960s, I had witnessed tremendous awakening in myself and others. Before this awakening, in my childhood and teens, there were few workable, sustainable answers to many of the world's most pressing problems. There were few non-polluting technologies to supply our energy, like wind and solar power. There were no health food stores or organic foods offering us healthy options to the unhealthy first-world diet. There was no natural childbirth classes offering organic ways to enter the planet or hospices offering us compassionate assistance upon leaving it.

In the mainstream society of my youth, there were no "self-help" sections at bookstores instructing us how to heal our bodies, minds and spirits without drugs or surgery or years of professional psychoanalysis. There was almost no yoga, no meditation, no tai-chi, no acupuncture, no massage therapies, no herbal cures offered in our society. There were few books on spirituality—other than those related to the traditional Western religions. Now there were thousands of books, revealing a myriad of other ways to seek—and find—God. The religions of our youths convinced us that we were all sinful children of a vengeful, angry God. Now, both ancient and modern truths were revealing that we are all uncorrupted souls created by an all-loving and compassionate Creator.

In the last few decades, through the efforts of people like Gandhi, Dr. King, Archbishop Tutu, Mandela, and others, we had witnessed the oppressed freed without a violent, armed conflict—the first time ever in the 5125-year "history" of the world. I had been born into a society that accepted—even embraced—the concept that blacks were not allowed in certain schools, restaurants, hotels or jobs and had watched my society rid itself of this prejudice to the point that our daughters' generations could hardly believe their country could ever be so cruel, so unconscious. In my twenties, I joined others as large parts of our population spoke out against our country's mistaken decision to go to war—something that was almost unheard of in *any* country before the Vietnam protests

All of this had happened in my lifetime—a brief second in humanity's walk on the planet. But could the pace of this expansion of consciousness accelerate beyond the pace of the growing unconsciousness of the media and the business and political leaders? Could it replace the ever-increasing control of the lobbyists and the military-industrial complex? Could it override the intense hype of this entertainment-addicted, consumerist society? Could it heal the seemingly-hopeless environmental damage already inflicted on the planet?

Like Tata Pedro, I knew this acceleration in awareness—this remembrance of who we *really* are and why we are here—could, but only through a mass change in consciousness. But how was this to occur? This awareness was growing but seemingly only in a tiny minority of people. Even Tata Pedro said only seven percent were even interested.

Chapter 10

Tikal Beckons Again

What is power? Has your idea of being powerful changed at all since we began this journey? To the world you created in your imagination, power is the ability to assert your will over another person or the environment itself. By now you have realized that everything this world claims to be true is actually the opposite of what is really true. The world's idea of power is in reality the definition of powerlessness, simply because it is based upon a false foundation: that you can decrease another person's power and, in doing so, increase your own. In reality, decreasing another person's power is the same as decreasing your own. Therefore, the opposite must be true: increasing another person's power increases yours.

You are now a powerful Spiritual Peacemaker because you have aligned your life with the Power of God, which only increases as it is shared. As you share your Light, Light increases all through the world. As you share your power, then the world and everything in it is empowered. What other reason but this leads to your decision to give everything to Everything? You are here to be truly happy, and that will only happen as you make others happy. Now you SEE with the eyes that were given you by God, rather than the eyes fashioned by the world that were made not to see at all . . . At last you are home, Beloved. At last you are able to See who you are, and to share that vision with everyone you meet.

-James F. Twyman, *The Art of Spiritual Peacemaking: Secret Teachings from Jeshua ben Joseph*

When we returned from San Pedro, I had thought this book was finished. We had discovered a Mayan message of unconditional love that was strong, clear and even came with an exact timeline to planetary remembrance. Over the spring and summer, I remained somewhat secluded myself. Punctuated by our visits to several local prisons and music festivals, I worked on this book.

We had never envisioned our message reaching into the prisons when we began our work. However, a year or so after *Rasta Heart* was released, we started getting letters from Rastafarian inmates and prison groups asking for copies of the book. After reading them, they would often write us letters—some of the most eloquent, heartfelt responses we have ever received. Julia and I started to make monthly visits to two of the groups at nearby prisons.

During that summer, we also hosted several prison-wide One Love Concerts featuring Laura Reed, a conscious recording artist from Asheville, North Carolina and her band, Deep Pocket. Our goal was to remind our incarcerated brothers that if you learn and teach love even behind prison walls, you are free—maybe freer than you were on the outside, perhaps freer than many people on the outside. I would remind them that when you teach and learn love—for yourself and others—you are heading Home, no matter what you did in your past or what was done to you. So that they would understand that their lives were not wasted, I reminded them that it is the Creator's will for *every* piece of the planet to be healed and that healing their piece "behind the fence" is as important as healing any other. Since many in the audience are lifers, I talked about how if they get up each day and love and forgive as much as they can, their life will be a mystical experience—even if they never leave prison.

Julia spoke to them about going within and finding peace and joy through meditation, a peace that is available to anyone, anywhere—even behind prison walls. She would encourage them to see their "cell" as their "chapel." Then Laura, with her conscious lyrics and electrifying stage presence, would take them directly to Zion. By the end of her first set, the audience would be on their feet. The response in the meetings and the concerts has been incredible—open-hearted, enthusiastic and healing. Following these concerts, our Rasta groups confirmed that things had truly changed in the yard for the better.

Also, during the warm months, we attended several of the many outdoor music festivals that spring up nationwide. We would set up our small booth, sell our books and reason with the festival-goers—mostly people in their teens and twenties. Sometimes we would be invited to speak from the stage. Since everyone camps at these festivals, everyday reality is suspended. For most of the attendees, except for those who come just to party, it is a chance to recharge by removing themselves from modern society. For three or four days, everyone leaves the high-tech, over-commercialized world behind and camps out in nature. There is no cell service, no Internet, no television, no media constantly trying to sell you something. It's just nature, friends and good music.

Most of these young people seem pretty relaxed in themselves, and with their peers, with little show of vanity or competitiveness. Even most of the courting rituals seem suspended and the women are dressed comfortably, seldom sexualizing themselves. Many of these young people are bright-eyed, optimistic and idealistic and perhaps more than any other group give me hope for the future.

What we notice, in festival after festival, is that when we share with others our viewpoint that each of us is only being asked to do *our* assignment by trying to love and forgive as much as possible and that the winds are finally, after 5125 years, shifting so as to support this effort, it is as if a long-awaited and long-hidden truth is being recognized deep within them. A light goes on in their eyes. "Wow, I really needed to hear that!" or "That makes me feel much more hopeful. I'll do my part to usher this in!" are common responses.

To me, it's important that the older generation not pass on a sense of hopelessness to the younger generations. Our disillusionment, our despair, and our sense of hopelessness is dissipated as we understand that we are not being asked to be *perfectly* loving or forgiving, but only to make it our *intention* everyday to love and forgive as much as we can. With this intention, the Creator will take it from there and use us as instruments of peace. It is the same for each person. We have not been given the task of healing *all* the problems in the world. The Creator has just given us the duty of healing the small piece of the planet we have been assigned to walk. What the other six billion people do is between them and their Creator. We are only responsible for our

181

individual assignment.

After the close of the festival season in September, we heard from Danny Diaz that two of the key organizers of Activation Maya, Aum-Rak and Anne Lossing, were going in different directions. Activation Maya was the gathering we first attended where Tata Pedro left because Aum-Rak had insisted he shorten his ceremonies. Anne, along with Chus, Louise and others in El Remate, were organizing a different event, called Unificación Maya, the inspiration of local Tikal guide Danilo Rodriguez. A Canadian who has lived in El Remate for 20 years with Enrique, her Guatemalan husband, the village's only doctor, Anne operates Project Ix-canaan, which serves the community through a clinic, and a women's library, computer and research center.

The event was to be held in the El Remate area on the 2007 Winter Solstice. Unlike Activation Maya, the event would be free. Both Anne and Aum-Rak invited us to join them and make a presentation to their groups. With limits on our time, money and energy, we declined.

However, a few weeks before the Winter Solstice, we got an email from Anne that she had just heard that over 2,500 Mayan *Sacerdotes* (priests) would be meeting in the Central Plaza of Tikal on the solstice to do a Fire Ceremony lasting the entire night. The Unificación Maya participants were invited to unite with them.

"I know we decided not to return to Tikal," I said to Julia after reading her the email, "but I'm thinking we should go. Closing the book with 2500 Mayan elders in Tikal on the Winter Solstice would be very powerful."

"I'm feeling the same," she responded enthusiastically. "I think we're meant to be there."

I contacted Anne and Aum-Rak and told them we were coming and would like to take them up on their earlier offer to make a presentation at their gatherings. I booked us a room in El Remate at the El Muelle, a quaint lakefront hotel.

On December 19, we flew to Cancun and from there, on to Flores, where Danny was to pick us up at the airport and drive us the 20 miles to El Remate. When we arrived, Danny was still stuck in Guatemala City repairing his truck, so two of his friends, Nancy and

Terry, met us. Over dinner at El Muelle, they told us the Unificación Maya had begun a few days earlier and things were going well.

After dinner, we all wandered down the lakefront road to the village center consisting of several *tiendas* and restaurants on one side of the road and a large open field on the lakefront side where several large party tents had been set up. The village is laid out on both sides of a quiet blacktop road that runs around Lake Petén Itza. Dramatic views are everywhere. On both sides of the road are small hotels, restaurants, cantinas and bars that are all geared toward the backpackers and eco-tourists. It is inviting and friendly, with a very rootsy, unassuming, peaceful quality to it.

A light rain was falling and a hundred or so locals and visitors had gathered under one of the tents to watch a performance of traditional Mayan dance. The dancing began with three Mayan women and two Mayan men, all dressed in traditional clothes. The Mayan men danced while holding a deer head with full antlers on their heads. Pablo Collado, an incredible native flute player from Belize, accompanied the dancers. Their ancient dance was slow and gentle—almost hypnotic—similar to the Hopi dances we had seen in Arizona. They took the audience into a peaceful, unhurried space— just what we needed after spending all day on planes and in airports.

The next morning, we joined Danilo, Anne and thirty or so others gathered at the lakefront for a quiet Pranic Healing Ceremony facilitated by Rosa Maria Gomar, founder of The Pranic Healing Society of Guatemala. Afterwards, Danilo and Anne handed out cereal and milk, provided by Rosa Maria, to many of the village children. Later in the afternoon, around ten people came to our presentation which we hosted in a thatched-roof hut at the end of the long pier in front of our hotel—a perfect place for storytelling. A light breeze was blowing and the humidity and temperature were just right as the group journeyed with us through Jamaica and the U.S.

That night we moved up to the Jungle Lodge, one of the three hotels inside Tikal Park. We were scheduled to do a presentation for Aum-Rak's Activation Maya group later that night at the hotel and we had to be at the park before dawn the next day for the solstice gathering of the elders.

After dinner at the lodge, where several of the Activation Maya group was staying, Aum-Rak hosted a documentary film, *Between Two Worlds*. The film featured Aum-Rak and several Mayan researchers including John Major Jenkins and Carl Calleman. It began by explaining the corrupting and disrupting influence of the standard Gregorian calendar created in 1582 by Pope Gregory XIII. Its 12 irregular months—based neither on logic, science nor nature—lacked connection to any natural cycles other than the 365-day solar year. Eighteen years later, in 1600, the first machine—the clock—was invented, separating time into 24-hour days, 60-minute hours and 60-second minutes which further separated humanity—and the conquered (indigenous) people on whom it was imposed—from the cycles of nature. Their year was the natural 13 "moons" of 28 days. This merged the monthly lunar cycle with the yearly solar cycle. It explained how over the centuries under this Gregorian system, we have forgotten that *we* are time and that time's cycles are within our bodies and within nature's daily rhythms and seasonal cycles. The film then explained the balancing influence of the more organic Mayan calendars.

After the film, I only had a few minutes to make my presentation before the hotel turned the electricity off for the night, so I decided to show everyone a few minutes of the footage of the elder Rastas in Jamaica. They carry the same message as the film—that love is expanding on the planet and we need only to open to it. Their joy—their "livity" as they call it—that they feel as they live their simple lives close to the land, was infectious. It was just what was needed before we retired.

∞∞∞

Julia and I got up around four in the morning and walked over to the guarded park entrance to meet Danilo who was leading the sunrise tour for the folks at Unificación Maya. Danilo, an articulate and warm-hearted Guatemalan, later told us, he and Luis are the only Tikal guides who offer a spiritual perspective to their tours.

A little before five he came up from El Remate with around 25 people. Everyone was looking forward to a peaceful half-hour stroll through the jungle in the dark followed by a flute concert by Pablo Collado as the sun rose over the Grand Plaza. The ceremony with thousands of Mayan elders would continue until sunrise the following morning. We quickly learned that Tikal had something quite different in store for us.

The first problem occurred as we tried to enter through the guarded entrance. A group called Fundación Kakulhaa had arranged for the group to get in free so everyone there assumed they would not have to come up with the usual tourist entrance fee of twenty dollars. However, it seemed that no one had told that to the several armed guards at the gate.

"It looks like all of us have to pay the entrance fee," Danilo said to our group. "The guards here were not told that we get in free and it's too early to contact the park manager. I'm sorry about the mix up so everyone get out their twenty bucks."

Immediately there was a collective groan from the group. Some didn't have the money with them so they had to borrow it from others. Finally, everyone paid and we headed up toward the Grand Plaza. It was still dark and the jungle was quiet except for the howler monkeys, who earned their names with their prehistoric-sounding, almost frightening, screams.

After a half-hour, we arrived at the Grand Plaza. With its beautiful grass center court, it is flanked on two sides by large low structures that are ancient burial vaults and on the other two sides by two magnificent stepped pyramids, one with three large levels and the other with nine steps. It was just starting to get light and everyone spread out over the steps of one of the pyramids while Pablo Collado, accompanied by a drummer wearing a beautiful Bob Marley shirt, began to play. For over an hour, as the sun rose over Tikal, Pablo, with his almost transcendent flute playing, took us all on a very peaceful mystical journey.

Julia and I had climbed to the top of one of the pyramids and sitting there on the Winter Solstice, with Pablo playing and thousands of Mayan elders soon to arrive for their ceremony, well, what can I say. You get the picture. It was a very, very nice way to spend a morning.

After Pablo's concert (which he later told us was the best one ever for him), Danilo gathered us together for a spiritual tour of Tikal, much as Luis had done with our family exactly a year earlier on the Winter Solstice in 2006. We had a few hours as the elders would be gathering at the gate to walk in procession to the Grand Plaza, where the ceremonies would begin at eleven and continue until dawn the next day.

"Mostly we have been seeing the Mayans from a Western perspective," Danilo said as he began the tour at the Grand Plaza. "Until recently, we didn't know anything about the Maya from *their* perspective. Now that information is coming back in a way that we are able to see them from their own perspective. That's what we are going to do through this tour."

"As a matter of fact the Star of David has the information of the behavior of the Universe. It represents a thousand years of light," he continues as he holds his hands together to form a triangle pointing up, "followed by a thousand years of darkness [he points his finger pyramid down]. Two thousand and twelve is the end of the cycle of darkness. This is a disintegrating, destructive cycle regulated by male energy. Maya believed in the constructive, natural cycle regulated by female energy which is why Venus is so important to the Maya. It is the morning star—the only planet we can see in the day. Venus is coming back to rule the new cycle. That is the discovery of Linda Schele [author of *A Forest of Kings:The Untold Story of the Ancient Maya*, *Maya Cosmos* and *Hidden Faces of the Maya*]. Linda used a computer program known as the Sky Globe that could tell you the location of the objects in the sky in Mayan times. She also used fine arts, astrology and philosophy to find out that Mayans were ruled by Venus. The rose in the DaVinci code, for example, uses the symbol of Venus.

"The result of breaking the harmony with nature, breaking the harmony of the Universe, is that we just limit ourselves to develop an economic system. I call it 'the wheel of the hamster.' It is just about how to earn money and how to spend it. When we are in it, it

186

is hard for us to get out of the wheel and stay still for a while and see what life is all about."

"The information is still here," he continued pointing toward the top of one of the pyramids. "In the light cycle we do changes from the inside to the outside. In the dark cycle, we put all the concepts upside down so the changes are done from the outside to the inside. That's why we are just living with the structures of society, just trying to reach a high economic level as an excuse not to change ourselves. Usually we try to change someone else rather than change ourselves. That is a particularity of the dark cycle.

"We have been ruled by the dark cycle. That's the discovery of Carl Calleman in his book *The Mayan Calendar and the Transformation of Consciousness*. He's been using information from the Mayan calendar. The information is also in the Bible but we decipher it in a different way depending on the time we are living in. Actually, when Jesus Christ was crucified, he was crucified at a time of a solar eclipse and an earthquake. That's our behavior. We always have a parallel relationship with astronomical events and natural disasters. That's why it's a surprise for us to talk about global warming, but when you are familiar with the Mayan calendar, that's not a surprise.

"We are getting to a point where this cycle is ending and a new cycle is starting. Some people call it a new age, but it is not a new age, but a repetition. We call it 'Cosmic Repetition.' Just like the Old Testament says, 'There is nothing new under the sun.' The cycle is just coming back again.

"They found on the other side of the planet from here a statue of Buddha in a triangle-shaped lotus position. It has the same measurements of this pyramid and it fits perfectly into this [he points toward the pyramid with the nine steps.]. This pyramid is a representation of ourselves sitting in a lotus position during meditation and going to a higher level of consciousness.

"For the Maya, from the doorway on top of the pyramid, there were nine negative levels to the underworld combined with nine positive levels to the upper world. This is represented by the snake with two heads that balances the negative and positive energy. Our minds work on these nine levels. This is what Einstein discovered in

187

relativism. But relative to what? Here we can see it is relative to the Absolute. The doorway at the top represents cosmic consciousness. The three level of this pyramid [he points toward the three-level pyramid] represents your mind, your body and your spirit. When we talk about the fight between evil and good, that's a lie. It's not an eternal fight. It's a fight for a thousand years. In the thousand years of light we balance positive and negative energy. That's the lion and the lamb being together. Like it says in the Bibles for God, one day is a thousand years and a thousand years is a day. I've been reading about the 5125-year cycle of no love but that cannot be possible. The Creation is held together by love, which is pure energy. What happens in a thousand years of darkness is we disintegrate the love but it is still there. Love is what keeps the atoms together."

We continued our tour around the Grand Plaza and Danilo pointed out several other references to Venus built into the structures.

"The Hopis also claim that Venus was the celestial object they used to indicate when they should continue their migrations," I said to Danilo. "Do you think that's why they were tracking it so closely here? Maybe they were watching to see when it was time to continue on and maybe that is why archeologists have never been able to explain why these Mayan ceremonial cities were abandoned?"

"Exactly," he answered. "Some of these people disappeared and some stayed to hold the Mayan information to the end of the Mayan civilization. The Hopis are credited with holding the Mayan information for centuries until the white buffalo was born in 1996, then they started publishing this information."

""We are now ending the disintegrated cycle where the information is spread out. Even your work," he said, pointing toward Julia and me, "is putting the information together to see the bigger puzzle to understand what is happening. We are coming from a time of exclusivity to inclusivity. The Universe is exposing the information to everyone. The Hopi hold specific prophecies. The prophecies are actually astronomical projections. That is the importance of the Mayan calendar. Even the *Book of Mormon* took some information from here to New York State. Around 1850, they deciphered that information and developed a whole religion. The names of Mayan kings also appear in the *Book of Mormon*."

"Were the gold tablets that the founder of the Mormons, John Smith, said he found, from here?" I asked.

"Yes. They were from here," Danilo replied, "and now new discoveries have been revealed. We used to talk about the Late Classic Period from 500AD to 830AD as being the flourishing time of the Maya. Recent discoveries put the date not at 830AD, but 909AD. Now with these new discoveries we are talking about the time from 200BC to 100BC as the time when the Mayans flourished. This is an earlier progression of the Mayan civilization. This reconfirms the information about Jesus Christ and the Maya. Robert, that was one of your questions that you asked Radford, the Hopi elder, in one of your videos that Luis gave me."

I had asked Radford if there is a Hopi legend about a white teacher of love visiting his tribe. Radford said the Hopis had no such legend but they still awaited the white brother or "white bahanna" to come with great wisdom. This bahanna would complete their spiritual understanding and usher in a period of global harmony.

However, a legend of this pale teacher with "eyes that looked forever" is found in many Native American tribes, including the Cherokee, Havasupai, Lakota, and many others. The legends say he carried no name but asked each tribe to name him. One tribe called him Chezoos. When he traveled on, he left twelve elders from the tribe to carry his wisdom.

There are other indications that the Christ spirit has manifested throughout history in other incarnations besides that of Jesus. Horus, the Egyptian Sun God who ruled around 3000BC, was born to a virgin on December 25. His birth was accompanied by a star in the east and three kings came to adorn him. By the age of 12 he was a teacher and he was initiated by Egyptian priests at 30 and began his ministry. He traveled with 12 disciples and performed miracles such as healing the sick and walking on water. After being betrayed, he was crucified, buried for three days and resurrected. Even the Biblical figure, Joseph, may have been a Christed-incarnation. He taught love by forgiving his brothers who sold him into slavery; he was one of 12 sons, was sold into slavery for 20 pieces of silver by his brother Judah and began his ministry at thirty.

"The Mormons say that Jesus Christ resurrected in North America and taught the native people their wisdom," Danilo continued. "I am finding information that that is backwards. Actually he *first* came here for the alignment and then he traveled to the Mid-East, to Jerusalem."

"So you think Jesus was here in Mayaland before he was in the Mid-East?" I asked just to be sure I understood him right.

"Yes," he answered. "Some investigations by linguistic experts of the words of Jesus Christ on the crucifix, especially regarding the last sentence, are revealing that it was not Aramaic Jesus spoke but Maya. They are translating that sentence into Maya and they are coming with a big surprise. In Aramaic it translates, 'God, why have you abandoned me?' but in Maya it translate more into the Buddhists' belief about the Ganges River delivering you into the ocean so that when you die you become part of everything, the ocean. The Sanskrit word is 'osho,' which means ocean.

"I'm sharing information that has taken me 27 years to develop. The sacrifices of the Maya in the ball court show that the Maya did a lot of preparation to die and to resurrect. [The Maya had a sacred ball game where, using only their hips and legs, they projected a ball through a small stone hoop sticking out of the ball field wall. Some researchers believe that the captain of the losing team was then willingly and proudly sacrificed; other researchers believe it was the captain of the winning team.] Like the sun, it sets and then rises. It travels the underworld and then resurrects again telling you how we resurrect eternally. What you see about the Maya is the whole message of Jesus Christ. During this disintegrated cycle, Christianity has branched off from the root of Jesus Christ into many branches, even more than the Muslims. There are many similarities between the message of Jesus Christ and the Mayan beliefs."

"Before I got into the Maya, I studied the Egyptians," Danilo continued. "When we talk about Maya, when we talk about Egyptians, we are not talking about a specific race or group. We are talking about a big cultural unification. On the back of the rattlesnake there is a pattern of diamond shapes. The diamond shape is information of the Mayan calendar. It talks about how we integrate, disintegrate and integrate again in the history of the different humanities [as he speaks he outlines diamond shapes with his hands showing them separating and then coming together again].

"When Bolivian President Evo Morales, an indigenous president, came to Guatemala, our indigenous people gave him a symbol of the fifth sun. Through Mayan unification we are preparing ourselves to welcome the fifth cycle that is coming, known as the 'Fifth Sun.' Ancient Mayans declared themselves as the 'Third Humanity.' This 'Fourth Humanity' is just about to end and we are going into the 'Fifth Humanity.'

"Einstein said that technology is going to go beyond humanity. We gave our power to the machines whereby we trust a piece of metal with wires more than we trust ourselves. That's how we gave our power to the machines. The whole mystery of the Maya was how they were balancing the positive and the negative energies. With the use of these temples, with the use of the principles of the pyramids and the use of the crystals, such as jade [he pulls a beautiful jade necklace he is wearing from underneath his shirt]. Don Juan, the Yaqui Indian shaman in Carlos Castaneda's books said they 'jump.' This jump is the extra amount of energy you need to change dimensions. All this has been proved by quantum physics. When we talk about 2012, it's known as the 'Quantum Jump.' It is also called 'Zero Year.' Even the Book of Revelation in the Bible talks of this."

(Though Darwin's theory of evolution has been taught as fact, most scientist knowledgeable on the subject now agree that there is *no* fossil or scientific evidence for Darwin's theory of a slow, orderly morphing from the simple amoeba to man. Instead there are "missing links" all over the evolutionary trail indicated that indeed "jumps" in evolution were—and are—the norm. Perhaps humanity becoming aware of its true Divine nature is the next jump.)

"When you go to a higher level of consciousness, you infuse yourself with white light," Danilo continued. "Savage is not a primitive state. It's a very high state of consciousness when you are unified with nature and the Universe represented by the eye in the top of the pyramid like you have on the one dollar bill. Mayans

191

sought balance, to have their heads in the clouds but their feet on the ground. From my Mayan investigations, I see the Universe as a big discotheque and God is the DJ. In the last five years, the process is accelerated, a lot of changes. We are in times of transition, from one cycle to another. To the Maya, the times we are living in is represented by the snake biting its own tail—Cosmic Repetition. It also means that this may be the last lifetime for people after many lifetimes—our last reincarnation. This cycle is known as the 'perfect imperfection.' The Mayan cycle and the next cycle is the 'imperfect perfection.' "

"These are some of the underground storage areas where the Maya stored the bread nuts," Danilo said as we wandered to an area of the path where we crossed over several small caves that appeared to be cut into solid rock. "The bread nut has sixteen percent more nutrition than corn. It was the main food of the Maya. Nothing has more nutrition than this. There was indigenous wheat that was good but long ago they modified it and then it started to lead to sickness like diabetes, depression."

"They developed that and then took away the dignity of the healers," Julia said. "The Egyptian healers would tell people not to eat that wheat."

"Exactly," Danilo said. "Here people don't eat wheat, only corn. That's why the Mayans believe people are made from corn; it represents that humanity can live in a symbiotic relationship with the earth like the Mayans did. Like humans, corn has teeth and hair."

"Also, let me show you how these cities were built," he continued picking up two small rocks off the ground and striking them together. "This rock is flint. It is very hard and the Mayans made axes from this flint. This rock is limestone and it is very soft and you can see how the flint cuts through the soft limestone— almost like butter [he cuts chips off the limestone with the flint rock]. This is the way the Mayans carved the blocks for the buildings. They made the plaster or stucco by burning the limestone."

"I've read that the ancient Mayans cut so many trees to burn the limestone for the temples," Julia said, "that maybe their decline was caused by an environmental disaster with the deforestation."

"Some scientists say that," Danilo responded, "but the Mayans only cut the dead trees out of the forest."

"Do the Mayan elders have any knowledge of the crystal skulls?" I asked.

"The elders hold that information," Danilo answered. "Many see that from a Western perspective. The crystal skull is a representation of ourselves, too. The name Christ comes from crystal. The skulls are like a battery that charges knowledge within us. With the coming alignment, you don't need too many external things. Soon, I'm going to get rid of this jade necklace I am wearing. We need these things for the jump, but after 2012, we will not even need language. These, and the ceremonies, are just devices to help us remember who we are.

"These pyramids were like the machine used in the movie *Contact*. In that movie, they used a machine to change dimensions. The chambers inside these pyramids were used for the same function. The Mayans had a technology to get out of the body. That's what we do when we die. When we die, we don't really die. We just change dimensions. The high priests would go out of the body to see what was in the other dimensions and then come back to the body again and then they would tell the people what was awaiting them in the other dimension so they would not be afraid of dying. This is similar to the information gathered by Dr. Elizabeth Kubler-Ross [the American doctor who researched death and dying by interviewing people who had near-death experiences]."

"Was the war here in El Remate?" I asked as we continued.

"Oh, yes," Danilo responded. "It was everywhere. The rebels even took over Tikal for a day and killed an employee. For five years, no tourists would come here. After the war, only 17 families were left in El Remate. The rest were killed or had fled. Then I made a promise. I said that I was not going to leave Guatemala again. In the 1970s, I was studying in the United States at the University of Alabama but I decided to return and to stay here because I wanted to know and help my people, my country. I returned in the middle of the war, in 1976. That's when I started my Mayan investigations. By staying here, I took a lot of risks without knowing what I was doing. I had a chance to go anywhere in the world because my father was a scientist, a doctor of chemistry and biology. He had the money, so we could go anywhere."

"And things seem to be getting better here," I commented. "Rigoberta Menchu didn't get elected, but what do you think of the new president?"

Alvaro Colom of the National Unity of Hope party had recently been elected. Colom, an engineer by profession, earned recognition through his work as director of the National Fund for Peace (FONAPAZ) and also for having negotiated the return of 45,000 Guatemalan refugees from Mexico. Colom is basing his plan of government on four fundamental issues: generating employment, fighting poverty, increasing productivity and governability.

"We are expecting a lot of changes for the positive with his election," he answered. "Colom says he is going to show the Mayan face of our country to the world. He is talking about Mayan unification. He is talking about One Love. Not that he uses that word but that is in his heart. I met with him. On March 21, the spring equinox, I was here in Tikal in a ceremony with White Eagle from Alaska. She brought the Grandmother Drum, a drum that was seven feet across. She had a vision in a dream to bring it here to complete a prophecy. The next day I met with Alvaro Colom in Guatemala City representing communities from here. I observed his energy close up. We are pleased that we are going to see a lot of changes. He is for all the people—not just a few. He has been declared a Mayan priest by the Mayan elders. In this cycle, the last will be first. We are seeing these changes. "

Don Alejandro Cirilo Perez Oxlaj, the head of the Mayan Council of Elders of Guatemala, initiated Colom as a Mayan Priest during Colom's inauguration ceremony in 2008. Don Alejandro spoke of the legend of the Quetzal bird of Central America uniting the Condors of the South and the Eagles of the North. Then he asked President Colom to make several public promises including to be the leader of *all* Guatemalans and to work for justice and equality and to not become "a servant to the powerful businesspeople and the dominant class." President Colom promised in agreement.

"You know, when I was on the top of the pyramid," I said, "I wondered if in ancient time only the nobility got to come up and have that view and the masses were always below. If so, that ceremonial city reinforced duality—kings and serfs, nobility and peons—not unity and therefore is it really sacred ground?"

"I have learned through my research," Danilo said, "that everyone here was a king or queen, prince or princess or a warrior and everyone could go anywhere in the city."

∞∞∞∞∞∞∞∞∞∞∞∞∞∞∞∞∞∞∞∞∞∞∞∞∞∞∞∞∞∞∞∞∞∞∞∞

It was now about 9:30 and some of us headed back to the Grand Plaza while others returned to the front gate. There, the elders would be starting a procession at ten to the Grand Plaza for the ceremony, scheduled to begin at eleven.

Julia and I walked to the plaza to await their arrival. I was looking forward to spending a few hours quietly in the plaza. It had really called to me. We walked over to find about thirty people milling around, a few tourists but mostly folks from Unificación Maya. Julia found a perch up high on one of the ancient structures and I laid flat on the grass in the center under a shade tree. Soon, we were both in very pleasant states.

By noon, Tata Pedro, Chus, Anne, Danny and Louise had not yet arrived in the plaza; nor had any of the 2500 elders. I spotted Danilo walking across the quad.

"Everyone is stuck at the gate," he told several of us as we gathered around. "The elders have not yet arrived and I don't think they are coming. Chus, Louise and Tata Pedro are working the Fundación Kakulhaa's people to get their people in and see if they can stay after closing and do their ceremony, but they're not having much luck so they're on their way up with Anne in the truck. There are some arguments going on. That's what I wanted to avoid this morning when we came in at dawn. In a while, they should be here."

No 2500 elders!! That's why we came! Last year, we came all this way to meet one elder, Tata Pedro, and he didn't show. This year it was to be with 2500 elders and now they're probably not going to show. What's going on here? What's the message from the Universe? My disappointment quickly gave way to my trust that

195

though I was writing this book, the Creator was shaping it. I laid back down and quickly fell asleep.

I awoke around an hour later and heard that everyone at the gate, including Tata Pedro, Chus, Louise, Anne and about forty others, were soon to arrive. The other 2500 elders were not coming, but Tata Pedro had brought two others with him, Tata Mariano de Leon Yac from Mazatenango and Nana Maria Juarez de Ramires from Huchuetenango. Danilo also told me Danny Diaz was still stuck in Guatemala City with truck problems and would not arrive until late that night.

Soon, the group finally arrived and after hellos and hugs, Tata Pedro began to set up his candles and incense. It was good to be in his presence again and experience the calm that always precedes his ceremonies. Pablo began playing his flute, accompanied on guitar by Terry, an American who ran a hotel in San Marcos.

When everything was ready, Chus called everyone together by blowing in a conch shell while Pablo blew into an amazing three-foot long twisted gourd. A hush came over the crowd as everyone gathered around in a large circle and held hands. Chus started to rhythmically beat a drum as Tata Pedro, Nana Maria and Tata Mariano continued placing candles and large balls of copal incense in a pattern in the fire pit in the middle of the Grand Plaza. When this was completed, silence came over the crowd and Tata Pedro asked the bare-chested men to please put on a shirt out of respect. Tata Mariano lit up a large ceremonial cigar and began rattling several three-foot long seed pods rhythmically.

When the vibe was set after a quiet group chant, Tata Pedro began speaking, translated by Louise, and later by Terry.

"We are looking for unification Maya," Tata Pedro began, dressed in his white ceremonial shirt and pants, brilliantly accented by his red sash and headdress. "We are looking for universal unity so that when we get to the Gregorian calendar date of 2012, we are united. We are of one spirit, of only one path. We all have different missions but we all have the same blood inside us. We have the same spirit inside us. We will be thinking about good things, about respect of our sacred bodies. We keep saying the body is sacred. Inside our body we have a Mayan calendar. Inside the calendar is the human body. Everything that we've talked about, humanity, is all inside Mother Earth, this planet.

"Thank you for coming. We want to be obedient to ourselves. Today we are here gathered together. The Winter Solstice unites us in this sacred site. It is okay for you to take notes, photos and videos so we can share this with others. You do not need to make apologies for this. We are going to honor the sun and keep calling to the spirits of the ruins for our Mayan descendants. This is a sacred temple of our ancestors. Here we can see here these large buildings, the strength, the cosmic strength our ancestors had. Today we say, 'Where did the Mayans go? Why today can we not do this? Where did our strength go?' The strength hasn't gone. It has not been hidden. The strength is here in our minds. Brothers and sisters, let's take a moment to concentrate within ourselves."

"Thank you for coming," Tata Pedro continued after a few minutes of silence. "In the name of our ancestors we give you welcome. Our arrival here was a little bit difficult, but here we are. We're always going to say thank you to the Creator and Former of the Universe. Each one of us has visions. We have ideas. What conclusions can we draw from this temple in front of us? What do we feel being in front of this sacred temple? It's not a ruin. If we keep calling it a ruin, it's because we are the ones who are ruining it. The sacred fire unites us. We are going to enter into our sacred ceremony. We begin with the first part, the invocation in the four directions. Later we'll be entering the second part."

Tata Pedro then began the ceremony, similar to the ones we had witnessed at the cave, the restaurant and at the Grandfather Trees. We prayed in the four directions, kissing the earth after each prayer. The ceremony continued for three to four hours. People seemed to be in a reverent, peaceful vibe, with no talking or distractions. Midway through, people broke out the musical instrument—drums, flutes, rattles and guitars—and began to gently play a meditative rhythm. Tata Pedro asked anyone needing a healing to come forward and he would offer a healing prayer for us individually.

Though it wasn't the 2500 elders we had expected, Tata Pedro's presence along with Tata Mariano's, Nana Maria's and the

197

other two hundred people assembled on this day and in this place, gave it a mystical sense of power.

Rumor was that we would all have to leave by the usual late afternoon closing. So, between that and the 4-hour sleep the night before, Julia and I headed out. The next morning, we wandered around the visitor's center before heading back to the El Muelle in El Remate for our last night.

"Well, I guess it was perfect, but not quite what I pictured," I said to Julia as we headed toward the visitor's center. "I had visions of ceremonies till dawn with thousands of Mayan elders."

"When you come to a place as powerful as Tikal," Julia said, "everyone has to confront their issues and their attachments. It's part of the needed cleansing. Everyone started out by looking at their money issues and their attachment to the ceremonies happening in a certain way. Maybe a couple of hundred of us in a four-hour ceremony was all that was meant to be."

"You're right. I had to let go of my expectations of what the last chapter of the book wants to be. I guess Unificación Maya is also part 'Purification Maya.' If we truly want to prepare ourselves for this leap into love coming in 2012, we are going to need to look at all our issues—fears, our greed, our blocks to love. It can be anything—a fear that we don't have enough money or not loving ourselves by eating badly or anything. And the times are quickening now so our issues are being revealed to us immediately and intensely. Also, I realized yesterday, when all the elders didn't show, that you really don't need to travel to any particular sacred spot to be with elders because the Creator is everywhere and every spot is sacred and you are always with elders. Even if you are alone in your house you are in a sacred spot with an elder. We are our own *tatas* and *nanas*."

As we were walking into the visitors' center, we ran into Saul from the group who had journeyed to Unificación Maya from Vera Cruz, Mexico. There, the Rainbow Family, whose non-commercial yearly gatherings draw thousands, had recently founded their first intentional community. As one of their unofficial (and *everything* is unofficial with the Rainbow Tribe) websites describes the family, "Some say we're the largest non-organization of non-members in the world. We have no leaders, and no organization. To be honest, the Rainbow Family means different things to different people. I think it's safe to say we're into intentional community building, non-violence, and alternative lifestyles. We also believe that Peace and Love are a great thing, and there isn't enough of that in this world. Many of our traditions are based on Native American traditions, and we have a strong orientation to take care of the Earth. We gather in the National Forests yearly to pray for peace on this planet."

"I loved your drumming yesterday," Julia said to him. "You were holding a nice vibration during the ceremony."

"Thanks. I usually hold the vibe at our ceremonies, but last night some of the younger people took it over," he said, his eyes glowing. "I'm just coming down from the Grand Plaza. We've been up there all night. A lot of people left early, but others came in and they didn't make us leave. After Tata Pedro's ceremony, a lot of the Rainbow Family people came up and started a ceremony. Then after dark, a group of Mayan youths arrived who going to a school in Guatemala where they teach traditional Mayan ways. They had come with some of the founders of Fundación Kakulhaa, who brought a couple of thousand Mayan elders here a few months ago. But those elders didn't make it for last night."

"So the ceremonies *did* continue until dawn?" I said, both disappointed we had missed them and yet glad the energy continued through the night.

"Absolutely!" Saul said. "It was awesome! They came in a bus jammed with people and on the top it was piled five feet high with baggage and they carried it all up from the gate to the plaza. It was full of food, wood, incense, musical instruments, a marimba, backpacks, everything for the ceremony. The ceremony went until just a little while ago. There was this young couple, Chris and Paula, there from the Rainbow Family and they held the whole ceremony. They were very solid. They just stood strongly by the fire pit and gathered everyone's energy together. It was the most powerful night of my life. They're camping over there by the restaurant in the campground. You want to meet them?"

"Absolutely!" I said and we all headed happily off.

We approached the campground, a beautiful open field with shade trees and open thatch-roofed huts with hammocks that rent for a few dollars a night. There were several groups camping together under some large shade trees and we wandered over.

We met up with Yannis, a thirty-something bearded man with bright eyes and a loving smile. He spoke English with a strong French accent. He had come from San Pedro with others in the bus the night before and was at the later ceremonies in the Grand Plaza. He was camping with several others including three beatific-looking young women and several children. They were all sitting on a blanket under the tree—tired but serene.

"What was the journey from San Pedro like?" I asked.

"It started on nineteenth of December and then we stopped and got the people from Fundación Kakulhaa in Los Ecuentros. That brought together a part of the Rainbow Family and the Mayan elders. We worked with them before at another gathering here in Guatemala. Then, we all came here and last night, in the big square of the Jaguar in Tikal, we came together for the first time and the Mayan elders and the Rainbow Family made a ceremony together. We brought some water from the Ganges River in India and the elders used that in the ceremony."

"And all of you came in one bus with 50 people and five feet of baggage?" I said. "What was that like?"

"It was packed. In four days, I slept one night for six hours in the bus," Yannis said laughing. "At the ceremony last night, it was very powerful for all of us, very strong. There were about a hundred of us. With the Rainbow Family, you never know how many we are. The Fundación brought a lot of incense and wood and we made a big pyramid in the shape of the Pyramid of the Jaguar next to the fire. It took two hours to build and we put four big crystals around it. After the pure Mayan ceremony, it was the time for the Rainbow Family, who were the keepers of the fire with the Mayan Nana and it was our job to put the offerings in the fire. It took hours! It burnt until this morning."

"Nice!" I said, just imagining the beauty of the night.

"We were in a big circle," Yannis continued. "Everybody in the circle made their own magic and if you are in the ceremony, you'll see the people. You'll see what's going on."

"We took the road of travels here, too," said another long-haired, bearded young man on the blanket. "It was not an easy road. Many things happened, but we always kept our spirit."

"All our issues will be coming up for us to heal now," I said, "but as we heal them, we do the work for everyone, for the whole planet."

"How is that?" one of the young women asked.

"I really didn't understand it either until I heard this story told by Dr. Elizabeth Kubler-Ross that really explains how as we free ourselves from our fears, we help many others free themselves from similar fears. Dr. Ross was the woman who spent years researching and writing on death and dying by interviewing people who had near-death experiences. The story is an example of how true peace—arrived at after a lifetime of struggle by one person—can be passed on to another in seconds.

"As Dr. Ross tells it, she was working at a large teaching hospital in Illinois where she noticed a change in her dying patients after a certain black cleaning woman entered their room to clean. After the cleaning woman's visits, the patients were calmer, no longer fearing death as they had shortly before her visit.

"Dr. Ross asked the cleaning woman to meet with her. Though at first mistrustful of Dr. Ross, the woman finally agreed to a meeting in a laundry room.

"Dr. Ross told her, 'I need to know what you are doing to my dying patients.' The woman began to tell Dr. Ross about her poverty-stricken life in the ghettos of Chicago. She told Dr. Ross painful story after painful story of her life in a cold-water flat where she watched friends and relatives suffer and die needlessly. Finally she told how her six-year old son died in her arms as she waited three hours in an emergency room in a county hospital.

"Dr. Ross at first did not understand what this had to do with her dying patients. As if the woman could read her mind, she stopped and said, 'You see, Dr. Ross, death is not a stranger to me any more. It's like an old friend. And sometimes when I enter their rooms, I see how afraid they are and I just go over and pat them and tell them it's not so bad.'

"This woman was able to pass on her lifetime struggle to come to peace with death to a perfect stranger in a three-second, four-word sentence. We've seen similar instantaneous changes in the inmates attending our prison concerts. They come in with a lifetime of issues and after a few hours with a handful of us reminding them that they can always claim their path of love, their hearts are open again—maybe for the first time since they were children. If you can get that powerful response from maximum-security inmates, you can get it from anyone. When you add this spiritual law to the reality that the winds are changing from duality to unity—from the love of power to the power of love—we can understand how quickly consciousness and love can—and is—expanding across the planet."

At this point, three of the organizers from Fundación Kakulhaa wandered over from the nearby camp site. They all seemed like very clear, calm spirits. I liked them immediately. As their brochure reads, "The Fundación is devoted to the "Cosmovision Maya al servicio de la humanidad."

"These are the people from the foundation," Yannis said introducing us. "This is Edmundo Chang, Carlos Perez Mendia and Victoria. Without them, we could not have made the ceremony we wanted. They are the magic connection to the government."

"What does your organization do?" I asked after the introductions and I explained a little of what we have been doing.

"We work with different Mayan organizations," Edmundo said, "and with different Mayan holy people. We are very interested in taking the Hopi elders to meet with them. Please extend an invitation to them on our behalf. If they come here, we will take them around Guatemala to meet with the elders here. It will be a very fruitful journey."

"I will certainly do that for you," I replied. By now, it was time for us to catch the bus to El Remate. We said goodbye, hoping that we would cross paths again.

Chapter 11

Visions
Staying Awake in a Sleeping World

You chose to be here and awake at this time so that the "Transition" may take place. And what is this Transition? It is as simple as opening your eyes and seeing what has been in front of you for so long, then gently touching the shoulder of others sleeping next to you, that they too may behold the presence of Joy. . . Now that you are awake, you can see that all Grace flows "through" and "as" you, for such is the will of the One who sent you into the World.

You are here to realize why you are here, then to fulfill it. Let this be the moment you recommit to this, for this is your function this and every moment—to remember why you are here.

-James F. Twyman, *The Art of Spiritual Peacemaking: Secret Teachings from Jeshua ben Joseph*

After checking into the El Muelle, we headed over to Gringo Perdido to touch base with Tata Pedro and Danny Diaz, who had finally arrived. We wanted to finalize arrangements with them for joining us in August for our next scheduled event. Called *The Gathering of the Peacemakers:Getting Ready for the Changes*, the event would be six days of conscious music and seven days of conscious instructions. Its genesis was a vision I had a few weeks before we flew to Tikal.

Late one night, I was reading my book *Memoirs of an Ex-Hippie*, which I had not read for almost eight years. The book chronicles my seven-year odyssey through the counterculture of the 1960s and 1970s, mostly living in a converted school bus and on communes in Oregon and North Carolina. The book ends with my leaving this nomadic life in 1979 and founding a non-profit institution in the San Francisco Bay Area called the Owner Builder Center. The institute taught housebuilding, design and remodeling classes in eight cities surrounding the Bay Area. The focus was on building passive solar, energy-efficient, minimum-polluting homes.

Each summer we held a housebuilding camp where people from all over would come for three weeks to learn how to build or contract their own homes. The camp, housed at a Quaker high school in Nevada City in the California Sierra Nevada Mountains, had a staff of 25, including teachers, cooks and social directors. I was the camp director.

My goal at the housebuilding camp, in addition to offering the obvious technical instructions while actually building two houses, was to remove everyone from their everyday reality and put them in a totally supportive and, for the most part, non-commercial and natural environment. After working at the site each day, everyone would swim in the clear Yuba River and then have a great meal followed by a movie, talent show or an evening in quaint Nevada City. The participants loved it and it has always been the benchmark of enjoyment and satisfaction in my work life. As an added benefit of my years at the Owner Builder Center, I met Julia. She was taking one of the classes I taught in her hometown of Palo Alto.

As I read this chapter of my book late that night, an idea came to me all at once—full and complete, just as the vision of the Owner Builder Center had come to me almost thirty years earlier. This new vision blended together my experience at the summer housebuilding camp, our One Love Events and our more recent participation at the summer music festivals.

As I finished the chapter, I thought, *Why not host a week-long summer camp where during the day people could learn much-needed life skills and at night enjoy conscious music?* The instruction would include workshops in all forms of appropriate, sustainable technology such as solar and wind energy, bio-diesel fuels, living off-the-grid, waste recycling, organic and bio-dynamic gardening, and other life skills including alternative and holistic healing techniques, co-housing and intentional communities, wilderness tracking and survival, yoga, meditation, building your own home, handling your money wisely, living on less, conscious parenting, creating and sustaining loving unions, and finding your mission in life. It would also include presentations on the Hopi and Mayan prophecies and the Mayan calendar. In the evening there would be live performances by conscious recording artists, followed by drumming circles, inspiring movies and talent shows.

Like most true visions, it brought together my best talents and passions, along with all we had learned after years of hosting events and going to festivals. I had longed for a self-sustaining, on-going vision. This was something we could do each summer. More than all this, it would allow us to more thoroughly do what we really wanted to do—prepare people physically, emotionally, mentally, and spiritually for the coming changes so that they could share this peace with others. Tata Pedro was to be our "Elder-in-Residence" at the first gathering. He would set the vibe with a lakeside ceremony each morning and address the gathering before the concert each night.

By dawn of the night of my vision, I was so excited I couldn't wait for Julia to wake up to share it with her. Julia loved the idea, too, but we've learned that just because we get excited about an idea doesn't always mean that we should enact it. Sometimes we can't afford it or don't have the time or energy. Sometimes it just loses its excitement or we put it on a shelf for awhile—maybe forever. Sometimes we see how the next few steps go to see if it feels right.

Within two days, we had located the perfect place—the 152-acre Holston Camp near our home in the North Carolina mountains. It was complete with a dining hall, a lodge, cabins, camping areas, fire circles, a swimming lake, a coffee shop, and a climbing wall.

We contacted Tata Pedro and he enthusiastically agreed to join us. Then we called Danny to come and be his interpreter. Danny also agreed. We contacted the best-known conscious recording artists in the Southeast and got them on board. Within a week of my vision, everything was set and our excitement kept growing.

At Gringo Perdido, we discussed the details with Tata Pedro and Danny and shared our vision in greater depth. Though tired, Tata Pedro was relaxed, having well completed his mission over the last few days. Soon, it was time for him to head out to begin his 24-hour journey by local transportation back to San Pedro. It would be a long, uncomfortable trip but it would be with his people, in his land.

After dinner that night at our hotel, Julia and I decided to wander over to the village center where a traveling carnival had set up on the large lakeside field where the traditional Mayan dancers had performed a few days earlier. It was a small enterprise—a large Ferris wheel, several smaller children's rides, a few food stands, gambling games and a beer garden set under several party tents.

From our hotel we could hear the loud music, mostly intense hip-hop and rap. As we approached the fair, it got so loud you could not even carry on a normal conversation as you wandered around. After a quick tour, we walked back to the hotel, glad the air conditioning would muffle the music that would blare until dawn.

The next morning, Danilo and Danny joined us before we had to catch our flight from nearby Flores to Cancun and from there on to North Carolina. We sat under the thatch-roofed hut on the pier for one last quiet reasoning together before all going our separate ways. It was good to be together—relaxed and drawing support and strength from each other's company. The carnival with its giant Ferris wheel was in the background—its music still blaring loudly.

"We wandered over to the carnival last night," I said to them. "It was a very intense vibe."

"That fair was sponsored by the Catholic church here," Danilo said. "They came to us and said we were doing such a good job organizing Unificación Maya, would we be willing to organize the fair for them, which we did. We thought it would be good for the people to have some recreation around Christmas. I just thought it would be generous on our part to help them."

"That's understandable," I said. "People who birth true visions, like all of you at Unificación Maya, are very inclusive, not exclusive. Julia and I have learned a lot about birthing visionary events. We made many mistakes in the beginning. People will be given many visions in the years to come but there is little

206

understanding available on how to best enact them."

"How do you handle situations where people want to be part of your vision without excluding them?" Danilo asked.

"I've realized that a true vision is not like a venture based on ego and money," I answered, "though those forces usually come into play. They still do with me but to a greatly diminished degree over the years. A vision usually comes to one person but sometimes to a couple or a small group. A vision is given *through* us by the Creator to be shared with all those drawn to it. Our loyalty must be to those to whom we offer it. We need to protect them from any discordant or divisive vibration that might interfere with the vision."

"How do you do that?" Danny asked.

"In the beginning, when I started writing our books and hosting our events," I answered, "the desire to be acknowledged and the hope of adding some money to the family funds were still in my heart and mind. We realized the events needed to be free.

"In 2002, our first event, *The Gathering of the Healers*, was held on Bob Marley's 57th birthday. We used the backyard of his home in Kingston, which is now a museum. It was one of the few times the Marley family let outsiders use his home. We invited six well-known Jamaican teachers of love—from reggae artists to a candidate for prime minister—to join us there for a press conference to invite the entire island to complete Bob's work of teaching love.

"The two-hour event went beautifully with only one discordant note. As we were getting ready to close, this Jamaican man came up and begged me to let him read his short poem. He said it was about One Love. I finally relented. The poem he read was more about his pain and anger. Though it didn't have a big effect on the gathering, it did break our stride. It taught us that it is essential that our vision not be affected by toxic influences or people.

"That taught me that all true visions are meant to teach unconditional love, no matter what form they may take. If that is where we want to take the people sharing our vision we have to be sure that whoever is on stage or is entrusted with the gathering's attention, their consciousness, is known by us, and perhaps even by the audience, as a teacher of love. Now we only allow people who are teaching love *fulltime* to speak or perform at our gatherings."

"So maybe I should have told the Catholic church that I would not help them?" Danilo said.

"Not necessarily," I said, "only if it means compromising the vision in any way. On Bob's 60th birthday in 2005, the Jamaican government asked us to combine our concert with theirs. We had already done 50 free concerts on the island and they didn't want to compete with ours because all of the conscious recording artists would appear for us at no charge. I told them we would, but *only* if everyone that appeared on stage was known to their people as a teacher of love. The government finally agreed to handle the infrastructure and let us take over who would appear on stage.

"The only exception was that Prime Minister Patterson would need to open the concert, which would be one of the biggest in the island's history. We agreed but the Prime Minister backed out the night before. When the concert began and there were tens of thousands of people in front of the stage in downtown Kingston and millions more watching on TV or listening on radio, instead of the country's prime minister opening the event, our daughter, Alicia, opened it. I had her scheduled to speak after the Prime Minister. When everyone was expecting Prime Minister Patterson to open the show, there was Alicia. We had never planned any of this but she said exactly what the country needed to hear that night."

"How so?" Danilo asked.

"She told the audience that she had been coming here since she was fourteen and she would always be a better person for having known the Jamaican people. They had shown us such love and had been so free of race prejudice or class prejudice, that they had taught her what really matters in life. She told them that the little things in life like clothes and cars and money will never mean as much to her after knowing them."

"I don't remember the rest," I continued, "but, with their economy and political system in disarray, with their poverty and potholes, here's this middle-class teenager from the wealthiest nation in the world telling them *they* have strengthened *her* faith in humanity. The next day a woman came up to us at the airport and told us that Alicia stole the show. She said she was watching the concert with her large family at home on TV and after Alicia spoke,

208

almost everyone was in tears. Only the Creator could have planned that. He'll use all our visions if we just let Him. I could never have thought that up. Like all our visions, this one turned out a little different than we envisioned it. The more we remembered this really wasn't *our* vision, but just coming *through* us, the more beautifully it unfolded. You can't get too attached to the outcome in this vision business. You just got to give it your best and see what it's meant to be."

(As I was making my final review of this chapter, Alicia located in her email the speech she gave that night three years earlier and we had never been able to find. She sent it to me on a lark. She had no idea I was talking about it in this book. It read, in part:

"Jamaica, today healers have gathered here to heal this country! The shattered state of your country in the last few years has become unacceptable. You must all rise up and take your destiny! Can anyone propose a better way to transform this colorful country than with love! Hatred and violence are not enjoyable states to be in, so why not move past those senseless sensations! Forgive and allow peace into your heart! I hear of the times when Jamaicans did not have to worry about the violence, theft, and corruption in their neighborhoods. I was not alive in these times, but I would like to be alive in this time when Jamaica becomes a violence-free country, unlike any other country in the world, Jamaica is special and every one of you needs to see your future not as a dangerous one, but as a peaceful one where love may prevail! So you may once again wander the streets without threats of violence or drugs looming in every dark corner! Allow all people, young and old, rich and poor, to unite in this One Love message and turn this country around! And as Bob Marley once said, 'Emancipate yourself from mental slavery. None but ourselves can free our mind!' ")

"I'm curious," Danny said. "Why did the Prime Minister decide not to speak at the last minute?"

"Actually that leads to something else we learned," I answered. "I think he didn't want to speak because he knew he would be the only person on stage that night that hadn't yet chosen to claim himself as a teacher of love. All the other recording artists and speakers we invited were known to their fellow Jamaicans for their message of love. He understood what our goal was—to have teachers of love invite others to join them. Two years before, in 2002, I had met with him, and the opposition leader, Edward Seaga, and invited them both to come to our first event on Bob's 57th birthday at Bob's house. I told them that I asked a lot of his people who taught love in his country and no one mentioned their names, but we wanted to have both of them come and hear from these teachers of love. Neither of them came."

"You said that to the Prime Minister of Jamaica!?" Danny said. "How did you even get to see him?"

"That was another lesson," I said laughing at how this reasoning was going. "A week before our first press conference at Bob's home on his 57th birthday, my Rasta friend Scram and I were staying in a hotel in Kingston, planning to spend the next day finalizing the plans for the event. As we were sitting out on the balcony of our room that night, Scram said, 'Ya, mon. We should invite Prime Minister Patterson and Mr. Seaga, to come to our press conference to hear from these great teachers of love. It may change their hearts. We should go to their offices in the morning and invite them.'

"I told Scram I thought there was little chance that a backcountry Rasta and an unknown American author could just drop by and see the top two leaders of his country and get a meeting unannounced, but he just said, 'Well, now, if JAH wants us to meet them now, they will have to see us.'

"The next morning, we got off the elevator in the crowded lobby of the hotel and this guy we knew, Horace Matthews, was walking across the lobby in front of us. Horace worked for Antonnette Haughton, who was running against Patterson and Seaga on a third party ticket. Antonnette was known for her message of love through her radio talk show and would be speaking at our press conference.

"As we fell in conversation with Horace, we walked down the corridor with the crowd. He turned into a large banquet room and gave the people at the door an invitation. We all walked in. We were so lost in the conversation, Scram and I barely noticed until we got inside and there was a breakfast set up for 400 people. It was the annual prayer breakfast for the top leaders in Jamaica and we had just wandered in! Scram and I sat at one of the tables, uninvited and looking like interlopers in our casual clothes among everyone in their best suits and dresses, all known to each other. And there at the head table were Patterson and Seaga!

"I looked over at Scram and he's laughing and says, 'Well, now, it looks like the Creator has set up our meeting. Now we must go up and tell them that we want to invite them to our gathering so we can big them up to teach love to their people. That is what every leader should do. And Jah didn't put us in this situation unless He wanted us to do what He sent us here to do.' So Scram and I went up to the head table and Scram talked to Seaga while I talked to Patterson and then we switched off and I talked to Seaga and Scram talked to Patterson.

"That day taught me that I would have to get over a lot of my fears and my discomfort in certain situations if I wanted to stay true to my vision. Whenever this comes up now, whenever I have to tell someone a truth that might hurt their feelings, such as they cannot perform or speak or work at our events, I remember that if I can tell the Prime Minister of Jamaica that he has not yet claimed himself as a teacher of love, I can tell anyone that. A true vision needs to surround itself with people who are fully committed to awakening, the path of a visionary can be lonely at time but more and more we are finding each other.

"And I think that is what you need to do next year. You need to be sure everyone who mixes their vibe with yours holds the same vision and sees it as purely. You can even use their misguided disruptive attempts to further the vision. They are looking for this same love, too. But they just don't know it yet."

"How can you do that?" Danilo asked.

"If the church wants you to organize the fair next year," I answered, "you could tell them you will, but *only* if you can control the music, as we did in Jamaica. Then, play Bob Marley and other conscious artists at a reasonable volume. Then, even if people come for the beer and gambling, the music will touch their hearts. If you played Bob Marley in El Remate for two days straight, it would change the vibes of the entire village. Maybe have Tata Pedro speak and show the DVD of our One Love Concerts."

"I really think that would be the best thing that could happen," Danny said smiling broadly. "I'm sick and tired of this unconscious, frantic music. If you go to the highlands, if you go to Guatemala City, it's there. It's everywhere."

"Most people do not really understand the impact of music and films," I said. "I was reading this book, *A Long Way Gone: Memoirs of a Boy Soldier*. It's about a boy in a village in Sierra Leone that is kidnapped by the army after the rebels killed his entire village. The army turns him into a vicious killer for three years. Part of the way they do that is every night they show the soldiers *Rambo* movies where the hero is a revenge-driven, violent killer. Finally, the boy is sent to a rehabilitation camp. It was run by a volunteer group that was trying to get the kids to be normal teenagers after years of being vicious killers. The way it happened for this kid is that a nurse gave him a Bob Marley cassette and he learned all the lyrics and started to sing Bob's music. It brought him back to himself again. So the media can be used for good or evil, Bob Marley or Rambo."

"That will happen," Danilo said. "I would like to make the changes you are talking about."

"We had a similar thing happen to us when we first started to do our concerts around Jamaica," I said. "This guy Roy tried to use our vision for his own gain. We had met him when we were writing *Rasta Heart*. When Roy heard we were doing these free concerts, he kept calling me in the States begging me to please do one in his village, saying that it would be the biggest event there ever. 'I just want to give a gift of One Love to my people,' he kept telling me.

"Finally, we got together with Abijah and Mackie Conscious, two well-known conscious Jamaican recording artists, and agreed to come up. When we arrived on the night of the concert, Roy was selling beer and white rum and he was playing slack music that was very demeaning to women. We quickly realized we had been used so he could draw a crowd and make some money. When Julia started walking toward the DJ, he switched to Bob Marley.

"All four of us got on the stage and explained that negative music causes a lot of pain in the world, as does the alcohol, and both undermined our message of One Love we had come all this way to deliver—and which we still planned to deliver. We let Bob do his magic for a while. Then Abijah and Mackie performed for two hours and totally transformed the vibe. Midway through the show, Roy got on stage and apologized to his people."

"It would be good to transform the energy at the fair," Danny said. "A lot of people came out for the fair."

"But even the numbers don't matter," I said. "It should be the same for the many or the few. We've done concerts for thousands, but our most moving was at a home for abandoned and abused boys in the Blue Hills of Jamaica. There were only twenty boys and five staff but there was so much love between them. Since the staff had all been raised in the home, too, they knew what the boys were going through. And this small home was a true vision. It touched only a few but its impact was very powerful. Visions don't have to be grand and public. Often they are modest and private—like a loving family life or a devoted teacher or healer.

"In 2003 we had another press conference in Jamaica and only one person came. We had the room set up for fifty. We even had refreshments laid out. We went ahead with the conference as if the room was full with Abijah, Julia, Alicia and me explaining the goal behind our upcoming concert tour. We didn't even know if this one guy worked for the press. When we finished, he just said, 'I'm amazed the press isn't covering this better,' and left. Turns out this was Bobby Stevens, a former Tourism Minister and a very high-minded and well-connected guy. A year later, it was Bobby who encouraged the government to work with us on producing Bob's 60th birthday concert, which was much bigger than it would have been if we had produced it ourselves. Later, he got the Jamaican Hotel Association to offer us free rooms and food so we could do more concerts there. Bobby had no ulterior motives but to help his people so he added to our vision rather than detracting from it.

"Other times we have said 'no' to working with others and doing our vision on a larger scale. When we were doing a concert in the Grand Canyon for the Havasupai tribe, a woman who was in charge of donating charitable funds for Reebok came and told us that Reebok might be interested in funding more of our concerts. All they would want was for the concerts to be branded with their name and logo. How can you have a One Love concert sponsored by a company that pays its employees wages that barely allow them to feed their family? We let that offer pass. We trusted that we would be given all the time, energy and money to enact our visions *without* compromise. You have to follow guidance and be sure you are not allowing someone to use your vision for selfish purposes."

"It just seems that it's been guided from the moment we chose it," Julia said. "It's been guided and we just trust in that. Sometimes one of us may forget and we remind each other because it can be disconcerting at times when you meet that dark side that wants to battle—you know, the ever-present fascination with good and evil. So many times in Jamaica we saw how love diffused the fight."

"Especially at one of the events we organized that was somewhat controversial," I said.

"What was that event?" Danny asked.

"It was called 'The Fires of Forgiveness' and we were asking Jamaicans to forgive as many people as they could, as much as they could and as soon as they could—even 400 years of African slavery. Remember Jamaica is a former slave colony and 96% of its population is descendants of African slaves. So, here comes this family from North Carolina—a former slave-holding state—asking *them* to forgive slavery, unilaterally and without reparations being offered. Needless to say, that event brought up some issues."

"What made you do that event?" Danny asked.

"There was a regatta of the tall-masted ships that summer in Jamaica," I said. "So Julia and Scram and I figured if the slave ships were returning to the former slave colony, we could use the event to heal this ancient wound. We organized a gathering and concert with Abijah in Port Antonio by the water so the ships would be in the background. After the concert, we lit a huge 'Fire of Forgiveness.'

"I arrived two months early and brought thousands of colorful 'Fires of Forgiveness' posters to put up around the island inviting people to join us that night in Port Antonio or to light their own fire or candle or a lamp at their home or community. I traveled throughout Jamaica asking people in small shops to put up these posters. Usually I would go into a shop where there might be a few people gathered and just my walking in often brought the place to a hush. They see few unfamiliar faces in these small shops and almost no white faces. I would ask the shop owners if they would mind putting up a 'Fires of Forgiveness' poster and forgive African slavery.

"At first there might be resistance. Often they would say that the U.S. and England should first beg for forgiveness and pay reparations before they would forgive. So I developed a five-minute reasoning on why we should forgive. I would remind them that people seldom ask for forgiveness or make amends and most of us aren't willing to forgive until that happens. And usually that just isn't going to happen.

"This is the main problem on our planet. It is keeping the world bound in a vicious cycle of revenge and retribution, of attack and counterattack, which must be broken. If we are going to wait to forgive those who hurt us personally, or even those who hurt or enslaved our ancestors, until they make it right, we are going to have a very long wait.

"And all during this wait, which may last a lifetime, we are going to have a bitter heart and that means less happiness, less peace of mind, less health. The only other option is to forgive others, even if they never ask us or make amends. Forgiveness doesn't mean we have to like them or be in their presence any longer. Or even tell them that we've forgiven. It just means we forgive them in our hearts. I know it is hard to forgive. It is the *second* hardest thing in the world to do. The only thing harder is to *not* forgive because you just keep reliving the attack and losing your peace of mind.

"Most people put up the posters, but there was this one well-known woman who stirred up a lot of anger on a radio show. She even got the government to rescind our permit to gather. The town cancelled their police protection at the last minute. Scram just said, 'JAH didn't get us this far to stop now.' So we told the mayor of Port Antonio we were going ahead and he could arrest us if he wanted. But I have to admit, I was really worried. I even told Alicia, who was only fourteen at the time, she might want to stay at the hotel because there was a threat of violence."

"What did Alicia say?" Danny asked.

"She said, 'Dad, I'm going. I'd be willing to die for this work

215

we are doing, but I hope I don't just get wounded and have to spend my life in a wheelchair.' It was one of my proudest moments."

"She's a warrior," Danilo said as Danny nodded in agreement.

"And everything went very smoothly that night," I said. "There were no problems and we never heard from that woman again because we just tried to send her love and not fight with her. And on Bob's 60th, we heard rumors that people planned to disrupt the concert. The government wanted to assign a detective to protect us, but the event went off with any problems and there were thousands of people in the streets.

"So those are some of the things we've learned about visions. If we're going to birth our visions, we have to take *total* responsibility for them. If an individual or group has been given a vision, we have to be responsible not only for the logistical and financial elements, but we have to be responsible for those we allow to share in its creation and be sure they hold the same intent as we do or it will weaken it. We have to be willing not to sacrifice our vision to avoid our discomfort or fear. Birthing a vision is very much a personal purification process. You have to constantly check yourself, constantly examine your motives and let go of your fears, your greed, and your need for acknowledgement. This takes blocking the world out on a regular basis and turning within and also surrounding yourself with conscious books and music, even if it's for a short time each day. You just have to discipline yourself to stop the messages from the commercial world and from constant contact with people still lost in it or it's very hard to remember who you are and why you are here.

"And you can't rush it. Some visions you can manifest in a short time; others may take years, even decades. It took Gandhi over four decades to get the British to quit India and Mandela 29 years in prison to birth his vision of an apartheid-free South Africa. Sometimes you can earn your living with your vision, like Bob Marley finally did and many of the conscious recording artists do now. However, that has not been the case with us. It's been just the opposite. Our visions have depleted our funds, but as the elders in Santiago Atitlan said when they spent their money to help the youths, 'Our poverty is our wealth.' "

"And when you birth a vision," Julia said, "you come from a state of 'My cup runneth over' and you want to share. Then what happens is the reverse with people who feel like they don't have enough, they feel like they have to take. It's the same thing with the whole monument over there in Tikal. The Spaniards felt they had to take it. It was a sacred place, but they wanted to take it just as the Catholics go to the Grandfather Tree shrine in San Pedro and build their altar on it."

"That's how it is in this destructive cycle that is now ending," Danilo said. "Now we can see how the Universe is doing the change from exclusivity to inclusivity again. It is like a tortilla flipping over. We are now working with a new program to put all these concepts the right side up. There is a book out called the *Knowledge of the Ka'kchiqueles.* It tried to get information from Mayan communities about what went on here in Mayan Golden Age. The only thing they remembered was a group coming and another group coming and another group coming so that this area was a huge cultural encounter, a cultural exchange. There was information about a ship with three sails that was left by the Mayans. Cultures came from the other side of the ocean. I see the Mayan civilization as a big cultural encounter. Cultures came and unified and condensed all the information available to humanity at the time, and that's what we call the Mayan civilization. Mayans developed on an *inclusive* basis. Then came the exclusive cycle and now we are going back to the inclusive cycle again."

"And you are learning here," I said, "in this remote area of Guatemala, how to transform a discordant vibe into love. Jesus was right when he said not to resist evil with evil, but with love. As Edgar Cayce once said, 'Evil is just under good, waiting to be lifted.' You are welcoming everyone into love and if discordant forces think they will transform you, it will really be *you* that transforms *them* because only *unity* is real. Duality is just an illusion."

It was now time to head to the airport. I think we all felt clear in understanding the gifts Unificación Maya had offered us—gifts quite different, perhaps, from what we expected, but just what we needed. We all hugged and, somewhat reluctantly, said goodbye.

217

Later that day, we found ourselves, once again, at the Cancun Airport. Though nothing like Tata Pedro's journey home, it was tiring—through customs in three countries, two flights, and a two-hour drive once we landed in Charlotte. And here we were for four hours in the massive shopping plaza in the Cancun Airport. We were tired and the noise, bright lights and competing smells of greasy airport food overwhelmed our senses which had been more accustomed to the Guatemalan lowlands.

We sat off to the side and while Julia read, I wandered around—past the fast-food court, past the duty-free shops, past the craft pavilion, past Margaritaville with Jimmy Buffett wailing "Wastin' Away Again in Margaritaville," his international, booze-glorifying hit from a time long passed. It all seemed rather depressing, so much 'maya bewilderment.' Then I heard music coming from The Hardrock Café gift shop—Bob Marley.

His video was playing on all five store monitors. One monitor was right on the edge of the shops so I stood in the plaza area watching him perform, my mood lifting. I soon realized the irony—during last year's Christmas season, only one person had outsold Bob Marley—Jimmy Buffett. As I looked around at the slick, corporate-created shopping plaza, only this—a dreadlock Rasta from the slums of Jamaica—exuded any heart, any livity. And, in the thirty minutes I stood there, as hundreds of passengers streamed by, only one young Japanese couple joined me to watch him. And yet, here he was like a jewel for all to see.

"Is this the *only* artist you play?" I asked the young Mexican man behind the counter. I noticed both him and his female co-worker were singing along with Bob, seeming to still enjoy him after listening to him for hours each day.

"Solamente!" he answered and with a bright smile, gave me a big two thumbs up.

The Gathering of the Peacemakers
Getting Ready for the Changes
(Our Summer Program in the Blue Ridge Mountains)

Every summer beginning in 2008, we are hosting this gathering. Our goal is to prepare ourselves mentally, physically, emotionally, and spiritually for the coming changes so that we might share this peace with others. The gathering will include 6 nights of live music and 7 days of conscious instruction. The event will be held at a Holston Camp in NC. Info at www.onelovepress.com.

Contact Information
Julia & Robert Roskind
One Love Press
P.O. Box 2142 Blowing Rock, NC 28605
(828) 295-4610 FAX: (828) 295-6901
Website: www.onelovepress.com Email: Roskind@boone.net

To contact **Tata Pedro** directly (in Spanish only):
Ajq'iij Pedro Cruz García,
3 Av. 6-71, Zona 1,
Cantón Pakucha',
San Pedro La Laguna,
Sololá, Guatemala, Central America.
Tel: (+00502) 52992726 or cell: (+00502) 50077843
E mail: juunimox9@yahoo.com

For English speakers who wish to contact Tata Pedro for workshops on Mayan energetic equilibrium, write to Louise Rothwell at holisticcentre@yahoo.com

Join Tata Pedro and other Mayan spiritual guides for seven days of Mayan fire ceremony at Unification Maya around Tikal, Peten, Guatemala, each December 15th - 21st 2007 -2012. Open to everyone. See: www.ixcanaan.com

For a useful, free download of Mayan Calendar Software see www.dearbrutus.com